"We may all be mighty fine fellows, but none of us can write like Hazlitt."

—*Stevenson*

WILLIAM HAZLITT—MAN OF MANY ROLES

CELEBRATED as one of the world's greatest essayists, who reacted to life in vivid prose.

ATTACKED as an "infernal" critic and ardent political radical.

ADMIRED as a journalist who became the Boswell of Regency England, ranging from politics and literature to the boxing ring.

FAMOUS as the middle-aged "fool of love" who penned a notorious account of his attachment to a young girl who scorned him.

ACCLAIMED as a brilliant commentator, a "writer's writer," whose appreciation of great literary figures forms a unique and readable history of English letters.

BELOVED for his companionable, forthright, human manner, his gusto and wit; he said, "Life is the art of being well deceived."

The Hazlitt Sampler

Selections from his Familiar, Literary, and Critical Essays

EDITED, WITH AN INTRODUCTION,

by Herschel M. Sikes, Ph.D.
HUNTER COLLEGE

GLOUCESTER, MASS.

PETER SMITH

1969

Contents

Introduction

"I said if there were three things superior in the modern world, they were 'The Excursion,' Haydon's pictures, and Hazlitt's depth of taste." Such was the judgment of the poet John Keats. The world no longer holds Wordsworth's long poem in this high acclaim and has lost enthusiasm for Haydon's vast canvases, but Hazlitt has attracted a far larger and certainly a more appreciative audience than he enjoyed in his own day. As a brilliant essayist and felicitous prose stylist he still wins the admiration of readers, and deepened interest in his more serious work has established him as one of the great critics in English literature along with Dryden, Johnson, Coleridge, and Arnold.

Part of Hazlitt's twentieth-century popularity may be attributed to our detachment from the literary squabbles and political battles which characterized the Romantic Age and often centered around him. Thus distracted, his contemporaries were dazzled or aggravated by the "infernal" critic and ardent political radical and were unwilling or unable to perceive his enduring merits. For Hazlitt was an original and independent thinker, an angry critic who lashed at the excesses of his times, ridiculed literary cliques and their vested interests, and ruthlessly exposed sham and pretentiousness wherever he found them. Today we savor the energy and flair even of what is ephemeral in the subjects upon which he wrote, and we more readily recognize that what seemed partisanship was really meant for mankind. Moreover, to his originality and honesty he added forcefulness and the versatility and clarity of a style which is ever fresh and vital. Together these qualities constitute his claim to fame—but especially his style. "We may all be mighty fine fellows," said Stevenson, "but none of us can write like Hazlitt."

The appealing personality of the man whom Charles Lamb considered "the best companion in the world" is impressed upon everything that he wrote. Apart from his own reactions to the world, his vigorous intellect, and strong human appeal—what he himself called "gusto" in Shakespeare and Fielding, and what Keats, in another brilliant flash, described as his "fiery laconicism"—Hazlitt was chiefly concerned with the creative experience. As a result, he has exerted a strong influence upon such later critics and writers as Matthew Arnold, whose theory of disinterestedness in literature owes a good deal to the earlier critic's essay on the subject. Thackeray considered him "one of the keenest and brightest critics that ever lived." More recently, W. Somerset Maugham, Christopher Morley, and J. B. Priestley, among others, have acknowledged their debt to Hazlitt while regarding his work as a model for the young writer.

William Hazlitt was born on April 10, 1778, at Maidstone, Kent. His father, a sturdy Unitarian minister and Liberal, was a friend of Joseph Priestley and Richard Price, ardent champions of American independence, and was acquainted with Benjamin Franklin during his English residence. Encouraged by them, the Hazlitts emigrated to America in 1783, settling first in Philadelphia and then at Boston, where Mr. Hazlitt founded the first Unitarian Church. But his religious views, too broad even for the New World, caused disputes with community leaders and hastened the family's return to England in 1787. Removing to a parish at Wem, Shropshire, William read in his father's library, attended the Grammar School, and developed that love of nature later echoed in such essays as *Why Distant Objects Please:*

> I see the beds of larkspur with purple eyes; tall holy-oaks, red and yellow; the broad sunflowers, caked in gold, with bees buzzing round them; wildernesses of pink, and hot-glowing peonies; poppies run to seed; the sugared lily, and faint mignionette, all ranged in order, and as thick as they can grow; the box-tree borders; the gravel-walks, the painted alcove, the confectionary, the clotted cream.

In 1793, at the age of fifteen, Hazlitt was sent to a Unitarian academy at Hackney, near London, which had been established as a charitable institution for the sons of dissenting preachers destined for the ministry. There he received an excellent education in the classics, modern languages, and philosophy, but "manifested an extreme distaste" for the religious life. Returning to Wem in 1796, he spent the next three years painting and reading, acquiring that immense knowledge of books and "the nature of realities" which so enriched his own writing. In 1798 occurred the famous meeting with Coleridge and, through him, the introduction to Wordsworth described in *My*

First Acquaintance with Poets. Although Hazlitt greatly admired the two authors and often wrote perceptively about their poems, they were not temperamentally suited for a lasting friendship. By 1803, primarily because of Hazlitt's zealous loyalty to Napoleon "even to the bitter end," his relationship with Coleridge and Wordsworth had soured into distrust. After Hazlitt's sensitive but unflattering review of *The Excursion* in 1814, Wordsworth, secure in the knowledge that his own illegitimate daughter was across the Channel, exaggerated and circulated the story of how Hazlitt some twelve years before had seduced a girl in the Lake District, thus arousing a mob from whose indignation he had to be extricated. This malice, combined with political differences, kept them estranged.

Still uncertain of his true talent, Hazlitt had traveled to Paris in 1802 to study painting and make copies of the old masters at the Louvre. Throughout his life he remained devoted to art, but soon found that literature and philosophy were his chief interests. His first book, *An Essay on the Principles of Human Action* (1805), begun while he was a student at the Unitarian New College, is a systematic defense of "the unity of the mind" against the prevalent emphasis on sense impressions, and contains the germ of an aesthetic theory based upon sympathy. From 1806 to 1812 Hazlitt struggled to become a writer, turning out a political pamphlet, *Free Thoughts on Public Affairs* (1806); short biographies of statesmen, *The Eloquence of the British Senate* (1807); a criticism of Thomas Malthus, *A Reply to the Essay on Population* (1807); and *A New and Improved Grammar of the English Tongue* (1810). With an appointment to *The Morning Chronicle* in 1812 as a reporter in the Press Gallery of Parliament, and dramatic critic the next year, his literary navvying came to an end. Soon he was writing in popular journals like the *Champion* and Leigh Hunt's *Examiner*. In 1814 he began to contribute to the *Edinburgh Review*, the most powerful liberal organ of the day, and in 1817 he became drama critic on *The Times* and, three years later, the celebrated "Table-Talk" essayist of *The London Magazine*.

A collection of essays and reviews culled from his newspaper and magazine writing appeared as *The Round Table* in 1817, but it was the *Characters of Shakespear's Plays*, published in the same year, which gained Hazlitt a reputation as a great critic. With its emphasis upon the plays themselves, character analysis, and psychological motivation, the *Characters of Shakespear's Plays* has directly influenced many dramatists and critics, such as Harley Granville-Barker and A. C. Bradley, as well as the acting and directing in the modern English and American theatre. That book was followed by penetrating analyses of Elizabethan dramas in the *Age of Elizabeth* (1820) and by discriminating studies of the great novelists and poets in *Lectures on the English Comic Writers* (1819) and *Lectures on the English Poets* (1818); both of them led to brutal personal attacks upon Hazlitt in the conservative *Blackwood's Magazine* and *Quarterly Review*.

In 1808 Hazlitt had married Sarah Stoddart, a friend of Charles and Mary Lamb. Sarah's cottage at Winterslow, near Salisbury Plain, became the author's favorite retreat and the setting for many of his essays. But the marriage was never a happy one, and in 1820, while separated from his wife and living in a London lodging house, Hazlitt fell hopelessly in love with Sarah Walker, the flirtatious daughter of his landlord. Despite little encouragement from the girl, Hazlitt persuaded his wife, who had borne him a son, to obtain a divorce in Scotland because English law forbade divorce to members of the professional classes. The difficulty and expense of the divorce and Sarah Walker's refusal to marry him threw Hazlitt into an emotional despair which temporarily disrupted his career; he found relief only in babbling about her to anybody who would listen—friends, strangers, even London whores. The intensity of his sufferings and the deceptions of his inamorata are self-consciously (and sometimes absurdly) detailed in *Liber Amoris, or the New Pygmalion,* a "confession" written "to burn her out of his thoughts," and published in 1823. But the most eloquent expression of his disappointment is contained in a short *apologia* in *My First Acquaintance with Poets:* "So have I loitered my life away, reading books, looking at pictures, going to plays, hearing, thinking, writing on what pleased me best. I have wanted only one thing to make me happy; but wanting that, have wanted everything!"

Many of Hazlitt's best essays were collected in *Table-Talk* (1821-22), and *The Plain Speaker* (1826). His masterpiece, *The Spirit of the Age,* a synthesis of the intellectual life of the Romantic era, containing his mature criticism of his contemporaries, appeared in 1825. In April of the previous year, Hazlitt had married his second wife, the widow of a lawyer, about whom little is known except that she was worth 300 pounds a year. Most of their short marriage was spent traveling on the continent, described in *Notes of a Journey Through France and Italy,* while Hazlitt collected material for his monumental, unsuccessful *Life of Napoleon* (1828-1830), which he considered his major work. He separated from his wife in 1827 and devoted his last years to writing the four-volume biography of his hero, "the child and champion of the Revolution." Hazlitt died of cancer in London on September 30, 1830.

Between 1812 and 1825 Hazlitt was the most productive critic and essayist in England. Because his interests ranged from acting, art, and athletics to philosophy, travel, and writing, his works cover a vast scope—autobiographical reminiscence of his serious, studious boyhood against the background of expansive countryside and frugal parish houses; sardonic sketches of tireless talkers and other worldlings at "evenings" in London; articles and books which grew out of his various careers as amateur philosopher, unsuccessful painter, journalist, biographer and, finally, distinguished critic who judged the works of the celebrated authors who were his contemporaries, namely Coleridge, Wordsworth, Shelley, Byron, and Keats, and who wrote vivid and penetrating analyses of their great predecessors, such as Shakespeare, Milton, and Pope. This book contains the outstanding criticism of both groups as well as the most representative familiar essays.

In the following selections, it will become clear to the reader that Hazlitt saw a unity of literature and life. "We are all Hamlet" and "we are all poets" are remarks that illustrate his tendency to see life in literature and literature in life. His ideas of sympathy (that is, empathy) and gusto (intense feeling or "energy") are expressive of his desire to relate the work of art to life, to the "common arena of mankind." Although the chief characteristic of his writing is an emphasis upon his own experience and the sympathy of the reader, it would be a mistake to overlook the consistency of principle, carefully reasoned philosophy, and earnest didacticism which underlie and give substance to his views. His criticism of Wordsworth's poetry, for example, is based upon a modified conception of classical organic wholeness, neo-classical "truth," or universal "unity of interest." Similarly, the unfavorable review of Shelley's poems is a result of the critic's emphasis upon a harmonious balance of inner and outer, discussed in terms of Bacon's distinction between "novelty" and "antiquity." In contrast, Keats' difficult bridging of the "golden mean" between disinterested objectivity and "a mind preying upon itself," as seen in *The Eve of St. Agnes,* led the critic to write that he "gave the greatest promise of genius of any poet of his day."

Hazlitt was the first major critic in English to represent a social group which was closer to the mass of the middle class than the criticism written by Oxford and Cambridge graduates, or others who voiced the opinions of the dominant classes. The fact that he was an enterprising, self-supporting writer does not mean, however, that he was a mere "taster" of literary jam. His essay on Milton, for example, which anticipated some critical "arguments" of this century, is a rich, sensitive, balanced appraisal of the poet's powers. If Hazlitt had to read while he ran, he wrote all the better and clearer for it. If there is occasionally a sense of hastiness in his works, he made up for it in the immediacy of his views and in the vitality of his style. Through his fusion of fiction and reality, which won him the admiration of Keats, Hazlitt chiefly endeavored to see literature and life enthusiastically, sympathetically, and totally. His ruling passion in literature, like Hamlet's admonition to the actors, was "to hold, as 't were, the mirror up to nature; to show virtue her own feature, scorn her own image, and the very age and body of the time his form and pressure."

HERSCHEL M. SIKES
Hunter College, New York

Herschel M. Sikes teaches English at Hunter College and is a Fellow of the Newberry Library. He attended the University of Florida and New York University, where he received a Ph.D. for a study of Hazlitt. He has written articles on Keats and Hazlitt, contributed to encyclopedias, and is the editor of a forthcoming volume of Hazlitt's letters.

On Shakespeare and Ben Jonson

Hazlitt's great enjoyment of the theatre was matched by his careful study of the drama, his sensitive analysis of character, language, and action. The essays on Shakespeare and Ben Jonson from On the English Poets, On the Comic Writers, *and* Characters of Shakespear's Plays *best illustrate these features as well as his contribution to psychological criticism.*

The striking peculiarity of Shakespeare's mind was its generic quality, its power of communication with all other minds—so that it contained a universe of thought and feeling within itself, and had no one peculiar bias, or exclusive excellence more than another. He was just like any other man, but that he was like all other men. He was the least of an egotist that it was possible to be. He was nothing in himself; but he was all that others were, or that they could become. He not only had in himself the germs of every faculty and feeling, but he could follow them by anticipation, intuitively, into all their conceivable ramifications, through every change of fortune or conflict of passion, or turn of thought. He had "a mind reflecting ages past," and present: all the people that ever lived are there. There was no respect of persons with him. His genius shone equally on the evil and on the good, on the wise and the foolish, the monarch and the beggar: "All corners of the earth, kings, queens, and states, maids, matrons, nay, the secrets of the grave," are hardly hid from his searching glance. He was like the genius of humanity, changing places with all of us at pleasure, and playing with our purposes as with his own. He turned the globe round for his amusement, and surveyed the generations of men, and the individuals as they passed, with their different concerns, passions, follies, vices, virtues, actions, and motives—as well those that they knew, as those which they did not know, or acknowledge to themselves. The dreams of childhood, the ravings of despair, were the toys of his fancy. Airy beings waited at his call, and came at his bidding. Harmless fairies "nodded to him, and did him courtesies": and the night-hag bestrode the blast at the

command of "his so potent art." The world of spirits lay
open to him, like the world of real men and women: and
there is the same truth in his delineations of the one as
of the other; for if the preternatural characters he describes could be supposed to exist, they would speak, and
feel, and act, as he makes them. He had only to think of
anything in order to become that thing, with all the circumstances belonging to it. When he conceived of a character, whether real or imaginary, he not only entered into
all its thoughts and feelings, but seemed instantly, and as
if by touching a secret spring, to be surrounded with all
the same objects, "subject to the same skyey influences,"
the same local, outward, and unforeseen accidents which
would occur in reality. Thus the character of Caliban not
only stands before us with a language and manners of its
own, but the scenery and situation of the enchanted island
he inhabits, the traditions of the place, its strange noises,
its hidden recesses, "his frequent haunts and ancient neigh-
bourhood," are given with a miraculous truth of nature,
and with all the familiarity of an old recollection. The
whole "coheres semblably together" in time, place, and
circumstance. In reading this author, you do not merely
learn what his characters say,—you see their persons. By
something expressed or understood, you are at no loss
to decipher their peculiar physiognomy, the meaning of a
look, the grouping, the by-play, as we might see it on the
stage. A word, an epithet paints a whole scene, or throws
us back whole years in the history of the person represented. So (as it has been ingeniously remarked) when
Prospero describes himself as left alone in the boat with
his daughter, the epithet which he applies to her, "Me and
thy *crying* self," flings the imagination instantly back from
the grown woman to the helpless condition of infancy,
and places the first and most trying scene of his misfortunes before us, with all that he must have suffered in
the interval. How well the silent anguish of Macduff is
conveyed to the reader, by the friendly expostulation of
Malcolm—"What! man, ne'er pull your hat upon your
brows!" Again, Hamlet, in the scene with Rosencrantz and
Guildenstern, somewhat abruptly concludes his fine soliloquy on life by saying, "Man delights not me, nor woman
neither, though by your smiling you seem to say so." Which
is explained by their answer—"My lord, we have no such
stuff in our thoughts. But we smiled to think, if you delight

not in man, what lenten entertainment the players shall receive from you, whom we met on the way": as if while Hamlet was making this speech, his two old school-fellows from Wittenberg had been really standing by, and he had seen them smiling by stealth, at the idea of the players crossing their minds. It is not "a combination and a form" of words, a set speech or two, a preconcerted theory of a character, that will do this: but all the persons concerned must have been present in the poet's imagination, as at a kind of rehearsal; and whatever would have passed through their minds on the occasion, and have been observed by others, passed through his, and is made known to the reader. I may add in passing that Shakespeare always gives the best directions for the costume and carriage of his heroes. The account of Ophelia's death begins thus:

> There is a willow hanging o'er a brook,
> That shows its hoary leaves in the glassy stream.

Now this is an instance of the same unconscious power of mind which is as true to nature as itself. The leaves of the willow are, in fact, white underneath, and it is this part of them which would appear "hoary" in the reflection in the brook. The same sort of intuitive power, the same faculty of bringing every object in nature, whether present or absent, before the mind's eye, is observable in the speech of Cleopatra, when conjecturing what were the employments of Antony in his absence: "He's speaking now, or murmuring, where's my serpent of old Nile?" How fine to make Cleopatra have this consciousness of her own character, and to make her feel that it is this for which Antony is in love with her! She says, after the battle of Actium, when Antony has resolved to risk another fight, "It is my birth-day; I had thought to have held it poor: but since my lord is Antony again, I will be Cleopatra." What other poet would have thought of such a casual resource of the imagination, or would have dared to avail himself of it? The thing happens in the play as it might have happened in fact. That which, perhaps, more than anything else distinguishes the dramatic productions of Shakespeare from all others, is this wonderful truth and individuality of conception. Each of his characters is as much itself, and as absolutely independent of the rest as well as of the author, as if they were living persons, not fictions of the mind. The poet may be said, for the time, to identify himself with the character he wishes to represent, and to pass from one to another, like the same soul successively animating different bodies. By an art like that of the ventriloquist, he throws his imagination out of himself, and makes every word appear to proceed from the mouth of the person in whose name it is given. His plays alone are properly expressions of the passions, not descriptions of them. His characters are real beings of flesh and blood; they speak like men, not like authors. One might suppose that he had stood by at the time, and overheard what passed. As in our dreams we hold conversations with ourselves, make remarks, or communicate intelligence, and have no idea of the answer which we shall receive, and which we ourselves make, till we hear it, so the dialogues in Shakespeare are carried on without any consciousness of what is to follow, without any appearance of preparation or premeditation. The gusts of passion come and go like sound of music borne on the wind. Nothing is made out by formal inference and analogy, by climax and antithesis: all comes, or seems to come, immediately from nature. Each object and circumstance exists in his mind, as it would have existed in reality: each several train of thought and feeling goes on of itself, without confusion or effort. In the world of his imagination, everything has a life, a place and being of its own!

Chaucer's characters are sufficiently distinct from one another, but they are too little varied in themselves, too much like identical propositions. They are consistent, but uniform; we get no new idea of them from first to last; they are not placed in different lights, nor are their subordinate traits brought out in new situations; they are like portraits or physiognomical studies, with the distinguishing features marked with inconceivable truth and precision, but that preserve the same unaltered air and attitude. Shakespeare's are historical figures, equally true and correct, but put into action, where every nerve and muscle is displayed in the struggle with others, with all the effect of collision and contrast, with every variety of light and shade. Chaucer's characters are narrative, Shakespeare's dramatic, Milton's epic. That is, Chaucer told only as much of his story as he pleased, as was required for a particular purpose. He answered for his characters himself. In Shakespeare they are introduced upon the stage, are liable to be asked all sorts of questions, and are forced to answer for themselves. In Chaucer we perceive a fixed essence of character. In Shakespeare there is a continual composition and decomposition of its elements, a fermentation of every particle in the whole mass, by its alternate affinity or antipathy to other principles which are brought in contact with it. Till the experiment is tried, we do not know the result, the turn which the character will take in its new circumstances. Milton took only a few simple principles of character, and raised them to the utmost conceivable grandeur, and refined them from every base alloy. His imagination, "nigh sphered in Heaven," claimed kindred only with what he saw from that height, and could raise to the same elevation with itself. He sat retired and kept his state alone, "playing with wisdom;" while Shakespeare mingled with the crowd, and played the host, "to make society the sweeter welcome."

The passion in Shakespeare is of the same nature as his delineation of character. It is not some one habitual feeling or sentiment preying upon itself, growing out of itself, and moulding everything to itself; it is passion modified by passion, by all the other feelings to which the individual is liable, and to which others are liable with him; subject to all the fluctuations of caprice and accident; calling into play all the resources of the understanding and all the energies of the will; irritated by obstacles or yielding to them; rising from small beginnings to its utmost height; now drunk with hope, now stung to madness, now sunk in despair, now blown to air with a breath, now raging like a torrent. The human soul is made the sport of fortune, the prey of adversity: it is stretched on the wheel of destiny, in restless ecstasy. The passions are in a state of projection. Years are melted down to moments, and every instant teems with fate. We know the results, we see the process. Thus after Iago has been boasting to himself of the effect of his poisonous suggestions on the mind of Othello, which "with a little act upon the blood, will work like mines of sulphur," he adds:

> *Look where he comes! not poppy, nor mandragora*
> *Nor all the drowsy syrups of the world,*
> *Shall ever medicine thee to that sweet sleep*
> *Which thou ow'dst yesterday.*

And he enters at this moment, like the crested serpent, crowned with his wrongs and raging for revenge! The whole depends upon the turn of a thought. A word, a look, blows the spark of jealousy into a flame; and the explosion is immediate and terrible as a volcano. The dialogues in Lear, in Macbeth, that between Brutus and Cassius, and nearly all those in Shakespeare, where the interest is wrought up to its highest pitch, afford examples of this dramatic fluctuation of passion. The interest in Chaucer is quite different; it is like the course of a river, strong, and full, and increasing. In Shakespeare, on the contrary, it is like the sea, agitated this way and that, and loud-lashed by furious storms; while in the still pauses of the blast we distinguish only the cries of despair, or the silence of death! Milton, on the other hand, takes the imaginative part of passion— that which remains after the event, which the mind reposes on when all is over, which looks upon circumstances from the remotest elevation of thought and fancy, and abstracts them from the world of action to that of contemplation. The objects of dramatic poetry affect us by sympathy, by their nearness to ourselves, as they take us by surprise, or force us upon action, "while rage with rage doth sympathise:" the objects of epic poetry affect us through the medium of the imagination, by magnitude and distance, by their permanence and universality. The one fills us with terror and pity, the other with admiration and delight. There are certain objects that strike the imagination, and inspire awe in the very idea of them, independently of any dramatic interest, that is, of any connection with the vicissitudes of human life. For instance, we cannot think of the pyramids of Egypt, of a Gothic ruin, or an old Roman encampment, without a certain emotion, a sense of power and sublimity coming over the mind. The heavenly bodies that hang over our heads wherever we go, and "in their untroubled element shall shine when we are laid in dust, and all our cares forgotten," affect us in the same way. Thus Satan's address to the Sun has an epic, not a dramatic interest; for though the second person in the dialogue makes no answer and feels no concern, yet the eye of that vast luminary is upon him, like the eye of Heaven, and seems conscious of what he says, like an universal presence. Dramatic poetry and epic in their perfection, indeed, approximate to and strengthen one another. Dramatic poetry borrows aid from the dignity of persons and things, as the heroic does from human passion; but in theory they are distinct. When Richard II calls for the looking glass to contemplate his faded majesty in it, and bursts into that affecting exclamation: "O that I were a mockery-king of snow, to melt away before the sun of Bolingbroke!" we have here the utmost force of human passion, combined with the ideas of regal splendor and fallen power.

Shakespeare's imagination is of the same plastic kind as his conception of character or passion. "It glances from heaven to earth, from earth to heaven." Its movement is rapid and devious. It unites the most opposite extremes; or, as Puck says, in boasting of his own feats, "puts a girdle round about the earth in forty minutes." He seems always hurrying from his subject, even while describing it; but the stroke, like the lightning's, is sure as it is sudden. He takes the widest possible range, but from that very range he has his choice of the greatest variety and aptitude of materials. He brings together images the most alike, but placed at the greatest distance from each other; that is, found in circumstances of the greatest dissimilitude. From the remoteness of his combinations, and the celerity with which they are effected, they coalesce the more indissolubly together. The more the thoughts are strangers to each other, and the longer they have been kept asunder, the more intimate does their union seem to become. Their felicity is equal to their force. Their likeness is made more dazzling by their novelty. They startle, and take the fancy prisoner in the same instant. Shakespeare's language and versification are like the rest of him. He has a magic power over words; they come winged at his bidding, and seem to know their places. They are struck out on the spur of the occasion, and have all the truth and vividness which arise from an actual impression of the objects. His epithets and single phrases are like sparkles, thrown off from an imagination fired by the whirling rapidity of its own motion. His language is hieroglyphical. It translates thoughts into visible images. It abounds in sudden transitions and elliptical expressions. This is the source of his mixed metaphors, which are only abbreviated forms of speech. These, however, give no pain from long custom. They have, in fact, become idioms in the language. They are the building, and not the scaffolding to thought. We take the meaning and effect of a well-known passage entire, and no more stop to scan and spell out the particular words and phrases than the syllables of which they are composed. In trying to recollect any other author, one sometimes stumbles, in case of failure, on a word as good. In Shakespeare, any other word but the true one is sure to be wrong. If anybody, for instance, could not recollect the words of the following description,

> *Light thickens, and the crow*
> *Makes wing to the rooky wood,*

he would be greatly at a loss to substitute others for them equally expressive of the feeling. These remarks, however, are strictly applicable only to the impassioned parts of Shakespeare's language, which flowed from the warmth and originality of his imagination, and were his own. The language used for prose conversation and ordinary business is sometimes technical, and involved in the affectation of the time. Compare, for example, Othello's Apology to the Senate, relating "his whole course of love," with some of the preceding parts relating to his appointment and the official dispatches from Cyprus. In this respect, "the business of the state does him offence." His versification is no less powerful, sweet, and varied.

It remains to speak of the faults of Shakespeare. They are not so many or so great as they have been represented; what there are, are chiefly owing to the following causes: the universality of his genius was, perhaps, a disadvantage to his single works; the variety of his resources, sometimes diverting him from applying them to the most effectual purposes. He might be said to combine the powers of Aeschylus and Aristophanes, of Dante and Rabelais, in his own mind. If he had been only half what he was, he would perhaps have appeared greater. The natural ease and indifference of his temper made him sometimes less scrupulous than he might have been. He is relaxed and careless in critical places; he is in earnest throughout only in Timon, Macbeth, and Lear. Again, he had no models of acknowledged excellence constantly in view to stimulate his efforts, and, by all that appears, no love of fame. He wrote for the "great vulgar and the small" in his time, not for posterity. If Queen Elizabeth and the maids of honor laughed heartily at his worst jokes, and the catcalls in the gallery were silent at his best passages, he went home satisfied, and slept the next night well. He did not trouble himself about Voltaire's criticisms. He was willing to take advantage of the ignorance of the age in many things; and if his plays pleased others, not to quarrel with them himself.

His very facility of production would make him set less value on his own excellences, and not care to distinguish nicely between what he did well or ill. His blunders in chronology and geography do not amount to above half a dozen, and they are offenses against chronology and geography, not against poetry. As to the unities, he was right in setting them at defiance. He was fonder of puns than became so great a man. His barbarisms were those of his age. His genius was his own. He had no objection to float down with the stream of common taste and opinion: he rose above it by his own buoyancy, and an impulse which he could not keep under, in spite of himself or others, and "his delights did show most dolphin-like."

In Ben Jonson we find ourselves generally in low company, and we see no hope of getting out of it. He is like a person who fastens upon a disagreeable subject and cannot be persuaded to leave it. His comedy in a word has not what Shakespeare somewhere calls "bless'd conditions." It is cross-grained, mean, and mechanical. It is handicraft wit. Squalid poverty, sheer ignorance, bare-faced impudence, or idiot imbecility are his dramatic commonplaces —things that provoke pity or disgust, instead of laughter. His portraits are caricatures by dint of their very likeness, being extravagant tautologies of themselves, as his plots are improbable by an excess of consistency; for he goes thorough-stitch with whatever he takes in hand, makes one contrivance answer all purposes, and every obstacle give way to a predetermined theory. For instance, nothing can be more incredible than the mercenary conduct of Corvino, in delivering up his wife to the palsied embraces of Volpone; and yet the poet does not seem in the least to boggle at the incongruity of it: but the more it is in keeping with the absurdity of the rest of the fable and the more it advances it to an incredible catastrophe, the more he seems to dwell upon it with complacency and a sort of willful exaggeration, as if it were a logical discovery or corollary from well-known premises. He would no more be baffled in the working out a plot than some people will be baffled in an argument. If to be wise were to be obstinate, our author might have laid signal claim to this title. Old Ben was of a scholastic turn, and he had dealt a little in the occult sciences and controversial divinity. He was a man of strong crabbed sense, retentive memory, acute observation, great fidelity of description and keeping in character, a power of working out an idea so as to make it painfully true and oppressive, and with great honesty and manliness of feeling as well as directness of understanding: but with all this, he wanted, to my thinking, that genial spirit of enjoyment and finer fancy which constitute the essence of poetry and of wit. The sense of reality exercised a despotic sway over his mind, and equally weighed down and clogged his perception of the beautiful or the ridiculous. He had a keen sense of what was true and false, but not of the difference between the agreeable and disagreeable; or if he had, it was by his understanding rather than his imagination, by rule and method, not by sympathy, or intuitive perception of the gayest, happiest attitude of things. There was nothing spontaneous, no impulse or ease about his genius; it was all forced, up-hill work, making a toil of pleasure. And hence his overweening admiration of his own works, from the effort they had cost him and the apprehension that they were not proportionably admired by others, who knew nothing of the pangs and throes of his Muse in child-bearing. In his satirical descriptions he seldom stops short of the lowest and most offensive point of meanness; and in his serious poetry he seems to repose with complacency only on the pedantic and far-fetched, the *ultima Thule* of his knowledge. . . . *The Silent Woman* is built upon the supposition of an old citizen disliking noise who takes to wife Epicene (a supposed young lady) for the reputation of her silence, and with a view to disinherit his nephew who has laughed at his infirmity; when the ceremony is no sooner over than the bride turns out a very shrew, his house becomes a very Babel of noises, and he offers his nephew his own terms to unloose the matrimonial knot, which is done by proving that Epicene is no woman. There is some humor in the leading character, but too much is made out of it, not in the way of Moliere's exaggerations, which, though extravagant, are fantastical and ludicrous, but of serious, plodding, minute prolixity. The first meeting between Morose and Epicene is well managed, and does not "o'erstep the modesty of nature," from the very restraint imposed by the situation of the parties—by the affected taciturnity of the one and the other's singular dislike of noise. The whole story, from the beginning to the end, is a gratuitous assumption and the height of improbability. The author, in sustaining the weight of his plot, seems like a balance-master who supports a number of people, piled one upon another, on his hands, his knees, his shoulders, but with a great effort on his own part, and with a painful effect to the beholders. The scene between Sir Amorous La Foole and Sir John Daw, in which they are frightened by a feigned report of each other's courage into a submission to all sorts of indignities, which they construe into flattering civilities, is the same device as that in *Twelfth Night* between Sir Andrew Aguecheek and Viola, carried to a paradoxical and revolting excess. Ben Jonson had no idea of decorum in his dramatic fictions, which Milton says is the principal thing, but went on caricaturing himself and others till he could go no farther in extravagance and sink no lower in meanness. The titles of his *dramatis personae,* such as Sir Amorous La Foole, Truewit, Sir John Daw, Sir Politic Would-be, which are significant and knowing, show his determination to overdo every thing by thus letting you into their characters beforehand, and afterwards proving their pretensions by their names. Thus Peregrine, in *Volpone,* says, "Your name, Sir?" "My name is Politick Would-be." To which Peregrine replies, "Oh, that speaks him." This play was Dryden's favorite. It is indeed full of sharp, biting sentences against the women, of whom he was fond. The following may serve as a specimen. Truewit says, "Did I not tell thee, Dauphine? Why, all their actions are governed by crude opinion, without reason or cause; they know not why they do anything; but, as they are informed, believe, judge, praise, condemn, love, hate, and in emulation one of another, do all these things alike. Only they have a natural inclination sways 'em generally to the worst when they are left to themselves." This is a cynical sentence and we may say of the rest of his opinions, that "even though we should hold them to be true, yet it is slander to have them so set down." The women in this play indeed justify the author's severity; they are altogether abominable. They have an utter want of principle and decency and are equally without a sense of pleasure, taste, or elegance. Madame Haughty, Madame Centaur, and Madame Mavis, form the College, as it is here pedantically called. They are a sort of candidates for being upon the town, but cannot find seducers, and a sort of blue-stockings, before the invention of letters. Mistress Epicene, the silent gentle-woman, turns out not to be a woman at all; which is not a very pleasant denouement of the plot, and is itself an incident apparently taken from the blundering blind-man's-buff conclusion of the *Merry Wives of Windsor*. What Shakespeare might introduce by an accident, and as a mere passing jest, Ben Jonson would set about building a whole play upon. The directions for making love given by Truewit, the author's favorite, discover great knowledge and shrewdness of observation mixed with the acuteness of malice, and approach to the best style of comic dialogue. But I must refer to the play itself for them.

The Fox, or *Volpone,* is his best play. It is prolix and improbable, but intense and powerful. It is written *con amore*. It is made up of cheats and dupes, and the author is at home among them. He shows his hatred of the one and contempt for the other, and makes them set one another off to great advantage. There are several striking dramatic contrasts in this play, where the Fox lies *perdue* to watch his prey, where Mosca is the dextrous go-between outwitting his gulls, his employer, and himself, and where each of the gaping legacy-hunters, the lawyer, the merchant, and the miser, eagerly occupied with the ridiculousness of the other's pretensions, is blind only to the absurdity of his own; but the whole is worked up too mechanically, and our credulity overstretched at last revolts into scepticism, and our attention overtasked flags into drowsiness. This play seems formed on the model of Plautus in unity of plot and interest; and Ben, in emulating his classic model, appears to have done his best. There is the same caustic unsparing severity in it as in his other works. His patience is tried to the utmost. His words drop gall. The scene between Volpone, Mosca, Voltore, Corvino, and Corbaccio, at the outset, will show the dramatic power in the conduct of his play, and will be my justification in what I have said of the literal tenaciousness of the author's imaginary descriptions.

Every Man in His Humour is a play well-known to the public. This play acts better than it reads. The pathos in the principal character, Kitely, is "as dry as the remainder biscuit after a voyage." There is, however, a certain good sense, discrimination, or logic of passion in the part, which affords excellent hints for an able actor, and which, if properly pointed, gives it considerable force on the stage. Bobadil is the only actually striking character in the play and the real hero of the piece. His well-known proposal for the pacification of Europe, by killing some twenty of them, each his man a day, is as good as any other that has been suggested up to the present moment. His extravagant affectation, his blustering and cowardice, are an entertaining medley; and his final defeat and exposure, though exceedingly humorous, are the most affecting part of the story. Brain-worm is a particularly dry and abstruse character. We neither know his business nor his motives: his plots are as intricate as they are useless, and as the ignorance of those he imposes upon is wonderful. This is the impression in reading it. Yet from the bustle and activity of this character on the stage, the changes of dress, the variety of affected tones and gipsy jargon, and the limping affected gestures, it is a very amusing theatrical exhibition. The rest, Master Matthew, Master Stephen, Cob and Cob's wife, were living in the sixteenth century. That is all we know of them. But from the very oddity of their appearance and behavior, they have a very droll and even picturesque effect when acted. It seems a revival of the dead. We believe in their existence when we see them. As an example of the power of the stage in giving reality and interest to what otherwise would be without it, I might mention the scene in which Brain-worm praises Master Stephen's leg. The folly here is insipid from its being seemingly carried to an excess, till we see it; and then we laugh the more at it, the more incredible we thought it before.

Bartholomew Fair is chiefly remarkable for the exhibition of odd humors and tumbler's tricks, and is on that account amusing to read once. *The Alchymist* is the most famous of this author's comedies, though I think it does not deserve its reputation. It contains all that is quaint, dreary, obsolete, and hopeless in this once-famed art, but not the golden dreams and splendid disappointments. We have the mere circumstantials of the sublime science, pots and kettles, aprons and bellows, crucibles and diagrams, all the refuse and rubbish, not the essence, the true *elixir vitae*. There is, however, one glorious scene between Surly and Sir Epicure Mammon, which is the finest example I know of dramatic sophistry, or of an attempt to prove the existence of a thing by an imposing description of its effects; but compared with this, the rest of the play is a *caput mortuum*.

Hamlet

This is that Hamlet the Dane, whom we read of in our youth, and whom we may be said almost to remember in our after-years; he who made that famous soliloquy on life, who gave the advice to the players, who thought "this goodly frame, the earth, a sterile promontory, and this brace o'er-hanging firmament, the air, this majestical roof fretted with golden fire, a foul and pestilent congregation of vapours"; whom "man delighted not, nor woman neither"; he who talked with the grave-diggers, and moralized on Yorick's skull; the school-fellow of Rosencrantz and Guildenstern at Wittenberg; the friend of Horatio; the lover of Ophelia; he that was mad and sent to England; the slow avenger of his father's death; who lived at the court of Horwendillus five hundred years before we were born, but all whose thoughts we seem to know as well as we do our own, because we have read them in Shakespeare.

Hamlet is a name; his speeches and sayings but the idle coinage of the poet's brain. What then, are they not real? They are as real as our own thoughts. Their reality is in the reader's mind. It is we who are Hamlet. This play has a prophetic truth, which is above that of history. Whoever has become thoughtful and melancholy through his own mishaps or those of others; whoever has borne about with him the clouded brow of reflection, and thought himself "too much i' th' sun"; whoever has seen the golden lamp of day dimmed by envious mists rising in his own breast, and could find in the world before him only a dull blank with nothing left remarkable in it; whoever has known "the pangs of despised love, the insolence of office, or the spurns which patient merit of the unworthy takes"; he who has felt his mind sink within him, and sadness cling to his heart like a malady, who has had his hopes blighted and his youth staggered by the apparitions of strange things; who cannot be well at ease, while he sees evil hovering near him like a spectre; whose powers of action have been eaten up by thought, he to whom the universe seems infinite, and himself nothing; whose bitterness of soul makes him careless of consequences, and who goes to a play as his best resource to shove off, to a second remove, the evils of life by a mock representation of them—this is the true Hamlet.

We have been so used to this tragedy that we hardly

know how to criticize it any more than we should know how to describe our own faces. But we must make such observations as we can. It is the one of Shakespeare's plays that we think of the oftenest, because it abounds most in striking reflections on human life, and because the distresses of Hamlet are transferred, by the turn of his mind, to the general account of humanity. Whatever happens to him we apply to ourselves, because he applies it so himself as a means of general reasoning. He is a great moralizer; and what makes him worth attending to is, that he moralizes on his own feelings and experience. He is not a commonplace pedant. If Lear is distinguished by the greatest depth of passion, Hamlet is the most remarkable for the ingenuity, originality, and unstudied development of character. Shakespeare had more magnanimity than any other poet, and he has shown more of it in this play than in any other. There is no attempt to force an interest; every thing is left for time and circumstances to unfold. The attention is excited without effort, the incidents succeed each other as matters of course, the characters think and speak and act just as they might do, if left entirely to themselves. There is no set purpose, no straining at a point. The observations are suggested by the passing scene—the gusts of passion come and go like sounds of music borne on the wind. The whole play is an exact transcript of what might be supposed to have taken place at the court of Denmark, at the remote period of time fixed upon, before the modern refinements in morals and manners were heard of. It would have been interesting enough to have been admitted as a bystander in such a scene, at such a time, to have heard and witnessed something of what was going on. But here we are more than spectators. We have not only "the outward pageants and the signs of grief"; but "we have that within which passes show." We read the thoughts of the heart, we catch the passions living as they rise. Other dramatic writers give us very fine versions and paraphrases of nature; but Shakespeare, together with his own comments, gives us the original text, that we may judge for ourselves. This is a very great advantage.

The character of Hamlet stands quite by itself. It is not a character marked by strength of will or even of passion, but by refinement of thought and sentiment. Hamlet is as little of the hero as a man can well be; but he is a young and princely novice, full of high enthusiasm and quick sensibility—the sport of circumstances, questioning with fortune and refining on his own feelings, and forced from the natural bias of his disposition by the strangeness of his situation. He seems incapable of deliberate action, and is only hurried into extremities on the spur of the occasion, when he has no time to reflect, as in the scene where he kills Polonius, and again, where he alters the letters which Rosencrantz and Guildenstern are taking with them to England, purporting his death. At other times, when he is most bound to act, he remains puzzled, undecided, and sceptical, dallies with his purposes, till the occasion is lost, and finds out some pretence to relapse into indolence and thoughtfulness again. For this reason he refuses to kill the King when he is at his prayers, and by a refinement in malice, which is in truth only an excuse for his own want of resolution, defers his revenge to a more fatal opportunity, when he shall be engaged in some act "that has no relish of salvation in it."

He is the prince of philosophical speculators; and because he cannot have his revenge perfect, according to the most refined idea his wish can form, he declines it altogether. So he scruples to trust the suggestions of the ghost, contrives the scene of the play to have surer proof of his uncle's guilt, and then rests satisfied with his confirmation of his suspicions, and the success of his experiment, instead of acting upon it. Yet he is sensible of his own weakness, taxes himself with it, and tries to reason himself out of it.

Still he does nothing; and this very speculation on his own infirmity only affords him another occasion for indulging it. It is not from any want of attachment to his father or of abhorrence of his murder that Hamlet is thus dilatory, but it is more to his taste to indulge his imagination in reflecting upon the enormity of the crime and refining on his schemes of vengeance, than to put them into immediate practice. His ruling passion is to think, not to act: and any vague pretext that flatters this propensity instantly diverts him from his previous purposes. . . .

Lear

To attempt to give a description of the play itself or of its effect upon the mind is mere impertinence. It is then the best of all Shakespeare's plays, for it is the one in which he was the most in earnest. He was here fairly caught in the web of his own imagination. The passion which he has taken as his subject is that which strikes its root deepest into the human heart; of which the bond is the hardest to be unloosed; and the canceling and tearing to pieces of which gives the greatest revulsion to the frame. This depth of nature, this force of passion, this tug and war of the elements of our being, this firm faith in filial piety, and the giddy anarchy and whirling tumult of the thoughts at finding this prop failing it, the contrast between the fixed, immovable basis of natural affection, and the rapid, irregular starts of imagination, suddenly wrenched from all its accustomed holds and resting-places in the soul, this is what Shakespeare has given, and what nobody else but he could give. So we believe. The mind of Lear, staggering between the weight of attachment and the hurried movements of passion, is like a tall ship driven about by the winds, buffeted by the furious waves, but that still rides above the storm, having its anchor fixed in the bottom of the sea; or it is like the sharp rock circled by the eddying whirlpool that foams and beats against it, or like the solid promontory pushed from its basis by the force of an earthquake.

The character of Lear itself is very finely conceived for the purpose. It is the only ground on which such a story could be built with the greatest truth and effect. It is his rash haste, his violent impetuosity, his blindness to everything but the dictates of his passions or affections, that produces all his misfortunes, that aggravates his impatience of them, that enforces our pity for him. The part which Cordelia bears in the scene is extremely beautiful: the story is almost told in the first words she utters. We see at once the precipice on which the poor old king stands from his own extravagant and credulous importunity, the indiscreet simplicity of her love (which, to be sure, has a little of her father's obstinacy in it) and the hollowness of her sisters' pretensions. Almost the first burst of that noble tide of passion, which runs through the play, is in the remonstrance of Kent to his royal master on the injustice of his sentence against his youngest daughter—"Be Kent unmannerly, when Lear is mad!" This manly plainness, which draws down on him the displeasure of the unadvised king, is worthy of the fidelity with which he adheres to his fallen fortunes. The true character of the two eldest daughters, Regan and Goneril (they are so thoroughly hateful that we do not even like to repeat their names) breaks out in their answer to Cordelia who desires them to treat their father well—"Prescribe not us our duties"— their hatred of advice being in proportion to their determination to do wrong, and to their hypocritical pretensions to do right. Their deliberate hypocrisy adds the last finishing to the odiousness of their characters. It is the absence of this detestable quality that is the only relief in the character of Edmund the Bastard, and that at times reconciles us to him. We are not tempted to exaggerate the guilt of his conduct, when he himself gives it up as a bad business, and writes himself down "plain villain." Nothing more can be said about it. His religious honesty in this respect is admirable. One speech of his is worth a million. His father, Gloucester, whom he has just deluded with a forged story of his brother Edgar's designs against his life, accounts for his unnatural behavior and the strange depravity of the times from the late eclipses in the sun and moon. Edmund, who is in the secret, says when he is gone —"This is the excellent foppery of the world, that when we are sick in fortune (often the surfeits of our own behavior) we make guilty of our disasters the sun, the moon, and stars: as if we were villains on necessity; fools by heavenly compulsion; knaves, thieves, and treacherous by spherical predominance; drunkards, liars, and adulterers by an enforced obedience of planetary influence; and all that we are evil in, by a divine thrusting on. An admirable evasion of whore-master man, to lay his goatish disposition on the charge of a star! My father compounded with my mother under the Dragon's tail, and my nativity was under Ursa Major: so that it follows, I am rough and lecherous. Tut! I should have been what I am, had the maidenliest star in the firmament twinkled on my bastardising." The whole character, its careless, light-hearted villainy, contrasted with the sullen, rancorous malignity of Regan and Goneril, its connection with the conduct of the under-plot, in which Gloucester's persecution of one of his sons and the ingratitude of another, form a counterpart to the mistakes and misfortunes of Lear,—his double amour with the two sisters, and the share which he has in bringing about the fatal catastrophe, are all managed with an uncommon degree of skill and power.

It has been said, and we think justly, that the third act of Othello and the three first acts of Lear, are Shakespeare's great masterpieces in the logic of passion: that they contain the highest examples not only of the force of individual passion, but of its dramatic vicissitudes and striking effects arising from the different circumstances and characters of the persons speaking. We see the ebb and flow of the feeling, its pauses and feverish starts, its impatience of opposition, its accumulating force when it has time to recollect itself, the manner in which it avails itself of every passing word or gesture, its haste to repel insinuation, the alternate contraction and dilatation of the soul, and all "the dazzling fence of controversy" in this mortal combat with poisoned weapons, aimed at the heart, where each wound is fatal. We have seen in Othello, how the unsuspecting frankness and impetuous passions of the Moor are played upon and exasperated by the artful dexterity of Iago. In the present play, that which aggravates the sense of sympathy in the reader, and of uncontrollable anguish in the swollen heart of Lear, is the petrifying indifference, the cold, calculating, obdurate selfishness of his daughters. His keen passions seem whetted on their stony hearts. The contrast would be too painful, the shock too great, but for the intervention of the Fool, whose well-timed levity comes in to break the continuity of feeling when it can no longer be borne, and to bring into play again the fibres of the heart just as they are growing rigid from over-strained excitement. The imagination is glad to take refuge in the half-comic, half-serious comments of the Fool, just as the mind under the extreme anguish of a surgical operation vents itself in sallies of wit. The character was also a grotesque ornament of the barbarous times, in which alone the tragic groundwork of the story could be laid. In another point of view it is indispensable, inasmuch as while it is a diversion to the too great intensity of our disgust, it carries the pathos to the highest pitch of which it is capable, by showing the pitiable weakness of the old king's conduct and its irretrievable consequences in the most familiar point of view. Lear may well "beat at the gate which let his folly in," after, as the Fool says, "he has made his daughters his mothers." The character is dropped in the third act to make room for the entrance of Edgar as Mad Tom, which well accords with the increasing bustle and wildness of the incidents; and nothing can be more complete than the distinction between Lear's real and Edgar's assumed madness, while the resemblance in the cause of their distresses, from the severing of the nearest ties of natural affection, keeps up a unity of interest. Shakespeare's mastery over his subject, if it was not art, was owing to a knowledge of the connecting links of the passions, and their effect upon the mind, still more wonderful than any systematic adherence to rules, and that anticipated and outdid all the efforts of the most refined art, not inspired and rendered instinctive by genius.

Falstaff

If Shakespeare's fondness for the ludicrous sometimes led to faults in his tragedies (which was not often the case) he has made us amends by the character of Falstaff. This is perhaps the most substantial comic character that ever was invented. Sir John carries a most portly presence in the mind's eye; and in him, not to speak it profanely, "we behold the fulness of the spirit of wit and humor bodily." We are as well acquainted with his person as his mind, and his jokes come upon us with double force and relish from the quantity of flesh through which they make their way, as he shakes his fat sides with laughter, or "lards the lean earth as he walks along." Other comic characters seem, if we approach and handle them, to resolve themselves into air, "into thin air"; but this is embodied and palpable to the grossest apprehension: it lies "three fingers deep upon the ribs," it plays about the lungs and the diaphragm with all the force of animal enjoyment. His body is like a good estate to his mind, from which he receives rents and revenues of profit and pleasure in kind, according to its extent, and the richness of the soil. Wit is often a meager substitute for pleasurable sensation; an effusion of spleen and petty spite at the comforts of others, from feeling none in itself. Falstaff's wit is an emanation of a fine constitution; an exuberance of good-humor and good-nature; an overflowing of his love of laughter and good-fellowship; a giving vent to his heart's ease, and over-contentment with himself and others. He would not be in character, if he were not so fat as he is; for there is the greatest keeping in the boundless luxury of his imagination and the pampered self-indulgence of his physical appetites. He manures and nourishes his mind with jests, as he does his body with sack and sugar. He carves out his jokes, as he would a capon or a haunch of venison, where there is *cut and come again;* and pours out upon them the oil of gladness. His tongue drops fatness, and in the chambers of his brain "it snows of meat and drink." He keeps up perpetual holiday and open house, and we live with him in a round of invitations to a rump and dozen.—Yet we are not to suppose that he was a mere sensualist. All this is as much in imagination as in reality. His sensuality does not engross and stupify his other faculties, but "ascends me into the brain, clears away all the dull, crude vapors that environ it, and makes it full of nimble, fiery, and delectable shapes." His imagination keeps up the ball after his senses have done with it. He seems to have even a greater enjoyment of the freedom from restraint, of good cheer, of his ease, of his vanity, in the ideal exaggerated description which he gives of them, than in fact. He never fails to enrich his discourse with allusions to eating and drinking, but we never see him at table. He carries his own larder about with him, and he is himself "a tun of man." His pulling out the bottle in the field of battle is a joke to show his contempt for glory accompanied with danger, his systematic adherence to his Epicurean philosophy in the most trying circumstances. Again, such is his deliberate exaggeration of his own vices, that it does not seem quite certain whether the account of his hostess's bill, found in his pocket, with such an out-of-the-way charge for capons and sack with only one halfpenny-worth of bread, was not put there by himself as a trick to humor the jest upon his favorite propensities, and as a conscious caricature of himself. He is represented as a liar, a braggart, a coward, a glutton, etc. and yet we are not offended but delighted with him; for he is all these as much to amuse others as to gratify himself. He openly assumes all these characters to show the humorous part of them. The unrestrained indulgence of his own ease, appetites, and convenience has neither malice nor hypocrisy in it. In a word, he is an actor in himself almost as much as upon the stage, and we no more object to the character of Falstaff in a moral point of view than we should think of bringing an excellent comedian, who should represent him to the life, before one of the police offices. We only consider the number of pleasant lights in which he puts certain foibles (the more pleasant as they are opposed to the received rules and necessary restraints of society) and do not trouble ourselves about the consequences resulting from them, for no mischievous consequences do result. Sir John is old as well as fat, which gives a melancholy restrospective tinge to the character; and by the disparity between his inclinations and his capacity for enjoyment, makes it still more ludicrous and fantastical.

The secret of Falstaff's wit is for the most part a masterly presence of mind, an absolute self-possession, which nothing can disturb. His repartees are involuntary suggestions of his self-love; instinctive evasions of everything that threatens to interrupt the career of his triumphant jollity and self-complacency. His very size floats him out of all his difficulties in a sea of rich conceits; and he turns round on the pivot of his convenience, with every occasion and at a moment's warning. His natural repugnance to every unpleasant thought or circumstance, of itself makes light of objections, and provokes the most extravagant and licentious answers in his own justification. His indifference to truth puts no check upon his invention, and the more improbable and unexpected his contrivances are, the more happily does he seem to be delivered of them, the anticipation of their effect acting as a stimulus to the gaiety of his fancy. The success of one adventurous sally gives him spirits to undertake another: he deals always in round numbers, and his exaggerations and excuses are "open, palpable, monstrous as the father that begets them." His dissolute carelessness of what he says discovers itself in the first dialogue with the Prince.

One of the topics of exulting superiority over others most common in Sir John's mouth is his corpulence and the exterior marks of good living which he carries about him, thus "turning his vices into commodity." He accounts for the friendship between the Prince and Poins, from "their legs being both of a bigness"; and compares Justice Shallow to "a man made after supper of a cheese-paring." There cannot be a more striking gradation of character than that between Falstaff and Shallow, and Shallow and Silence. It seems difficult at first to fall lower than the squire; but this fool, great as he is, finds an admirer and humble foil in his cousin Silence. Vain of his acquaintance with Sir John, who makes a butt of him, he exclaims, "Would, cousin Silence, that thou had'st seen that which this knight and I have seen!"—"Aye, Master Shallow, we have heard the chimes at midnight," says Sir John. To Falstaff's observation "I did not think Master Silence had been a man of this mettle," Silence answers, "Who, I? I have been merry twice and once ere now." What an idea is here conveyed of a prodigality of living? What good husbandry and economical self-denial in his pleasures? What a stock of lively recollections? It is curious that Shakespeare has ridiculed in Justice Shallow, who was "in some authority under the king," that disposition to unmeaning tautology which is the regal infirmity of later times, and which, it may be supposed, he acquired from talking to his cousin Silence, and receiving no answers. . . .

The true spirit of humanity, the thorough knowledge of

the stuff we are made of, the practical wisdom with the seeming fooleries in the whole of the garden-scene at Shallow's country-seat, and just before in the exquisite dialogue between him and Silence on the death of old Double, have no parallel anywhere else. In one point of view, they are laughable in the extreme; in another they are equally affecting, if it is affecting to show *what a little thing is human life*, what a poor forked creature man is!

The heroic and serious part of these two plays founded on the story of Henry IV. is not inferior to the comic and farcical. The characters of Hotspur and Prince Henry are two of the most beautiful and dramatic, both in themselves and from contrast, that ever were drawn. They are the essence of chivalry. We like Hotspur the best upon the whole, perhaps because he was unfortunate.—The characters of their fathers, Henry IV. and old Northumberland, are kept up equally well. Henry naturally succeeds by his prudence and caution in keeping what he has got; Northumberland fails in his enterprise from an excess of the same quality, and is caught in the web of his own cold, dilatory policy. Owen Glendower is a masterly character. It is as bold and original as it is intelligible and thoroughly natural. The disputes between him and Hotspur are managed with infinite address and insight into nature. . . .

The peculiarity and the excellence of Shakespeare's poetry is, that it seems as if he made his imagination the hand-maid of nature, and nature the plaything of his imagination. He appears to have been all the characters, and in all the situations he describes. It is as if either he had had all their feelings, or had lent them all his genius to express themselves. There cannot be stronger instances of this than Hotspur's rage when Henry IV. forbids him to speak of Mortimer, his insensibility to all that his father and uncle urge to calm him, and his fine abstracted apostrophe to honor, "By heaven methinks it were an easy leap to pluck bright honor from the moon," etc. After all, notwithstanding the gallantry, generosity, good temper, and idle freaks of the mad-cap Prince of Wales, we should not have been sorry, if Northumberland's force had come up in time to decide the fate of the battle at Shrewsbury; at least, we always heartily sympathize with Lady Percy's grief, when she exclaims, "Had my sweet Harry had but half their numbers, to-day might I (hanging on Hotspur's neck) have talked of Monmouth's grave."

The Tempest

There can be little doubt that Shakespeare was the most universal genius that ever lived. "Either for tragedy, comedy, history, pastoral, pastoral-comical, historical-pastoral, scene individable or poem unlimited, he is the only man. Seneca cannot be too heavy, nor Plautus too light for him." He has not only the same absolute command over our laughter and our tears, all the resources of passion, of wit, of thought, of observation, but he has the most unbounded range of fanciful invention, whether terrible or playful, the same insight into the world of imagination that he has into the world of reality; and over all there presides the same truth of character and nature, and the same spirit of humanity. His ideal beings are as true and natural as his real characters; that is, as consistent with themselves, or if we suppose such beings to exist at all, they could not act, speak, or feel otherwise than as he makes them. He has invented for them a language, manners, and sentiments of their own, from the tremendous imprecations of the Witches in *Macbeth*, when they do "a deed without a name," to the sylph-like expressions of Ariel, who "does his spiriting gently"; the mischievous tricks and gossiping of Robin Goodfellow, or the uncouth gabbling and emphatic gesticulations of Caliban in this play.

The Tempest is one of the most original and perfect of Shakespeare's productions, and he has shown in it all the variety of his powers. It is full of grace and grandeur. The human and imaginary characters, the dramatic and the grotesque, are blended together with the greatest art, and without any appearance of it. Though he has here given "to airy nothing a local habitation and a name," yet that part which is only the fantastic creation of his mind has the same palpable texture, and coheres "semblably" with the rest. As the preternatural part has the air of reality, and almost haunts the imagination with a sense of truth, the real characters and events partake of the wildness of a dream. The stately magician, Prospero, driven from his dukedom, but around whom (so potent is his art) airy spirits throng numberless to do his bidding; his daughter Miranda ("worthy of that name") to whom all the power of his art points, and who seems the goddess of the isle; the princely Ferdinand, cast by fate upon the haven of his happiness in this idol of his love; the delicate Ariel; the savage Caliban, half brute, half demon; the drunken ship's crew—are all connected parts of the story, and can hardly be spared from the place they fill. Even the local scenery is of a piece and character with the subject. Prospero's enchanted island seems to have risen up out of the sea; the airy music, the tempest-tost vessel, the turbulent waves, all have the effect of the landscape background of some fine picture. Shakespeare's pencil is (to use an allusion of his own) "like the dyer's hand, subdued to what it works in." Everything in him, though it partakes of "the liberty of wit," is also subjected to "the law" of the understanding. For instance, even the drunken sailors, who are made reeling-ripe, share, in the disorder of their minds and bodies, in the tumult of the elements, and seem on shore to be as much at the mercy of chance as they were before at the mercy of the winds and waves. These fellows with their sea-wit are the least to our taste of any part of the play: but they are as like drunken sailors as they can be, and are an indirect foil to Caliban, whose figure acquires a classical dignity in the comparison.

The character of Caliban is generally thought (and justly so) to be one of the author's masterpieces. It is not indeed pleasant to see this character on the stage any more than it is to see the god Pan personated there. But in itself it is one of the wildest and most abstracted of all Shakespeare's characters, whose deformity whether of body or mind is redeemed by the power and truth of the imagination displayed in it. It is the essence of grossness, but there is not a particle of vulgarity in it. Shakespeare has described the brutal mind of Caliban in contact with the pure and original forms of nature; the character grows out of the soil where it is rooted, uncontrolled, uncouth and wild, uncramped by any of the meannesses of custom. It is "of the earth, earthy." It seems almost to have been dug out of the ground, with a soul instinctively superadded to it answering to its wants and origin. Vulgarity is not natural coarseness, but conventional coarseness, learnt from others, contrary to, or without an entire conformity of natural power and disposition; as fashion is the common-place affectation of what is elegant and refined without any feeling of the essence of it. Schlegel, the admirable German critic on Shakespeare, observes that Caliban is a poetical character, and "always speaks in blank verse." . . .

Shakespeare has, as it were by design, drawn off from

Caliban the elements of whatever is ethereal and refined, to compound them in the unearthly mold of Ariel. Nothing was ever more finely conceived than this contrast between the material and the spiritual, the gross and delicate. Ariel is imaginary power, the swiftness of thought personified. When told to make good speed by Prospero, he says, "I drink the air before me." This is something like Puck's boast on a similar occasion, "I'll put a girdle round about the earth in forty minutes." But Ariel differs from Puck in having a fellow feeling in the interests of those he is employed about. How exquisite is the following dialogue between him and Prospero!

> '*Ariel.* Your charm so strongly works 'em,
> That if you now beheld them, your affections
> Would become tender.
> *Prospero.* Dost thou think so, spirit?
> *Ariel.* Mine would, sir, were I human.
> *Prospero.* And mine shall.
> Hast thou, which art but air, a touch, a feeling
> Of their afflictions, and shall not myself,
> One of their kind, that relish all as sharply,
> Passion'd as they, be kindlier moved than thou art?'

The courtship between Ferdinand and Miranda is one of the chief beauties of this play. It is the very purity of love. The pretended interference of Prospero with it heightens its interest, and is in character with the magician, whose sense of preternatural power makes him arbitrary, tetchy, and impatient of opposition.

The Tempest is a finer play than the *Midsummer Night's Dream,* which has sometimes been compared with it; but it is not so fine a poem. There are a greater number of beautiful passages in the latter. Two of the most striking in *The Tempest* are spoken by Prospero. The one is that admirable one when the vision which he has conjured up disappears, beginning "The cloud-capp'd towers, the gorgeous palaces," etc., which has been so often quoted, that every school-boy knows it by heart; the other is that which Prospero makes in abjuring his art.

The Age of Elizabeth

The first lecture from The Dramatic Literature of the Age of Elizabeth *(1820) presents a "general view of the subject," the milieu of dramatists and poets like Marlowe, whose works are then appraised.*

The age of Elizabeth was distinguished beyond perhaps any other in our history by a number of great men, famous in different ways, and whose names have come down to us with unblemished honors; statesmen, warriors, divines, scholars, poets, and philosophers, Raleigh, Coke, Hooker, and higher and more sounding still, and still more frequent in our mouths, Shakespeare, Spenser, Sidney, Bacon, Jonson, Beaumont and Fletcher, men whom fame has eternalized in her long and lasting scroll, and who, by their words and acts, were benefactors of their country and ornaments of human nature. Their attainments of different kinds bore the same general stamp and it was sterling: what they did had the mark of their age and country upon it. Perhaps the genius of Great Britain (if I may so speak without offense or flattery) never shone out fuller or brighter or looked more like itself than at this period. Our writers and great men had something in them that savored of the soil from which they grew: they were not French, they were not Dutch, or German, or Greek, or Latin; they were truly English. They did not look out of themselves to see what they should be; they sought for truth and nature, and found it in themselves. There was no tinsel, and but little art; they were not the spoiled children of affectation and refinement, but a bold, vigorous, independent race of thinkers, with prodigious strength and energy, with none but natural grace and heartfelt unobtrusive delicacy. They were not at all sophisticated. The mind of their country was great in them, and it prevailed. With their learning and unexampled acquirements, they did not forget that they were men: with all their endeavors after excellence, they did not lay aside the strong original bent and character of their minds. What they performed was chiefly nature's handy-work; and time has claimed it for his own. To these, however, might be added others not less learned, nor with a scarce less happy vein, but less fortunate in the event, who, though as renowned in their day, have sunk into "mere oblivion," and of whom the only record (but that the noblest) is to be found in their works. Their works and their names, "poor, poor dumb names," are all that remain of such men as Webster, Dekker, Marston, Marlowe, Chapman, Heywood, Middleton, and Rowley! "How lov'd, how honor'd once, avails them not": though they were the friends and fellow-laborers of Shakespeare, sharing his fame and fortunes with him, the rivals of Jonson, and the masters of Beaumont and Fletcher's well-sung woes! They went out one by one unnoticed, like evening lights; or were swallowed up in the headlong torrent of puritanic zeal which succeeded and swept away everything in its unsparing course, throwing up the wrecks of taste and genius at random, and at long fitful intervals amidst the painted gew-gaws and foreign frippery of the reign of Charles II and from which we are only now recovering the scattered fragments and broken images to erect a temple to true Fame! How long before it will be completed?

If I can do anything to rescue some of these writers from hopeless obscurity, and to do them right, without prejudice to well-deserved reputation, I shall have succeeded in what I chiefly propose. I shall not attempt, indeed, to adjust the spelling, or restore the pointing, as if the genius of poetry lay hid in errors of the press, but leaving these weightier matters of criticism to those who are more able and willing to bear the burden, try to bring out their real beauties to the eager sight, "draw the curtain of Time, and show the picture of Genius," restraining my own admiration within reasonable bounds!

There is not a lower ambition, a poorer way of thought, than that which would confine all excellence, or arrogate its final accomplishment to the present or modern times. We ordinarily speak and think of those who had the misfortune to write or live before us, as laboring under very singular privations and disadvantages in not having the benefit of those improvements which we have made, as buried in the grossest ignorance, or the slaves of "poring pedantry"; and we make a cheap and infallible estimate of their progress in civilization upon a graduated scale of perfectibility calculated from the meridian of our own times. If we have pretty well got rid of the narrow bigotry that would limit all sense or virtue to our own country, and have fraternized, like true cosmopolites, with our neighbors and contemporaries, we have made our self-love amends by letting the generation we live in engross nearly all our admiration and by pronouncing a sweeping sentence of barbarism and ignorance on our ancestry backwards, from the commencement (as near as can be) of the nineteenth or the latter end of the eighteenth century. From thence we date a new era, the dawn of our own intellect and that of the world, like "the sacred influence of light" glimmering on the confines of Chaos and old night; new manners rise and all the cumbrous "pomp of elder days" vanishes, and is lost in worse than Gothic darkness. Pavilioned in the glittering pride of our superficial accomplishments and upstart pretensions, we fancy that everything beyond that magic circle is prejudice and error; and all, before the present enlightened period, but a dull and useless blank in the great map of time. . . . A falser inference could not be drawn, nor one more contrary to the maxims and cautions of a wise humanity. "Think," says Shakespeare, the prompter of good and true feelings, "there's livers out of Britain." So there have been thinkers, and great and sound ones, before our time. They had the same capacities that we have, sometimes greater motives for their exertion, and, for the most part, the same subject-matter to work upon. What we learn from nature, we may hope to do as well as they; what we learn from them, we may in general expect to do worse. What is, I think, as likely as anything to cure us of this overweening admiration of the present and unmingled contempt for past times is the looking at the finest old pictures; at Raphael's heads, at Titian's faces, at Claude's landscapes. We have there the evidence of the senses, without the alterations of opinion or disguise of language. We there see the blood circulate through the veins, the same red and white "by nature's own sweet and cunning hand laid on," the same thoughts passing through the mind and seated on the lips, the same blue sky and glittering sunny vales, "where Pan, knit with the Graces and the Hours in dance, leads on the eternal spring." And we begin to feel that nature and the mind of man are not a thing of yesterday, as we had been led to suppose; and that "there are more things between heaven and earth than were ever dreamt of in our philosophy." . . .

It is the present fashion to speak with veneration of old English literature; but the homage we pay to it is more akin to the rites of superstition than the worship of true religion. Our faith is doubtful; our love cold; our knowledge little or none. We now and then repeat the names of some of the old writers by rote; but we are shy of looking into their works. Though we seem disposed to think highly of them, and to give them every credit for a masculine and original vein of thought, as a matter of literary courtesy and enlargement of taste, we are afraid of coming to the proof, as too great a trial of our candor and patience. . . .

One cause that might be pointed out here, as having contributed to the long-continued neglect of our earlier writers, lies in the very nature of our academic institutions, which unavoidably neutralizes a taste for the productions of native genius, estranges the mind from the history of our own literature, and makes it in each successive age like a book sealed. The Greek and Roman classics are a sort of privileged text-books, the standing order of the day, in a University education, and leave little leisure for a competent acquaintance with, or due admiration of, a whole host of able writers of our own, who are suffered to molder in obscurity on the shelves of our libraries, with a decent reservation of one or two top-names, that are cried up for form's sake, and to save the national character. Thus we keep a few of these always ready in capitals, and strike off the rest, to prevent the tendency to a superfluous population in the republic of letters; in other words, to prevent the writers from becoming more numerous than the readers. The ancients are become effete in this respect, they no longer increase and multiply; or if they have imitators among us, no one is expected to read, and still less to admire them. It is not possible that the learned professors and the reading public should clash in this way, or necessary for them to use any precautions against each other. But it is not the same with the living languages, where there is danger of being overwhelmed by the crowd of competitors; and pedantry has combined with ignorance to cancel their unsatisfied claims.

We affect to wonder at Shakespeare, and one or two more of that period, as solitary instances upon record; whereas it is our own dearth of information that makes the waste; for there is no time more populous of intellect, or more prolific of intellectual wealth, than the one we are speaking of. Shakespeare did not look upon himself in this light, as a sort of monster of poetical genius, or on his contemporaries as "less than smallest dwarfs," when he speaks with true, not false modesty, of himself and them, and of his wayward thoughts, "desiring this man's art, and that man's scope." We fancy that there were no such men that could either add to or take any thing away from him, but such there were. He indeed overlooks and commands the admiration of posterity, but he does it from the *tableland* of the age in which he lived. He towered above his fellows, "in shape and gesture proudly eminent"; but he was one of a race of giants, the tallest, the strongest, the most graceful, and beautiful of them; but it was a common and a noble brood. He was not something sacred and aloof from the vulgar herd of men, but shook hands with nature and the circumstances of the time, and is distinguished from his immediate contemporaries not in kind but in degree and greater variety of excellence. He did not form a class or species by himself, but belonged to a class or species. His age was necessary to him; nor could he have been wrenched from his place in the edifice of which he was so conspicuous a part, without equal injury to himself and it. Mr. Wordsworth says of Milton, "that his soul was like a star, and dwelt apart." This cannot be said with any propriety of Shakespeare, who certainly moved in a constellation of bright luminaries, and "drew after him a third part of the heavens." With the exception of a single writer, Otway, and of a single play of his (*Venice Preserved*) there is nobody in tragedy and dramatic poetry (I do not here speak of comedy) to be compared to the great men of the age of Shakespeare and immediately after. They are a mighty phalanx of kindred spirits closing him round, moving in the same orbit, and impelled by the same causes in their whirling and eccentric career. They had the same faults and the same excellences; the same strength and depth and richness, the same truth of character, passion, imagination, thought and language, thrown, heaped, massed together without careful polishing or exact method, but poured out in unconcerned profusion from the lap of nature and genius in boundless and unrivalled magnificence. The sweetness of Dekker, the thought of Marston, the gravity of Chapman, the grace of Fletcher and his young-eyed wit, Jonson's learned sock, the flowing vein of Middleton, Heywood's ease, the pathos of Webster, and Marlowe's deep designs, add a double lustre to the sweetness, thought, gravity, grace, wit, artless nature, copiousness, ease, pathos, and sublime conceptions of Shakespeare's Muse. For such an extraordinary combination and development of fancy and genius many causes may be assigned; and we may seek for the chief of them in religion, in politics, in the circumstances of the time, the recent diffusion of letters, in local situation, and in the character of the men who adorned that period.

The first cause I shall mention as contributing to this general effect was the Reformation, which had just then taken place. This event gave a mighty impulse and increased activity to thought and inquiry, and agitated the inert mass of accumulated prejudices throughout Europe. The effect of the concussion was general; but the shock was greatest in this country. It toppled down the full-grown, intolerable abuses of centuries at a blow; heaved the ground from under the feet of bigoted faith and slavish obedience; and the roar and dashing of opinions, loosened from their accustomed hold, might be heard like the noise of an angry sea, and has never yet subsided. . . . The translation of the Bible was the chief engine in the great work. It threw open, by a secret spring, the rich treasures of religion and morality, which had been there locked up as in a shrine. It revealed the visions of the prophets, and conveyed the lessons of inspired teachers to the meanest of the people. It gave them a common interest in the common cause. Their hearts burnt within them as they read. It gave a *mind* to the people by giving them common subjects of thought and feeling. . . . There have been persons who, being sceptics as to the divine mission of Christ, have taken an unaccountable prejudice to his doctrines, and have been disposed to deny the merit of his character; but this was not the feeling of the great men in the age of Elizabeth, one of whom says of him, with a boldness equal to its piety:

> The best of men
> That e'er wore earth about him was a sufferer;
> A soft, meek, patient, humble, tranquil spirit;
> The first true gentleman that ever breathed.

This was old honest Dekker, and the lines ought to embalm his memory to every one who has a sense of religion, or philosophy, or humanity, or true genius. Nor can I help thinking that we may discern the traces of the influence exerted by religious faith in the spirit of the poetry of the age of Elizabeth, in the means of exciting terror and pity, in the delineation of the passions of grief, remorse, love, sympathy, the sense of shame, in the fond desires, the longings after immortality, in the heaven of hope, and the abyss of despair it lays open to us.

The effects of the Reformation on politics and philosophy may be seen in the writings and history of the next and of the following ages. They are still at work and will continue to be so. The effects on the poetry of the time were chiefly confined to the molding of the character, and giving a powerful impulse to the intellect of the country.

For much about the same time, the rich and fascinating stores of the Greek and Roman mythology, and those of the romantic poetry of Spain and Italy, were eagerly explored by the curious, and thrown open in translations to the admiring gaze of the vulgar. This last circumstance could hardly have afforded so much advantage to the poets of the day, who were themselves the translators. . . . There were translations of Tasso by Fairfax, and of Ariosto by Harrington, of Homer and Hesiod by Chapman, and of Virgil long before, and Ovid soon after; there was Sir Thomas North's translation of Plutarch, of which Shakespeare has made such admirable use in his *Coriolanus* and *Julius Caesar* and Ben Jonson's tragedies of *Catiline* and *Sejanus* may themselves be considered as almost literal translations into verse of Tacitus, Sallust, and Cicero's orations in his consulship. Boccacio, Petrarch, Dante, the satirist Aretine, Machiavel, Castiglione, and others, were familiar to our writers, and they make occasional mention of some few French authors, as Ronsard and Du Bartas. . . .

What also gave an unusual impetus to the mind of man at this period was the discovery of the New World, and the reading of voyages and travels. Green islands and golden sands seemed to arise, as by enchantment, out of the bosom of the watery waste, and invite the cupidity, or wing the imagination of the dreaming speculator. Fairy land was realized in new and unknown worlds. The people, the soil, the clime, everything gave unlimited scope to the curiosity of the traveler and reader. Other manners might be said to enlarge the bounds of knowledge, and new mines of wealth were tumbled at our feet. It is from a voyage to the Straits of Magellan that Shakespeare has taken the hint of Prospero's Enchanted Island, and of the savage Caliban with his god Setebos. Spenser seems to have had the same feeling in his mind in the production of his *Faery Queen,* and vindicates his poetic fiction on this very ground of analogy. . . . Again, the heroic and martial spirit which breathes in our elder writers was yet in considerable activity in the reign of Elizabeth. "The age of chivalry was not then quite gone, nor the glory of Europe extinguished for ever." Jousts and tournaments were still common with the nobility in England and in foreign countries: Sir Philip Sidney was particularly distinguished for his proficiency in these exercises (and indeed fell a martyr to his ambition as a soldier)—and the gentle Surrey was still more famous, on the same account, just before him. It is true, the general use of firearms gradually superseded the necessity of skill in the sword, or bravery in the person; and as a symptom of the rapid degeneracy in this respect, we find Sir John Suckling soon after boasting of himself as one—

> *Who prized black eyes, and a lucky hit*
> *At bowls, above all the trophies of wit.*

Lastly, to conclude this account; what gave a unity and common direction to all these causes was the natural genius of the country, which was strong in these writers in proportion to their strength. We are a nation of islanders and we cannot help it; nor mend ourselves if we would. We are something in ourselves, nothing when we try to ape others. Music and painting are not our *forte*: for what we have done in that way has been little, and that borrowed from others and with great difficulty. But we may boast of our poets and philosophers. That's something. We have had strong heads and sound hearts among us.

Marlowe

Marlowe is a name that stands high, and almost first in this list of dramatic worthies. He was a little before Shakespeare's time, and has a marked character both from him and the rest. There is a lust of power in his writings, a hunger and thirst after unrighteousness, a glow of the imagination, unhallowed by any thing but its own energies. His thoughts burn within him like a furnace with bickering flames; or throwing out black smoke and mists, that hide the dawn of genius, or like a poisonous mineral, corrode the heart. His *Life and Death of Doctor Faustus*, though an imperfect and unequal performance, is his greatest work. Faustus himself is a rude sketch, but it is a gigantic one. This character may be considered as a personification of the pride of will and eagerness of curiosity, sublimed beyond the reach of fear and remorse. He is hurried away, and, as it were, devoured by a tormenting desire to enlarge his knowledge to the utmost bounds of nature and art, and to extend his power with his knowledge. He would realize all the fictions of a lawless imagination, would solve the most subtle speculations of abstract reason; and for this purpose, sets at defiance all mortal consequences, and leagues himself with demoniacal power, with "fate and metaphysical aid." The idea of witchcraft and necromancy, once the dread of the vulgar and the darling of the visionary recluse, seems to have had its origin in the restless tendency of the human mind to conceive of and aspire to more than it can achieve by natural means. Such is the foundation of the present story. Faustus, in his impatience to fulfil at once and for a moment, for a few short years, all the desires and conceptions of his soul, is willing to give in exchange his soul and body to the great enemy of mankind. Whatever he fancies becomes by this means present to his sense; whatever he commands is done. He calls back time past and anticipates the future: the visions of antiquity pass before him, Babylon in all its glory, Paris and Oenone: all the projects of philosophers, or creations of the poet pay tribute at his feet: all the delights of fortune, of ambition, of pleasure, and of learning are centered in his person; and from a short-lived dream of supreme felicity and drunken power, he sinks into an abyss of darkness and perdition. This is the alternative to which he submits; the bond which he signs with his blood! As the outline of the character is grand and daring, the execution is abrupt and fearful. The thoughts are vast and irregular; and the style halts and staggers under them, "with uneasy steps." There is a little fustian and incongruity of metaphor now and then, which is not very injurious to the subject.

I do not think the *Rich Jew of Malta* so characteristic a specimen of this writer's powers. It has not the same fierce glow of passion or expression. It is extreme in act and outrageous in plot and catastrophe; but it has not the same vigorous filling up. The author seems to have relied on the horror inspired by the subject, and the national disgust excited against the principal character, to rouse the feelings of the audience: for the rest, it is a tissue of gratuitous, unprovoked, and incredible atrocities, which are committed, one upon the back of the other, by the parties concerned, without motive, passion, or object. There are, notwithstanding, some striking passages in it, as Barabbas's description of the bravo, Philia Borzo; the relation of his own unaccountable villainies to Ithamore; his rejoicing over his recovered jewels "as the morning lark sings over her young"; and the backwardness he declares in himself to forgive the Christian injuries that are offered him, which may have given the idea of one of Shylock's speeches, where he ironically disclaims any enmity to the merchants on the same account.

Edward II is, according to the modern standard of composition, Marlowe's best play. It is written with few offenses against the common rules, and in a succession of smooth and flowing lines. The poet however succeeds less in the voluptuous and effeminate descriptions which he here attempts than in the more dreadful and violent bursts of passion. *Edward II* is drawn with historic truth, but without much dramatic effect. The management of the plot is feeble and desultory; little interest is excited in the various turns of fate; the characters are too worthless, have too little energy, and their punishment is, in general, too well deserved to excite our commiseration; so that this play will bear, on the whole, but a distant comparison with Shakespeare's *Richard II* in conduct, power, or effect. But the death of Edward II in Marlowe's tragedy is certainly superior to that of Shakespeare's King; and in heart-breaking distress, and the sense of human weakness, claiming pity from utter helplessness and conscious misery, is not surpassed by any writer whatever.

On Reading Old Books

Hazlitt's wit, clarity of style, and "love of paradoxes" are characteristic of his familiar essays, such as the following, which first appeared in the London Magazine *(February, 1821).*

I hate to read new books. There are twenty or thirty volumes that I have read over and over again, and these are the only ones that I have any desire ever to read at all. It was a long time before I could bring myself to sit down to the *Tales of My Landlord,* but now that author's works have made a considerable addition to my scanty library. I am told that some of Lady Morgan's are good, and have been recommended to look into *Anastasius;* but I have not yet ventured upon that task. A lady, the other day, could not refrain from expressing her surprise to a friend, who said he had been reading *Delphine:*—she asked,—If it had not been published some time back? Women judge of books as they do of fashions or complexions, which are admired only "in their newest gloss." That is not my way. I am not one of those who trouble the circulating libraries much, or pester the booksellers for mail-coach copies of standard periodical publications. I cannot say that I am greatly addicted to black-letter, but I profess myself well versed in the marble bindings of Andrew Millar in the middle of the last century; nor does my taste revolt at Thurlow's *State Papers,* in russia leather; or an ample impression of Sir William Temple's *Essays,* with a portrait after Sir Godfrey Kneller in front. I do not think altogether the worse of a book for having survived the author a generation or two. I have more confidence in the dead than the living. Contemporary writers may generally be divided into two classes—one's friends or one's foes. Of the first we are compelled to think too well, and of the last we are disposed to think too ill, to receive much genuine pleasure from the perusal, or to judge fairly of the merits of either. One candidate for literary fame, who happens to be of our acquaintance, writes finely, and like a man of genius; but unfortunately has a foolish face, which spoils a delicate passage:—another inspires us with the highest respect for his personal talents and character, but does not quite come up to our expectations in print. All these con-

tradictions and petty details interrupt the calm current of
our reflections. If you want to know what any of the
authors were who lived before our time, and are still objects of anxious inquiry, you have only to look into their
works. But the dust and smoke and noise of modern literature have nothing in common with the pure, silent air of
immortality.

When I take up a work that I have read before (the
oftener the better) I know what I have to expect. The
satisfaction is not lessened by being anticipated. When the
entertainment is altogether new, I sit down to it as I should
to a strange dish,—turn and pick out a bit here and there,
and am in doubt what to think of the composition. There
is a want of confidence and security to second appetite.
New-fangled books are also like made-dishes in this respect, that they are generally little else than hashes and
rifaccimenti of what has been served up entire and in a
more natural state at other times. Besides, in thus turning
to a well-known author, there is not only an assurance
that my time will not be thrown away, or my palate nau-
seated with the most insipid or vilest trash,—but I shake
hands with, and look an old, tired, and valued friend in
the face,—compare notes, and chat the hours away. It is
true, we form dear friendships with such ideal guests—
dearer, alas! and more lasting, than those with our most
intimate acquaintance. In reading a book which is an old
favorite with me (say the first novel I ever read) I not
only have the pleasure of imagination and of a critical
relish of the work, but the pleasures of memory added to
it. It recalls the same feelings and associations which I had
in first reading it, and which I can never have again in
any other way. Standard productions of this kind are links
in the chain of our conscious being. They bind together the
different scattered divisions of our personal identity. They
are landmarks and guides in our journey through life.
They are pegs and loops on which we can hang up, or
from which we can take down, at pleasure, the wardrobe
of a moral imagination, the relics of our best affections,
the tokens and records of our happiest hours. They are
"for thoughts and for remembrance!" They are like For-
tunatus's Wishing-Cap—they give us the best riches—
those of Fancy; and transport us, not over half the globe,
but (which is better) over half our lives, at a word's
notice!

My father Shandy solaced himself with Bruscambille. Give me for this purpose a volume of *Peregrine Pickle* or *Tom Jones*. Open either of them anywhere—at the Memoirs of Lady Vane, or the adventures at the masquerade with Lady Bellaston, or the disputes between Thwackum and Square, or the escape of Molly Seagrim, or the incident of Sophia and her muff, or the edifying prolixity of her aunt's lecture—and there I find the same delightful, busy, bustling scene as ever, and feel myself the same as when I was first introduced into the midst of it. Nay, sometimes the sight of an odd volume of these good old English authors on a stall, or the name lettered on the back among others on the shelves of a library, answers the purpose, revives the whole train of ideas, and sets "the puppets dallying." Twenty years are struck off the list, and I am a child again. A sage philosopher, who was not a very wise man, said, that he should like very well to be young again, if he could take his experience along with him. This ingenious person did not seem to be aware, by the gravity of his remark, that the great advantage of being young is to be without this weight of experience, which he would fain place upon the shoulders of youth, and which never comes too late with years. Oh! what a privilege to be able to let this hump, like Christian's burthen, drop from off one's back, and transport oneself, by the help of a little musty duodecimo, to the time when "ignorance was bliss," and when we first got a peep at the raree-show of the world, through the glass of fiction—gazing at mankind, as we do at wild beasts in a menagerie, through the bars of their cages,— or at curiosities in a museum, that we must not touch! For myself, not only are the old ideas of the contents of the work brought back to my mind in all their vividness, but the old associations of the faces and persons of those I then knew, as they were in their life-time—the place where I sat to read the volume, the day when I got it, the feeling of the air, the fields, the sky—return, and all my early impressions with them. This is better to me— those places, those times, those persons, and those feelings that come across me as I retrace the story and devour the page, are to me better far than the wet sheets of the last new novel from the Ballantyne press, to say nothing of the Minerva press in Leadenhall Street. It is like visiting the scenes of early youth. I think of the time "when I was in my father's house, and my path ran down with butter and honey,"—when I was a little, thoughtless child, and had no other wish or care but to con my daily task, and be happy!—*Tom Jones,* I remember, was the first work that broke the spell. It came down in numbers once a fortnight, in Cooke's pocket-edition, embellished with cuts. I had hitherto read only in school-books, and a tiresome ecclesiastical history (with the exception of Mrs. Radcliffe's *Romance of the Forest*): but this had a different relish with it,—"sweet in the mouth," though not "bitter in the belly." It smacked of the world I lived in, and in which I was to live—and showed me groups, "gay creatures" not "of the element," but of the earth; not "living in the clouds," but travelling the same road that I did;—some that had passed on before me, and others that might soon overtake me. My heart had palpitated at the thoughts of a boarding-school ball, or gala-day at Midsummer or Christmas: but the world I had found out in Cooke's edition of the *British Novelists* was to me a dance through life, a perpetual gala-day. The sixpenny numbers of this work regularly contrived to leave off just in the middle of a sentence, and in the nick of a story, where Tom Jones discovers Square behind the blanket; or where Parson Adams, in the inextricable confusion of events, very undesignedly gets to bed to Mrs. Slip-slop. Let me caution the reader against this impression of Joseph Andrews; for there is a picture of Fanny in it which he should not set his heart on, lest he should never meet with anything like it; or if he should, it would, perhaps, be better for him that he had not. It was just like —— ——! With what eagerness I used to look forward to the next number, and open the prints! Ah! never again shall I feel the enthusiastic delight with which I gazed at the figures, and anticipated the story and adventures of Major Bath and Commodore Trunnion, of Trim and my Uncle Toby, of Don Quixote and Sancho and Dapple, of Gil Blas and Dame Lorenza Sephora, or Laura and the fair Lucretia, whose lips open and shut like buds of roses. To what nameless ideas did they give rise,— with what airy delights I filled up the outlines, as I hung in silence over the page!—Let me still recall them, that they may breathe fresh life into me, and that I may live that birthday of thought and romantic pleasure over again! Talk of the *ideal!* This is the only true ideal—the heavenly tints of Fancy reflected in the bubbles that float upon the spring-tide of human life. . . .

On the Metaphysical Poets

Although Hazlitt disliked Donne's "oblique and forced construction," his criticism of the Metaphysical Poets in On the English Comic Writers *(1819) is in general sympathetic, and forms an interesting contrast to his treatment of Milton.*

The metaphysical poets or wits of the age of James and Charles I, whose style was adopted and carried to a more dazzling and fantastic excess by Cowley in the following reign, after which it declined and gave place almost entirely to the poetry of observation and reasoning, are thus happily characterized by Dr. Johnson:

> The metaphysical poets were men of learning, and to show their learning was their whole endeavor: but unluckily resolving to show it in rhyme, instead of writing poetry, they only wrote verses, and very often such verses as stood the trial of the finger better than of the ear; for the modulation was so imperfect, that they were only found to be verses by counting the syllables.

The writers here referred to (such as Donne, Davies, Crashaw, and others) not merely mistook learning for poetry—they thought anything was poetry that differed from ordinary prose and the natural impression of things, by being intricate, far-fetched, and improbable. Their style was not so properly learned as metaphysical; that is to say, whenever, by any violence done to their ideas, they could make out an abstract likeness or possible ground of comparison, they forced the image, whether learned or vulgar, into the service of the Muses. Anything would do to "hitch into a rhyme," no matter whether striking or agreeable, or not, so that it would puzzle the reader to discover the meaning, and if there was the most remote circumstance, however trifling or vague, for the pretended comparison to hinge upon. They brought ideas together not the most, but the least like; and of which the collision produced not light, but obscurity—served not to strengthen, but to confound. Their mystical verses read like riddles or an allegory. They neither belong to the class of lively or severe poetry. They have not the force of the one, nor the gaiety of the other; but are an ill-assorted, unprofitable union of the two together, applying to serious subjects that quaint and partial

54

style of allusion which fits only what is light and ludicrous, and building the most labored conclusions on the most fantastical and slender premises. The object of the poetry of imagination is to raise or adorn one idea by another more striking or more beautiful: the object of these writers was to match any one idea with any other idea, for better for worse, as we say, and whether anything was gained by the change of condition or not. The object of the poetry of the passions again is to illustrate any strong feeling, by showing the same feeling as connected with objects or circumstances more palpable and touching; but here the object was to strain and distort the immediate feeling into some barely possible consequence or recondite analogy, in which it required the utmost stretch of misapplied ingenuity to trace the smallest connection with the original impression. In short, the poetry of this period was strictly the poetry not of ideas, but of *definitions*: it proceeded in mode and figure, by *genus* and specific difference; and was the logic of the schools, or an oblique and forced construction of dry, literal matter-of-fact, decked out in a robe of glittering conceits and clogged with the halting shackles of verse. The imagination of the writers, instead of being conversant with the face of nature, or the secrets of the heart, was lost in the labyrinths of intellectual abstraction, or entangled in the technical quibbles and impertinent intricacies of language. The complaint so often made, and here repeated, is not of the want of power in these men, but of the waste of it; not of the absence of genius, but the abuse of it. They had (many of them) great talents committed to their trust, richness of thought, and depth of feeling; but they chose to hide them (as much as they possibly could) under a false show of learning and unmeaning subtlety. From the style which they had systematically adopted, they thought nothing done till they had perverted simplicity into affectation, and spoiled nature by art. They seemed to think there was an irreconcilable opposition between genius as well as grace and nature; tried to do without, or else constantly to thwart her; left nothing to her outward impress, or spontaneous impulses, but made a point of twisting and torturing almost every subject they took in hand till they had fitted it to the mold of their self-opinion and the previous fabrications of their own fancy, like those who pen acrostics in the shape of pyramids, and cut out trees into the shape of peacocks.

Their chief aim is to make you wonder at the writer, not to interest you in the subject; and by an incessant craving after admiration, they have lost what they might have gained with less extravagance and affectation. Donne, who was considerably before Cowley, is without his fancy, but was more recondite in his logic and rigid in his descriptions. He is hence led, particularly in his satires, to tell disagreeable truths in as disagreeable a way as possible, or to convey a pleasing and affecting thought (of which there are many to be found in his other writings) by the harshest means and with the most painful effort. His Muse suffers continual pangs and throes. His thoughts are delivered by the Caesarean operation. The sentiments, profound and tender as they often are, are stifled in the expression; and "heaved pantingly forth" are "buried quick again" under the ruins and rubbish of analytical distinctions. It is like poetry waking from a trance: with an eye bent idly on the outward world and half-forgotten feelings crowding about the heart; with vivid impressions, dim notions, and disjointed words. The following may serve as instances of beautiful or impassioned reflections losing themselves in obscure and difficult applications. He has some lines to a Blossom, which begin thus:

> *Little think'st thou, poor flow'r,*
> *Whom I have watched six or seven days,*
> *And seen thy birth, and seen what every hour*
> *Gave to thy growth, thee to this height to raise,*
> *And now dost laugh and triumph on this bough,*
> > *Little think'st thou*
> *That it will freeze anon, and that I shall*
> *To-morrow find thee fall'n, or not at all.*

This simple and delicate description is only introduced as a foundation for an elaborate metaphysical conceit as a parallel to it, in the next stanza.

> *Little think'st thou (poor heart*
> *That labour'st yet to nestle thee,*
> *And think'st by hovering here to get a part*
> *In a forbidden or forbidding tree,*
> *And hop'st her stiffness by long siege to bow:)*
> > *Little think'st thou,*
> *That thou to-morrow, ere the sun doth wake,*
> *Must with this sun and me a journey take.*

This is but a lame and impotent conclusion from so delightful a beginning. He thus notices the circumstance of
his wearing his late wife's hair about his arm, in a little
poem which is called the Funeral:

> *Whoever comes to shroud me, do not harm*
> > *Nor question much*
> *That subtle wreath of hair, about mine arm;*
> *The mystery, the sign you must not touch.*

The scholastic reason he gives quite dissolves the charm
of tender and touching grace in the sentiment itself—

> *For 'tis my outward soul,*
> *Viceroy to that, which unto heaven being gone,*
> > *Will leave this to control,*
> *And keep these limbs, her provinces, from dissolution.*

Again, the following lines, the title of which is Love's
Deity, are highly characteristic of this author's manner, in
which the thoughts are inlaid in a costly but imperfect
mosaic work.

> *I long to talk with some old lover's ghost,*
> *Who died before the God of Love was born:*
> *I cannot think that he, who then lov'd most,*
> *Sunk so low, as to love one which did scorn.*
> *But since this God produc'd a destiny,*
> *And that vice-nature, custom, lets it be;*
> *I must love her that loves not me.*

The stanza in the Epithalamion on a Count Palatine of
the Rhine, has been often quoted against him, and is an
almost irresistible illustration of the extravagances to which
this kind of writing, which turns upon a pivot of words
and possible allusions, is liable. Speaking of the bride and
bridegroom he says, by way of serious compliment—

> *Here lies a she-Sun, and a he-Moon there,*
> *She gives the best light to his sphere;*
> *Or each is both and all, and so*
> *They unto one another nothing owe.*

His love-verses and epistles to his friends give the most

favorable idea of Donne. His satires are too clerical. He shows, if I may so speak, too much disgust, and, at the same time, too much contempt for vice. His dogmatical invectives hardly redeem the nauseousness of his descriptions, and compromise the imagination of his readers more than they assist their reason. The satirist does not write with the same authority as the divine, and should use his poetical privileges more sparingly. "To the pure all things are pure" is a maxim which a man like Dr. Donne may be justified in applying to himself; but he might have recollected that it could not be construed to extend to the generality of his readers, *without benefit of clergy.* . . .

Crashaw was a writer of the same ambitious stamp whose imagination was rendered still more inflammable by the fervors of fanaticism, and who having been converted from Protestantism to Popery (a weakness to which the "seething brains" of the poets of this period were prone) by some visionary appearance of the Virgin Mary, poured out his devout raptures and zealous enthusiasm in a torrent of poetical hyperboles. The celebrated Latin Epigram on the miracle of our Saviour, "The water blushed into wine," is in his usual *hectic* manner. His translation of the contest between the Musician and the Nightingale is the best specimen of his powers. . . .

On Milton

In attempting to restore Milton's "force of imagina-
tion" to the summit of English poetry, Hazlitt in-
fluenced the revival of interest in the epic genre, while
his criticism, with its emphasis on the poetry itself,
remains uniquely modern. It was published in Lectures
on the English Poets.

Shakespeare discovers in his writings little religious enthusiasm, and an indifference to personal reputation; he
had none of the bigotry of his age; and his political prejudices were not very strong. In these respects, as well as
in every other, he formed a direct contrast to Milton. Milton's works are a perpetual invocation to the Muses, a
hymn to Fame. He had his thoughts constantly fixed on the
contemplation of the Hebrew theocracy, and of a perfect
commonwealth; and he seized the pen with a hand just
warm from the touch of the ark of faith. His religious zeal
infused its character into his imagination; so that he de-
votes himself with the same sense of duty to the cultivation
of his genius, as he did to the exercise of virtue or the good
of his country. The spirit of the poet, the patriot, and the
prophet vied with each other in his breast. His mind appears to have held equal communion with the inspired
writers, and with the bards and sages of ancient Greece
and Rome. He had a high standard with which he was
always comparing himself, nothing short of which could
satisfy his jealous ambition. He thought of nobler forms
and nobler things than those he found about him. He lived
apart in the solitude of his own thoughts, carefully exclud-
ing from his mind whatever might distract its purposes,
or alloy its purity, or damp its zeal. "With darkness and
with dangers compassed round," he had the mighty models
of antiquity always present to his thoughts, and determined
to raise a monument of equal height and glory; "piling up
every stone of lustre from the brook," for the delights and
wonder of posterity. He had girded himself up, and, as it
were, sanctified his genius to this service from his youth.
He adorns and dignifies his subject to the utmost: he surrounds it with every possible association of beauty or
grandeur, whether moral, intellectual, or physical. He refines on his descriptions of beauty, loading sweets on sweets,
till the sense aches at them, and raises his images of terror

to a gigantic elevation, that "makes Ossa like a wart." In Milton, there is always an appearance of effort: in Shakespeare, scarcely any.

Milton has borrowed more than any other writer, and exhausted every source of imitation, sacred or profane; yet he is perfectly distinct from every other writer. He is a writer of centos, and yet in originality scarcely inferior to Homer. The power of his mind is stamped on every line. The fervor of his imagination melts down and renders malleable, as in a furnace, the most contradictory materials. In reading his works, we feel oursevles under the influence of a mighty intellect that, the nearer it approaches to others, becomes more distinct from them. The quantity of art in him shows the strength of his genius: the weight of his intellectual obligations would have oppressed any other writer. Milton's learning has the effect of intuition. He describes objects, of which he could only have read in books, with the vividness of actual observation. His imagination has the force of nature. He makes words tell as pictures:

> *Him followeth Rimmon, whose delightful seat*
> *Was fair Damascus, on the fertile banks*
> *Of Abbana and Pharphar, lucid streams.*

The word lucid here gives to the idea all the sparkling effect of the most perfect landscape.

We might be tempted to suppose that the vividness with which he describes visible objects was owing to their having acquired an unusual degree of strength in his mind after the privation of his sight; but we find the same palpableness and truth in the descriptions which occur in his early poems. In *Lycidas,* he speaks of "the great vision of the guarded mount," with that preternatural weight of impression with which it would present itself suddenly to "the pilot of some small night-foundered skiff:" and the lines in the *Penseroso,* describing "the wandering moon,"

> *Riding near her highest noon,*
> *Like one that hath been led astray*
> *Through the heaven's wide pathless way,*

are as if he had gazed himself blind in looking at her. There is also the same depth of impression in his descriptions of the objects of all the different senses, whether colors, or sounds, or smells—the same absorption of his mind in whatever engaged his attention at the time. It has been indeed objected to Milton by a common perversity of criticism, that his ideas were musical rather than picturesque, as if, because they were in the highest degree musical, they must be (to keep the sage critical balance even, and to allow no one man to possess two qualities at the same time) proportionably deficient in other respects. But Milton's poetry is not cast in any such narrow, commonplace mold: it is not so barren of resources; his worship of the Muse was not so simple or confined. A sound arises "like a steam of rich distilled perfumes;" we hear the pealing organ; but the incense on the altars is also there, and the statues of the gods are ranged around! The ear indeed predominates over the eye, because it is more immediately affected, and because the language of music blends more immediately with, and forms a more natural accompaniment to, the variable and indefinite associations of ideas conveyed by words. But where the associations of the imagination are not the principal thing, the individual object is given by Milton with equal force and beauty. The strongest and best proof of this, as a characteristic power of his mind, is that the persons of Adam and Eve, of Satan, are always accompanied, in our imagination, with the grandeur of the naked figure; they convey to us the ideas of sculpture.

Again, nothing can be more magnificent than the portrait of Beelzebub:

> *With Atlantean shoulders fit to bear*
> *The weight of mightiest monarchies:*

Or the comparison of Satan, as he "lay floating many a rood," to "that sea beast,"

> *Leviathan, which God of all his works*
> *Created hugest that swim the ocean-stream!*

What a force of imagination is there in this last expression! What an idea it conveys of the size of that hugest of created beings, as if it shrunk up the ocean to a stream, and took up the sea in its nostrils as a very little thing! Force of style is one of Milton's greatest excellences.

Hence, perhaps, he stimulates us more in the reading, and less afterwards. The way to defend Milton against all impugners is to take down the book and read it.

Milton's blank verse is the only blank verse in the language (except Shakespeare's) that deserves the name of verse. Dr. Johnson, who had modelled his ideas of versification on the regular sing-song of Pope, condemns *Paradise Lost* as harsh and unequal. I shall not pretend to say that this is not sometimes the case; for where a degree of excellence beyond the mechanical rules of art is attempted, the poet must sometimes fail. But I imagine that there are more perfect examples in Milton of musical expression, or of an adaptation of the sound and movement of the verse to the meaning of the passage, than in all our other writers, whether of rhyme or blank verse, put together (with the exception already mentioned). Spenser is the most harmonious of our stanza writers, as Dryden is the most sounding and varied of our rhymists. But in neither is there anything like the same ear for music, the same power of approximating the varieties of poetical to those of musical rhythm, as there is in our great epic poet. The sound of his lines is molded into the expression of the sentiment, almost of the very image. They rise or fall, pause or hurry rapidly on with exquisite art, but without the least trick or affectation, as the occasion seems to require. . . .

To proceed to a consideration of the merits of *Paradise Lost*, in the most essential point of view, I mean as to the poetry of character and passion. I shall say nothing of the fable, or of other technical objections or excellences; but I shall try to explain at once the foundation of the interest belonging to the poem. I am ready to give up the dialogues in Heaven where, as Pope justly observes, "God the Father turns a school divine;" nor do I consider the battle of the angels as the climax of sublimity, or the most successful effort of Milton's pen. In a word, the interest of the poem arises from the daring ambition and fierce passions of Satan, and from the account of the paradisaical happiness, and the loss of it by our first parents. Three-fourths of the work are taken up with these characters, and nearly all that relates to them is unmixed sublimity and beauty. The two first books alone are like two massy pillars of solid gold.

Satan is the most heroic subject that ever was chosen

for a poem; and the execution is as perfect as the design is lofty. He was the first of created beings who, for endeavoring to be equal with the highest, and to divide the empire of heaven with the Almighty, was hurled down to hell. His aim was no less than the throne of the universe; his means, myriads of angelic armies bright, the third part of the heavens, whom he lured after him with his countenance, and who durst defy the Omnipotent in arms. His ambition was the greatest, and his punishment was the greatest; but not so his despair: for his fortitude was as great as his sufferings. His strength of mind was matchless as his strength of body; the vastness of his designs did not surpass the firm, inflexible determination with which he submitted to his irreversible doom and final loss of all good. His power of action and of suffering was equal. He was the greatest power that was ever overthrown, with the strongest will left to resist or to endure. He was baffled, not confounded. . . .

He was still surrounded with hosts of rebel angels, armed warriors, who own him as their sovereign leader, and with whose fate he sympathizes as he views them round, far as the eye can reach; though he keeps aloof from them in his own mind, and holds supreme counsel only with his own breast. An outcast from Heaven, Hell trembles beneath his feet, Sin and Death are at his heels, and mankind are his easy prey,

> *All is not lost; th' unconquerable will,*
> *And study of revenge, immortal hate,*
> *And courage never to submit or yield,*
> *And what else is not to be overcome,*

are still his. The sense of his punishment seems lost in the magnitude of it; the fierceness of tormenting flames is qualified and made innocuous by the greater fierceness of his pride; the loss of infinite happiness to himself is compensated in thought by the power of inflicting infinite misery on others. Yet Satan is not the principle of malignity, or of the abstract love of evil, but of the abstract love of power, of pride, of self-will personified, to which last principle all other good and evil, and even his own, are subordinate. From this principle he never once flinches. His love of power and contempt for suffering are never once relaxed from the highest pitch of intensity. His thoughts burn like a hell within him; but the power of thought holds dominion in his mind over every other consideration. The consciousness of a determined purpose, of "that intellectual being, those thoughts that wander through eternity," though accompanied with endless pain, he prefers to nonentity, to "being swallowed up and lost in the wide womb of uncreated night." He expresses the sum and substance of all ambition in one line: "Fallen cherub, to be weak is miserable, doing or suffering!" After such a conflict as his and such a defeat, to retreat in order to rally, to make terms, to exist at all, is something; but he does more than this: he founds a new empire in hell, and from it conquers this new world, whither he bends his undaunted flight, forcing his way through nether and surrounding fires. The poet has not in all this given us a mere shadowy outline; the strength is equal to the magnitude of the conception. The Achilles of Homer is not more distinct; the Titans were not more vast; Prometheus chained to his rock was not a more terrific example of suffering and of crime. Wherever the figure of Satan is introduced, whether he walks or flies, "rising aloft incumbent on the dusky air," it is illustrated with the most striking and appropriate images: so that we see it always before us, gigantic, irregular, portentous, uneasy, and disturbed: but dazzling in its faded splendor, the clouded ruins of a god. The deformity of Satan is only in the depravity of his will; he has no bodily deformity to excite our loathing or disgust. The horns and tail are not there, poor emblems of the unbending, unconquered spirit, of the writhing agonies within. Milton was too magnanimous and open an antagonist to support his argument by the by-tricks of a hump and cloven foot; to bring into the fair field of controversy the good old catholic prejudices of which Tasso and Dante have availed themselves, and which the mystic German critics would restore. He relied on the justice of his cause, and did not scruple to give the devil his due. Some persons may think that he has carried his liberality too far, and injured the cause he professed to espouse by making him the chief person in his poem. Considering the nature of his subject, he would be equally in danger of running into this fault, from his faith in religion and his love of rebellion; and perhaps each of these motives had its full share in determining the choice of his subject.

The whole of the speeches and debates in Pandemonium

are well worthy of the place and the occasion—with gods for speakers, and angels and archangels for hearers. There is a decided manly tone in the arguments and sentiments, an eloquent dogmatism, as if each person spoke from thorough conviction; an excellence which Milton probably borrowed from his spirit of partisanship or else his spirit of partisanship from the natural firmness and vigor of his mind. That approximation to the severity of impassioned prose which has been made an objection to Milton's poetry, and which is chiefly to be met with in these bitter invectives, is one of its great excellences. The rout in heaven is like the fall of some mighty structure, nodding to its base "with hideous ruin and combustion down." But, perhaps, of all the passages in *Paradise Lost,* the description of the employments of the angels during the absence of Satan, some of whom "retreated in a silent valley, sing with notes angelical to many a harp their own heroic deeds and hapless fall by doom of battle," is the most perfect example of mingled pathos and sublimity. . . .

Of Adam and Eve it has been said, that the ordinary reader can feel little interest in them, because they have none of the passions, pursuits, or even relations of human life, except that of man and wife, the least interesting of all others, if not to the parties concerned, at least to the bystanders. The preference has on this account been given to Homer, who, it is said, has left very vivid and infinitely diversified pictures of all the passions and affections, public and private, incident to human nature—the relations of son, of brother, parents, friend, citizen, and many others. Longinus preferred the *Iliad* to the *Odyssey,* on account of the greater number of battles it contains; but I can neither agree to his criticism nor assent to the present objection. It is true, there is little action in this part of Milton's poem; but there is much repose and more enjoyment. . . . In their first false step we trace "all our future woe, with loss of Eden." But there was a short and precious interval between, like the first blush of morning before the day is overcast with tempest, the dawn of the world, the birth of nature from "the unapparent deep," with its first dews and freshness on its cheek, breathing odors. Theirs was the first delicious taste of life, and on them depended all that was to come of it. In them hung trembling all our hopes and fears. They were as yet alone in the world, in the eye of nature, wondering at their new being, full of enjoyment

and enraptured with one another, with the voice of their
Maker walking in the garden, and ministering angels at-
tendant on their steps, winged messengers from heaven
like rosy clouds descending in their sight. Nature played
around them her virgin fancies wild, and spread for them
a repast where no crude surfeit reigned. Was there nothing
in this scene, which God and nature alone witnessed, to
interest a modern critic? What need was there of action,
where the heart was full of bliss and innocence without it!
They had nothing to do but feel their own happiness, and
"know to know no more." "They toiled not, neither did
they spin; yet Solomon in all his glory was not arrayed
like one of these." All things seemed to acquire fresh sweetness, and to be clothed with fresh beauty in their sight.
They tasted as it were for themselves and us of all that
there ever was pure in human bliss. "In them the burthen
of the mystery, the heavy and the weary weight of all this
unintelligible world, is lightened." They stood awhile perfect; but they afterwards fell, and were driven out of
Paradise, tasting the first fruits of bitterness as they had
done of bliss. But their pangs were such as a pure spirit
might feel at the sight, their tears "such as angels weep."
The pathos is of that mild contemplative kind which arises
from regret for the loss of unspeakable happiness, and
resignation to inevitable fate. There is none of the fierceness of intemperate passion, none of the agony of mind and
turbulence of action, which is the result of the habitual
struggles of the will with circumstances, irritated by repeated disappointment, and constantly setting its desires
most eagerly on that which there is an impossibility of at-
taining. This would have destroyed the beauty of the whole
picture. They had received their unlooked-for happiness as
a free gift from their Creator's hands, and they submitted
to its loss, not without sorrow, but without impious and
stubborn repining.

On Old English Writers
and Speakers

Those "superior, happy spirits who slid through life on the rollers of learning" are the subject of the next essay, which was written in Paris and published in the New Monthly Magazine *(January, 1825).*

When I see a whole row of standard French authors piled up on a Paris book-stall, to the height of twenty or thirty volumes, showing their mealy coats to the sun, pink, blue, and yellow, they seem to me a wall built up to keep out the intrusion of foreign letters. There is scarcely such a thing as an English book to be met with, unless, perhaps, a dusty edition of *Clarissa Harlowe* lurks in an obscure corner, or a volume of the *Sentimental Journey* perks its well-known title in your face. But there is a huge column of Voltaire's works complete in sixty volumes, another (not so frequent) of Rousseau's in fifty, Racine in ten volumes, Molière in about the same number, La Fontaine, Marmontel, *Gil Blas,* for ever; Madame Sevigné's *Letters,* Pascal, Montesquieu, Crebillon, Marivaux, with Montaigne, Rabelais, and the grand Corneille more rare; and eighteen full-sized volumes of La Harpe's criticism, towering vaingloriously in the midst of them, furnishing the streets of Paris with a graduated scale of merit for all the rest, and teaching the very *garçons perruquiers* how to measure the length of each act of each play by a stop-watch, and to ascertain whether the angles at the four corners of each classic volume are right ones. How climb over this lofty pile of taste and elegance to wander down into the bogs and wastes of English or of any other literature, "to this obscure and wild?" Must they "on that fair mountain leave to feed, to batten on this moor?" Or why should they? Have they not literature enough of their own, and to spare, without coming to us? Is not the public mind crammed, choked with French books, pictures, statues, plays, operas, newspapers, parties, and an incessant farrago of words, so that it has not a moment left to look at home into itself, or abroad into nature? Must they cross the Channel to increase the vast stock of impertinence, to acquire foreign tastes, suppress native prejudices, and reconcile the opinions of the *Edinburgh* and *Quarterly Reviews?* It is quite needless. There is a project at present entertained in certain circles, to give the French a taste for Shakespeare. They should really begin with the English. Many of their own best authors are neglected; others, of whom new Editions have been printed, lie heavy on the booksellers' hands. It is by an especial dispensation of Providence that languages wear out; as otherwise we should be buried alive under a load of books and knowledge. People talk of a philosophical and universal language. We have enough to do to understand our own, and to read a thousandth part (perhaps not the best) of what is written in it. It is ridiculous and monstrous vanity. We would set up a standard of general taste and of immortal renown; we would have the benefits of science and of art universal, because we suppose our own capacity to receive them unbounded; and we would have the thoughts of others never die, because we flatter ourselves that our own will last for ever; and like the frog imitating the ox in the fable, we burst in the vain attempt. Man, whatever he may think, is a very limited being; the world is a narrow circle drawn about him; the horizon limits our immediate view; immortality means a century or two. Languages happily restrict the mind to what is of its own native growth and fitted for it, as rivers and mountains bound countries; or the empire of learning, as well as states, would become unwieldy and overgrown. A little importation from foreign markets may be good; but the home production is the chief thing to be looked to. . . .

There was advertised not long ago in Paris an Elegy on the Death of Lord Byron, by his friend Sir Thomas More, —evidently confounding the living bard with the old statesman. It is thus the French in their light, salient way transpose everything. The mistake is particularly ludicrous to those who have ever seen Mr. Moore, or Mr. Shee's portrait of him in Mr. Hookham's shop, and who chance to see Holbein's head of Sir Thomas More in the Louvre. There is the same difference that there is between a surly English mastiff and a little lively French pug. Mr. Moore's face is gay and smiling enough, old Sir Thomas's is severe, not to say sour. It seems twisted awry with difficult questions, and bursting asunder with a ponderous load of meaning. Mr. Moore has nothing of this painful and puritanical cast. He floats idly and fantastically on the top of the literature of his age; his renowned and almost forgotten namesake has nearly sunk to the bottom of his. The Author of *Utopia* was no flincher, he was a martyr to his opinions, and was burnt to death for them—the most heroic action of Mr. Moore's life is, the having burnt the Memoirs of his friend!

The expression in Holbein's pictures conveys a faithful but not very favorable notion of the literary character of that period. It is painful, dry, and labored. Learning was then an ascetic, but recluse and profound. You see a weight of thought and care in the studious heads of the time of the Reformation, a sincerity, an integrity, a sanctity of purpose, like that of a formal dedication to a religious life, or the inviolability of monastic vows. They had their work to do; we reap the benefits of it. We skim the surface, and travel along the high road. They had to explore dark recesses, to dig through mountains, and make their way through pathless wildernesses. It is no wonder they looked grave upon it. The seriousness, indeed, amounts to an air of devotion; and it has to me something fine, manly, and *old English* about it. There is a heartiness and determined resolution; a willingness to contend with opposition; a superiority to ease and pleasure; some sullen pride, but no trifling vanity. They addressed themselves to study as to a duty, and were ready to "leave all and follow it." In the beginning of such an era, the difference between ignorance and learning, between what was commonly known and what was possible to be known, would appear immense; and no pains or time would be thought too great to master the difficulty. Conscious of their own deficiencies and the scanty information of those about them, they would be glad to look out for aids and support, and to put themselves apprentices to time and nature. This temper would lead them to exaggerate rather than to make light of the difficulties of their undertaking; and would call forth sacrifices in proportion. Feeling how little they knew, they would be anxious to discover all that others had known, and instead of making a display of themselves, their first object would be to dispel the mist and darkness that surrounded them. They did not cull the flowers of learning, or pluck a leaf of laurel for their own heads, but tugged at the roots and very heart of their subject, as the woodman tugs at the roots of the gnarled oak. The sense of the arduousness of their enterprise braced their courage, so that they left nothing half done. They inquired *de omne scibile et quibusdam aliis.*

They ransacked libraries, they exhausted authorities. They acquired languages, consulted books, and deciphered manuscripts. They devoured learning, and swallowed antiquity whole, and (what is more) digested it. They read incessantly, and remembered what they read, from the zealous interest they took in it. Repletion is only bad when it is accompanied with apathy and want of exercise. They labored hard, and showed great activity both of reasoning and speculation. Their fault was that they were too prone to unlock the secrets of nature with the key of learning, and often to substitute authority in the place of argument. They were also too polemical; as was but naturally to be expected in the first breaking up of established prejudices and opinions. It is curious to observe the slow progress of the human mind in loosening and getting rid of its trammels, link by link, and how it crept on its hands and feet, and with its eyes bent on the ground, out of the cave of Bigotry, making its way through one dark passage after another; those who gave up one half of an absurdity contending as strenuously for the remaining half, the lazy current of tradition stemming the tide of innovation, and making an endless struggle between the two. But in the dullest minds of this period there was a deference to the opinions of their leaders; an imposing sense of the importance of the subject, of the necessity of bringing all the faculties to bear upon it; a weight either of armor or of internal strength, a zeal either *for* or *against;* a head, a heart, and a hand, a holding out to the death for conscience' sake, a strong spirit of proselytism—no flippancy, no indifference, no compromising, no pert shallow scepticism, but truth was supposed indissolubly knit to good, knowledge to usefulness, and the temporal and eternal welfare of mankind to hang in the balance. The pure springs of a lofty faith (so to speak) had not then descended by various gradations from their skyey regions and cloudy height, to find their level in the smooth, glittering expanse of modern philosophy, or to settle in the stagnant pool of stale hypocrisy! A learned man of that day, if he knew no better than others, at least knew all that they did. He did not come to his subject, like some dapper barrister who has never looked at his brief, and trusts to the smartness of his wit and person for the agreeable effect he means to produce, but like an old and practiced counsellor, covered over with the dust and cobwebs of the law. If it was a speaker in

Parliament, he came prepared to handle his subject, armed with cases and precedents, the constitution and history of Parliament from the earliest period, a knowledge of the details of business and the local interests of the country; in short, he had taken up *the freedom of the House,* and did not treat the question like a cosmopolite, or a writer in a Magazine. If it were a divine, he knew the Scriptures and the Fathers, and the Councils and the Commentators by heart, and thundered them in the ears of his astonished audience. Not a trim essay or a tumid oration, patronizing religion by modern sophisms, but the Law and the Prophets, the chapter and the verse. If it was a philosopher, Aristotle and the Schoolmen were drawn out in battle-array against you:—if an antiquarian, the Lord bless us! There is a passage in Selden's notes on Drayton's *Poly-Olbion,* in which he elucidates some point of topography by a reference not only to Stowe and Holinshed and Camden and Saxo-Grammaticus and Dugdale and several other authors that we are acquainted with, but to twenty obscure names, that no modern reader ever heard of; and so on through the notes to a folio volume, written apparently for relaxation. Such were the intellectual amusements of our ancestors! Learning then ordinarily lay-in of folio volumes: now she litters octavos and duodecimos, and will soon, as in France, miscarry of half sheets! Poor Job Orton! why should I not record a jest of his (perhaps the only one he ever made), emblematic as it is of the living and the learning of the good old times? The Rev. Job Orton was a Dissenting Minister in the middle of the last century, and had grown heavy and gouty by sitting long at dinner and at his studies. He could only get downstairs at last by spreading the folio volumes of Caryl's *Commentaries upon Job* on the steps and sliding down them. Surprised one day in his descent, he exclaimed, "You have often heard of Caryl upon Job—now you see Job upon Caryl!" This same quaint-witted gouty old gentleman seems to have been one of those "superior, happy spirits," who slid through life on the rollers of learning, enjoying the good things of the world and laughing at them, and turning his infirmities to a livelier account than his patriarchal name-sake. Reader, didst thou ever hear either of Job Orton or of Caryl on Job? I daresay not. Yet the one did not therefore slide down his theological staircase the less pleasantly; nor did the other compile his Commentaries in vain! For myself, I

should like to browse on folios, and have to deal chiefly
with authors that I have scarcely strength to lift, that are
as solid as they are heavy, and if dull, are full of matter.
It is delightful to repose on the wisdom of the ancients; to
have some great name at hand, besides one's own initials
always staring one in the face: to travel out of one's self
into the Chaldee, Hebrew, and Egyptian characters; to have
the palm-trees waving mystically in the margin of the page,
and the camels moving slowly on in the distance of three
thousand years. In that dry desert of learning, we gather
strength and patience, and a strange and insatiable thirst
of knowledge . . . .

Learning is its own exceeding great reward; and at the
period of which we speak, it bore other fruits, not unworthy of it. Genius, when not smothered and kept down
by learning, blazed out triumphantly over it; and the Fancy
often rose to a height proportioned to the depth to which
the Understanding had struck its roots. After the first
emancipation of the mind from the trammels of Papal
ignorance and superstition, people seemed to be in a state
of breathless wonder at the new light that was suffered
to break in upon them. They were startled as "at the birth
of nature from the unapparent deep." They seized on all
objects that rose in view with a firm and eager grasp, in
order to be sure whether they were imposed upon or not.
The mind of man, "pawing to get free" from custom and
prejudice, struggled and plunged, and like the fabled Peg-
asus, opened at each spring a new source of truth. Images
were piled on heaps, as well as opinions and facts, the
ample materials for poetry and prose, to which the bold
hand of enthusiasm applied its torch, and kindled it into a
flame. The accumulation of past records seemed to form
the framework of their prose, as the observation of external
objects did of their poetry—

"Whose body nature was, and man the soul."

Among poets they have to boast such names, for instance,
as Shakespeare, Spenser, Beaumont and Fletcher, Marlowe,
Webster, Dekker, and soon after, Milton; among prose-
writers, Selden, Bacon, Jeremy Taylor, Baxter, and Sir
Thomas Browne; for patriots they have such men as
Pym, Hampden, Sydney; and for a witness of their zeal
and piety, they have Fox's *Book of Martyrs,* instead of

which we have Mr. Southey's *Book of the Church,* and a
whole host of renegades! Perhaps Jeremy Taylor and also
Beaumont and Fletcher may be mentioned as rather exceptions to the gravity and severity I have spoken of as
characteristic of our earlier literature. It is true, they are
florid and voluptuous in their style, but they still keep their
state apart, and there is an eloquence of the heart about
them, which seems to gush from the "pure well of English
undefiled." The one treats of sacred things with a vividness and fervor as if he had a revelation of them: the others
speak of human interests with a tenderness as if man's
nature were divine. Jeremy Taylor's pen seems to have been
guided by the very spirit of joy and youth, but yet with a
sense of what was due to the reverence of age, and "tears
of pious awe, that feared to have offended." Beaumont and
Fletcher's love-scenes are like the meeting of hearts in
Elysium. Let any one have dwelt on any object with the
greatest fondness, let him have cherished the feeling to the
utmost height, and have it put to the test in the most trying
circumstances, and he will find it described to the life in
Beaumont and Fletcher . . . Words and paper, each *couleur
de rose,* are the two requisites of a fashionable style. But
the glossy splendor, the voluptuous glow of the obsolete,
old-fashioned writers just mentioned has nothing artificial,
nothing meretricious in it. It is the luxuriance of natural
feeling and fancy. I should as soon think of accusing the
summer-rose of vanity for unfolding its leaves to the dawn,
or the hawthorn that puts forth its blossoms in the genial
warmth of spring, of affecting to be fine. We have heard
a good deal of the pulpit-eloquence of Bossuet and other
celebrated preachers of the time of Fenelon; but I doubt
much whether all of them together could produce any
number of passages to match the best of those in the *Holy
Living and Dying,* or even Baxter's severe but thrilling
denunciations of the insignificance and nothingness of life
and the certainty of a judgment to come. There is a fine
portrait of this last-named powerful controversialist, with
his high forehead and black velvet cap, in Calamy's *Non-
Conformist's Memorial,* containing an account of the Two
Thousand Ejected Ministers at the Restoration of Charles
II. This was a proud list for Old England; and the account
of their lives, their zeal, their eloquence and sufferings for
conscience' sake, is one of the most interesting chapters in
the history of the human mind. How high it can soar in

faith! How nobly it can arm itself with resolution and fortitude! How far it can surpass itself in cruelty and fraud! How incapable it seems to be of good, except as it is urged on by the contention with evil! The retired and inflexible descendants of the Two Thousand Ejected Ministers and their adherents are gone with the spirit of persecution that gave a soul and body to them; and with them, I am afraid, the spirit of liberty, of manly independence, and of inward self-respect is nearly extinguished in England. There appears to be no natural necessity for evil, but that there is a perfect indifference to good without it. One thing exists and has a value set upon it only as it has a foil in some other; learning is set off by ignorance, liberty by slavery, refinement by barbarism. The cultivation and attainment of any art or excellence is followed by its neglect and decay; and even religion owes its zest to the spirit of contradiction; for it flourishes most from persecution and hostile factions. Mr. Irving speaks of the great superiority of religion over every other motive, since it enabled its professors to "endure having hot molten lead poured down their throats." He forgets that it was religion that poured it down their throats, and that this principle, mixed with the frailty of human passion, has often been as ready to inflict as to endure. I could make the world good, wise, happy tomorrow, if, when made, it would be contented to remain so without the alloy of mischief, misery, and absurdity: that is, if every possession did not require the principle of contrast, contradiction, and excess, to enliven and set it off and keep it at a safe distance from sameness and insipidity.

The different styles of art and schools of learning vary and fluctuate on this principle. After the restoration of Charles, the grave, enthusiastic, puritanical, "prick-eared" style became quite exploded, and a gay and piquant style, the reflection of courtly conversation and polished manners, and borrowed from the French, came into fashion, and lasted till the Revolution. Some examples of the same thing were given in the time of Charles I by Sir J. Suckling and others, but they were eclipsed and overlaid by the prevalence and splendor of the opposite examples. It was at its height, however, in the reign of the restored monarch, and in the witty and licentious writings of Wycherley, Congreve, Rochester, and Waller. Milton alone stood out as a partisan of the old Elizabethan school. Out of compliment, I suppose, to the Houses of Orange and Hanover, we sobered down, after the Revolution, into a strain of greater demureness, and into a Dutch and German fidelity of imitation of domestic manners and individual character, as in the periodical essayists, and in the works of Fielding and Hogarth. Yet, if the two last-named painters of manners are not English, who are so? I cannot give up my partiality to them for the fag-end of a theory. They have this mark of genuine English intellect, that they constantly combine truth of external observation with strength of internal meaning. The Dutch are patient observers of nature, but want character and feeling. The French, as far as we have imitated them, aim only at the pleasing, and glance over the surfaces of words and things. Thus has our literature descended (according to the foregoing scale) from the tone of the pulpit to that of the court or drawing-room, from the drawing-room into the parlor, and from thence, if some critics say true, into the kitchen and ale-house. It may do even worse than that!

On Dryden and Pope

In spite of the prevailing opposition to neo-classic literature, Hazlitt admired Dryden and Pope as poets of art, personality, and the "polished life." The following extracts from Lectures on the English Poets *illustrate a judicious and sincere criticism.*

Dryden was a better prose-writer, and a bolder and more varied versifier than Pope. He was a more vigorous thinker, a more correct and logical declaimer, and had more of what may be called strength of mind than Pope; but he had not the same refinement and delicacy of feeling. Dryden's eloquence and spirit were possessed in a higher degree by others, and in nearly the same degree by Pope himself; but that by which Pope was distinguished was an essence which he alone possessed, and of incomparable value on that sole account. Dryden's *Epistles* are excellent, but inferior to Pope's, though they appear (particularly the admirable one to Congreve) to have been the model on which the latter formed his. His *Satires* are better than Pope's. His *Absalom and Achitophel* is superior, both in force of invective and discrimination of character, to anything of Pope's in the same way. The character of Achitophel is very fine, and breathes, if not a sincere love for virtue, a strong spirit of indignation against vice.

MacFlecknoe is the origin of the idea of the *Dunciad;* but it is less elaborately constructed, less feeble, and less heavy. The difference between Pope's satirical portraits and Dryden's appears to be this in a good measure, that Dryden seems to grapple with his antagonists, and to describe real persons; Pope seems to refine upon them in his own mind, and to make them out just what he pleases, till they are not real characters, but the mere driveling effusions of his spleen and malice. Pope describes the thing, and then goes on describing his own description, till he loses himself in verbal repetitions. Dryden recurs to the object often, takes fresh sittings of nature, and gives us new strokes of character as well as of his pencil. The *Hind and Panther* is an allegory as well as a satire, and so far it tells less home; the battery is not so point-blank. But otherwise it has more genius, vehemence, and strength of description than any other of Dryden's works, not excepting the *Absalom and Achitophel*. It also contains the finest examples of varied and sounding versification.

The *Annus Mirabilis* is a tedious performance; it is a tissue of far-fetched, heavy, lumbering conceits, and in the worst style of what has been denominated metaphysical poetry. His *Odes* in general are of the same stamp; they are the hard-strained offspring of a meagre, meretricious fancy. The famous *Ode on St. Cecilia* deserves its reputation; for, as a piece of poetical mechanism to be set to music, or recited in alternate strophe and antistrophe, with classical allusions and flowing verse, nothing can be better. It is equally fit to be said or sung; it is not equally good to read. It is lyrical without being epic or dramatic. For instance, the description of Bacchus—

> *The jolly god in triumph comes,*
> *Sound the trumpets, beat the drums:*
> *Flush'd with a purple grace,*
> *He shows his honest face—*

does not answer, as it ought, to our idea of the god, returning from the conquest of India, with satyrs and wild beasts that he had tamed, following in his train: crowned with vine leaves, and riding in a chariot drawn by leopards —such as we have seen him painted by Titian or Rubens! Lyrical poetry, of all others, bears the nearest resemblance to painting; it deals in hieroglyphics and passing figures, which depend for effect, not on the working out, but on the selection. It is the dance and pantomine of poetry. In variety and rapidity of movement, the *Alexander's Feast* has all that can be required in this respect; it only wants loftiness and truth of character.

Dryden's plays are better than Pope could have written; for though he does not go out of himself by the force of imagination, he goes out of himself by the force of commonplaces and rhetorical dialogue. On the other hand, they are not so good as Shakespeare's; but he has left the best character of Shakespeare that has ever been written.

Pope

Pope was not distinguished as a poet of lofty enthusiasm, of strong imagination, with a passionate sense of the beauties of nature, or a deep insight into the workings of the heart; but he was a wit and a critic, a man of sense, of observation, and the world, with a keen relish for the elegances of art, or of nature when embellished by art, a quick tact for propriety of thought and manners as established by the forms and customs of society, a refined sympathy with the sentiments and habitudes of human life, as he felt them within the little circle of his family and friends. He was, in a word, the poet, not of nature, but of art; and the distinction between the two, as well as I can make it out, is this: the poet of nature is one who, from the elements of beauty, of power, and of passion in his own breast, sympathizes with whatever is beautiful, and grand, and impassioned in nature, in its simple majesty, in its immediate appeal to the senses, to the thoughts and hearts of all men; so that the poet of nature, by the truth, and depth, and harmony of his mind, may be said to hold communion with the very soul of nature; to be identified with, and to foreknow, and to record the feelings of all men at all times and places, as they are liable to the same impressions, and to exert the same power over the minds of his readers that nature does. He sees things in their eternal beauty, for he sees them as they are; he feels them in their universal interest, for he feels them as they affect the first principles of his and our common nature. Such was Homer, such was Shakespeare, whose works will last as long as nature, because they are a copy of the indestructible forms and everlasting impulses of nature, welling out from the bosom as from a perennial spring, or stamped upon the senses by the hand of their Maker. The power of the imagination in them is the representative power of all nature. It has its center in the human soul, and makes the circuit of the universe.

Pope was not assuredly a poet of this class, or in the first rank of it. He saw nature only dressed by art; he judged of beauty by fashion; he sought for truth in the opinions of the world; he judged of the feelings of others by his own. The capacious soul of Shakespeare had an intuitive and mighty sympathy with whatever could enter into the heart of man in all possible circumstances: Pope had an exact knowledge of all that he himself loved or hated, wished or wanted. Milton has winged his daring flight from heaven to earth, through Chaos and old Night. Pope's Muse never wandered with safety but from his library to his grotto, or from his grotto into his library back again. His mind dwelt with greater pleasure on his own garden than on the garden of Eden; he could describe the faultless whole-length mirror that reflected his own person better than the smooth surface of the lake that reflects the face of heaven, a piece of cut glass or a pair of paste buckles with more brilliance and effect than a thousand dew-drops glittering in the sun. He would be more delighted with a patent lamp than with "the pale reflex of Cynthia's brow," that fills the skies with its soft silent lustre, that trembles through the cottage window, and cheers the watchful mariner on the lonely wave. In short, he was the poet of personality and of polished life. That which was nearest to him was the greatest: the fashion of the day bore sway in his mind over the immutable laws of nature. He preferred the artificial to the natural in external objects, because he had a stronger fellow-feeling with the self-love of the maker or proprietor of a gewgaw than admiration of that which was interesting to all mankind. He preferred the artificial to the natural in passion, because the involuntary and uncalculating impulses of the one hurried him away with a force and vehemence with which he could not grapple; while he could trifle with the conventional and superficial modifications of mere sentiment at will, laugh at or admire, put them on or off like a masquerade dress, make much or little of them, indulge them for a longer or a shorter time, as he pleased; and because, while they amused his fancy and exercised his ingenuity, they never once disturbed his vanity, his levity or indifference. His mind was the antithesis of strength and grandeur; its power was the power of indifference. He had none of the enthusiasm of poetry; he was in poetry what the sceptic is in religion.

The Rape of the Lock is a double-refined essence of wit and fancy, as the *Essay on Criticism* is of wit and sense. The quantity of thought and observation in this work, for so young a man as Pope was when he wrote it, is wonderful: unless we adopt the supposition, that most men of genius spend the rest of their lives in teaching others what they themselves have learned under twenty. The conciseness and felicity of the expression are equally remarkable. Thus in reasoning on the variety of men's opinion, he says;

> *'Tis with our judgments, as our watches; none*
> *Go just alike, yet each believes his own.*

Nothing can be more original and happy than the general remarks and illustrations in the *Essay*: the critical rules laid down are too much those of a school, and of a confined one. There is one passage in the *Essay on Criticism* in which the author speaks with that eloquent enthusiasm of the fame of ancient writers, which those will always feel who have themselves any hope or chance of immortality.

There is a cant in the present day about genius as everything in poetry: there was a cant in the time of Pope about sense, as performing all sorts of wonders. It was a kind of watchword, the shibboleth of a critical party of the day. As a proof of the exclusive attention which it occupied in their minds, it is remarkable that in the *Essay on Criticism* (not a very long poem) there are no less than half a score of successive couplets rhyming to the word sense.

I have mentioned this the more for the sake of those critics who are bigoted idolizers of our author, chiefly on the score of his correctness. These persons seem to be of opinion that "there is but one perfect writer, even Pope." This is, however, a mistake: his excellence is by no means faultlessness. If he had no great faults, he is full of little errors. His grammatical construction is often lame and imperfect. In the Abelard and Eloise, he says:

> *There died the best of passions, Love and Fame.*

This is not a legitimate ellipsis. Fame is not a passion, though love is: but his ear was evidently confused by the meeting of the sound "love and fame," as if they of themselves immediately implied "love, and love of fame." Pope's rhymes are constantly defective, being rhymes to the eye instead of the ear. The praise of his versification must be confined to its uniform smoothness and harmony. In the translation of the *Iliad,* which has been considered as his masterpiece in style and execution, he continually changes the tenses in the same sentence for the purpose of the rhyme, which shows either a want of technical resources, or great inattention to punctilious exactness.

The epistle of *Eloise to Abelard* is the only exception I

can think of to the general spirit of the foregoing remarks; and I should be disingenuous not to acknowledge that it is an exception. The foundation is in the letters themselves of Abelard and Eloise, which are quite as impressive, but still in a different way. It is fine as a poem: it is finer as a piece of high-wrought eloquence. No woman could be supposed to write a better love-letter in verse. Besides the richness of the historical materials, the high gusto of the original sentiments which Pope had to work upon, there were perhaps circumstances in his own situation which made him enter into the subject with even more than a poet's feeling. The tears shed are drops gushing from the heart: the words are burning sighs breathed from the soul of love. Perhaps the poem to which it bears the greatest similarity in our language is Dryden's *Tancred and Sigismunda,* taken from Boccaccio. Pope's *Eloise* will bear this comparison; and after such a test, with Boccaccio for the original author, and Dryden for the translator, it need shrink from no other.

The *Essay on Man* is not Pope's best work. It is a theory which Bolingbroke is supposed to have given him, and which he expanded into verse. But "he spins the thread of his verbosity finer than the staple of his argument." All that he says, "the very words, and to the self-same tune," would prove just as well that whatever is, is wrong, as that whatever is, is right. The *Dunciad* has splendid passages, but in general it is dull, heavy, and mechanical.

The finest piece of personal satire in Pope (perhaps in the world) is his character of Addison; and this, it may be observed, is of a mixed kind, made up of his respect for the man, and a cutting sense of his failings. The other finest one is that of Buckingham, and the best part of that is the pleasurable.

Among his happiest and most inimitable effusions are the Epistles to Arbuthnot and to Jervas the painter: amiable patterns of the delightful unconcerned life, blending ease with dignity, which poets and painters then led.

Of Persons One Would Wish to Have Seen

"Of Persons One Would Wish to Have Seen" is Hazlitt's immortal portrait of the literati who often met at Lamb's rooms in Mitre-Court to exchange the brilliant talk recorded in this dialogue. The Speakers, whose names were disguised for publication in the New Monthly Magazine (January, 1826), are William Ayrton, musician and critic; Mary Lamb ("Mrs. Reynolds"); John Rickman ("H"), a political economist and litterateur; Edward Phillips ("Erasmus"), his secretary; Captain James Burney, Fanny Burney's brother, and his son Martin; Barron Field, critic and lawyer; and George Dyer ("G. J."), the poet. The person with a "shrill, querulous voice" who wishes to call up Don Quixote is the author.

Lamb it was, I think, who suggested this subject, as well as the defence of Guy Faux, which I urged him to execute. As, however, he would undertake neither, I suppose I must do both, a task for which he would have been much fitter, no less from the temerity than the felicity of his pen—

> *"Never so sure our rapture to create*
> *As when it touched the brink of all we hate."*

Compared with him, I shall, I fear, make but a commonplace piece of business of it; but I should be loth the idea was entirely lost, and besides I may avail myself of some hints of his in the progress of it. I am sometimes, I suspect, a better reporter of the ideas of other people than expounder of my own. I pursue the one too far into paradox or mysticism; the others I am not bound to follow farther than I like, or than seems fair and reasonable.

On the question being started, A[yrton] said, "I suppose the two first persons you would choose to see would be the two greatest names in English literature, Sir Isaac Newton and Mr. Locke?" In this A[yrton], as usual, reckoned without his host. Every one burst out a laughing at the expression of Lamb's face, in which impatience was restrained by courtesy. "Yes, the greatest names," he stammered out hastily, "but they were not persons—not persons."—"Not persons?" said A[yrton], looking wise and foolish at the same time, afraid his triumph might be premature. "That is," rejoined Lamb, "not characters, you know. By Mr.

82

Locke and Sir Isaac Newton, you mean the *Essay on the Human Understanding,* and the *Principia,* which we have to this day. Beyond their contents there is nothing personally interesting in the men. But what we want to see any one *bodily* for, is when there is something peculiar, striking in the individuals, more than we can learn from their writings, and yet are curious to know. I dare say Locke and Newton were very like Kneller's portraits of them. But who could paint Shakespeare?"—"Ay," retorted A[yrton], "there it is; then I suppose you would prefer seeing him and Milton instead?"—"No," said Lamb, "neither. I have seen so much of Shakespeare on the stage and on book-stalls, in frontis-pieces and on mantel-pieces, that I am quite tired of the everlasting repetition: and as to Milton's face, the impressions that have come down to us of it I do not like; it is too starched and puritanical; and I should be afraid of losing some of the manna of his poetry in the leaven of his countenance and the precisian's band and gown."—"I shall guess no more," said A[yrton]. "Who is it, then, you would like to see 'in his habit as he lived,' if you had your choice of the whole range of English literature?" Lamb then named Sir Thomas Browne and Fulke Greville, the friend of Sir Philip Sidney, as the two worthies whom he should feel the greatest pleasure to encounter on the floor of his apartment in their nightgown and slippers, and to exchange friendly greetings with them. At this A[yrton] laughed outright, and conceived Lamb was jesting with him; but as no one followed his example, he thought there might be something in it, and waited for an explanation in a state of whimsical suspense. Lamb then (as well as I can remember a conversation that passed twenty years ago—how time slips!) went on as follows. "The reason why I pitch upon these two authors is, that their writings are riddles, and they themselves the most mysterious of personages. They resemble the soothsayers of old, who dealt in dark hints and doubtful oracles; and I should like to ask them the meaning of what no mortal but themselves, I should suppose, can fathom. There is Dr. Johnson: I have no curiosity, no strange uncertainty about him; he and Boswell together have pretty well let me into the secret of what passed through his mind. He and other writers like him are sufficiently explicit: my friends whose repose I should be tempted to disturb (were it in my power), are implicit, inextricable, inscrutable.

"When I look at that obscure but gorgeous prose-composition, the *Urn-burial,* I seem to myself to look into a deep abyss, at the bottom of which are hid pearls and rich treasure; or it is like a stately labyrinth of doubt and withering speculation, and I would invoke the spirit of the author to lead me through it. Besides, who would not be curious to see the lineaments of a man who, having himself been twice married, wished that mankind were propagated like trees! As to Fulke Greville, he is like nothing but one of his own 'Prologues spoken by the ghost of an old king of Ormus,' a truly formidable and inviting personage: his style is apocalyptical, cabalistical, a knot worthy of such an apparition to untie; and for the unravelling a passage or two, I would stand the brunt of an encounter with so portentous a commentator!"—"I am afraid, in that case," said A[yrton], "that if the mystery were once cleared up, the merit might be lost"; and turning to me, whispered a friendly apprehension, that while Lamb continued to admire these old crabbed authors, he would never become a popular writer. Dr. Donne was mentioned as a writer of the same period, with a very interesting countenance, whose history was singular, and whose meaning was often quite as *uncomeatable,* without a personal citation from the dead, as that of any of his contemporaries. The volume was produced; and while some one was expatiating on the exquisite simplicity and beauty of the portrait prefixed to the old edition, A[yrton] got hold of the poetry, and exclaiming "What have we here?" read the following:

> "Here lies a shee Sunne and a hee Moone here,
> She gives the best light to his Spheare,
> Or each is both, and all, and so
> They unto one another nothing owe."

There was no resisting this, till Lamb, seizing the volume, turned to the beautiful *Lines to his Mistress,* dissuading her from accompanying him abroad, and read them with suffused features and a faltering tongue. . . .

Some one then inquired of Lamb if we could not see from the window the Temple walk in which Chaucer used to take his exercise; and on his name being put to the vote, I was pleased to find that there was a general sensation in his favor in all but A[yrton], who said something about the ruggedness of the metre, and even objected to the quaint-

ness of the orthography. I was vexed at this superficial
gloss, pertinaciously reducing everything to its own trite
level, and asked "if he did not think it would be worth
while to scan the eye that had first greeted the Muse in that
dim twilight and early dawn of English literature; to see
the head round which the visions of fancy must have played
like gleams of inspiration or a sudden glory; to watch those
lips that 'lisped in numbers, for the numbers came'—as by
a miracle, or as if the dumb should speak? Nor was it
alone that he had been the first to tune his native tongue
(however imperfectly to modern ears); but he was himself a noble, manly character, standing before his age and
striving to advance it; a pleasant humorist withal, who
has not only handed down to us the living manners of his
time, but had, no doubt, store of curious and quaint
devices, and would make as hearty a companion as Mine
Host of the Tabard. His interview with Petrarch is fraught
with interest. Yet I would rather have seen Chaucer in
company with the author of the *Decameron,* and have
heard them exchange their best stories together—the
Squire's Tale against the *Story of the Falcon,* the *Wife of
Bath's Prologue* against the *Adventures of Friar Albert.*
How fine to see the high mysterious brow which learning
then wore, relieved by the gay, familiar tone of men of the
world, and by the courtesies of genius! Surely, the thoughts
and feelings which passed through the minds of these great
revivers of learning, these Cadmuses who sowed the teeth
of letters, must have stamped an expression on their features as different from the moderns as their books, and well
worth the perusal. Dante," I continued, "is as interesting a
person as his own Ugolino, one whose lineaments curiosity
would as eagerly devour in order to penetrate his spirit,
and the only one of the Italian poets I should care much
to see. There is a fine portrait of Ariosto by no less a hand
than Titian's; light, Moorish, spirited, but not answering
our idea. The same artist's large colossal profile of Peter
Aretine is the only likeness of the kind that has the effect
of conversing with 'the mighty dead'; and this is truly
spectral, ghastly, necromantic." Lamb put it to me if I
should like to see Spenser as well as Chaucer; and I
answered, without hesitation, "No; for that his beauties
were ideal, visionary, not palpable or personal, and therefore connected with less curiosity about the man. His
poetry was the essence of romance, a very halo round the

bright orb of fancy; and the bringing in the individual might dissolve the charm. No tones of voice could come up to the mellifluous cadence of his verse; no form but of a winged angel could vie with the airy shapes he has described. He was (to my apprehension) rather a 'creature of the element, that lived in the rainbow and played in the plighted clouds,' than an ordinary mortal. Or if he did appear, I should wish it to be as a mere vision, like one of his own pageants, and that he should pass by unquestioned like a dream or sound—

> ——'That *was Arion crown'd:*
> *So went he playing on the wat'ry plain.'* "

Captain [Burney] muttered something about Columbus, and M[artin Burney] hinted at the Wandering Jew; but the last was set aside as spurious, and the first made over to the New World.

"I should like," said [Mrs. Reynolds], "to have seen Pope talk with Patty Blount; and I *have* seen Goldsmith." Every one turned round to look at [Mrs. Reynolds], as if by so doing they could get a sight at Goldsmith.

"Where," asked a harsh, croaking voice, "was Dr. Johnson in the years 1745-6? He did not write anything that we know of, nor is there any account of him in Boswell during those two years. Was he in Scotland with the Pretender? He seems to have passed through the scenes in the Highlands in company with Boswell, many years after, 'with lack-lustre eye,' yet as if they were familiar to him, or associated in his mind with interests that he durst not explain. If so, it would be an additional reason for my liking him; and I would give something to have seen him seated in the tent with the youthful Majesty of Britain, and penning the Proclamation to all true subjects and adherents of the legitimate Government."

"I thought," said A[yrton], turning short round upon Lamb, "that you of the Lake School did not like Pope?" —"Not like Pope! My dear sir, you must be under a mistake—I can read him over and over for ever!"—"Why, certainly, the *Essay on Man* must be allowed to be a masterpiece."—"It may be so, but I seldom look into it."—"Oh! then it's his *Satires* you admire?"—"No, not his *Satires,* but his friendly *Epistles* and his compliments."—"Compliments! I did not know he ever made any."—"The finest," said Lamb, "that were ever paid by the wit of man. Each of them is worth an estate for life—nay, is an immortality. There is that superb one to Lord Cornbury:

> *'Despise low joys, low gains;*
> *Disdain whatever Cornbury disdains;*
> *Be virtuous, and be happy for your pains.'*

Was there ever more artful insinuation of idolatrous praise? And then that noble apotheosis of his friend Lord Mansfield (however little deserved), when, speaking of the House of Lords, he adds:

> *'Conspicuous scene! another yet is nigh,*
> *(More silent far) where kings and poets lie;*
> *Where Murray (long enough his country's pride)*
> *Shall be no more than Tully or than Hyde.'*

And with what a fine turn of indignant flattery he addresses Lord Bolingbroke:

> *'Why rail they then, if but one wreath of mine,*
> *Oh! all accomplish'd St. John, deck thy shrine?'*

Or turn," continued Lamb, with a slight hectic on his cheek and his eyes glistening, "to his list of early friends:

> *'But why then publish? Granville the polite,*
> *And knowing Walsh, would tell me I could write;*
> *Well-natured Garth inflamed with early praise,*
> *And Congreve loved, and Swift endured my lays;*
> *The courtly Talbot, Somers, Sheffield read,*
> *Ev'n mitred Rochester would nod the head;*
> *And St. John's self (great Dryden's friend before)*
> *Received with open arms one poet more.*
> *Happy my studies, if by these approved!*
> *Happier their author, if by these beloved!*
> *From these the world will judge of men and books,*
> *Not from the Burnets, Oldmixons, and Cooks.'* "

Here his voice totally failed him, and throwing down the books, he said, "Do you think I would not wish to have been friends with such a man as this?"

"What say you to Dryden?"—"He rather made a show

of himself, and courted popularity in that lowest temple of fame, a coffee-shop, so as in some measure to vulgarize one's idea of him. Pope, on the contrary, reached the very *beau ideal* of what a poet's life should be; and his fame while living seemed to be an emanation from that which was to circle his name after death. He was so far enviable (and one would feel proud to have witnessed the rare spectacle in him) that he was almost the only poet and man of genius who met with his reward on this side of the tomb, who realized in friends, fortune, the esteem of the world, the most sanguine hopes of a youthful ambition, and who found that sort of patronage from the great during his lifetime which they would be thought anxious to bestow upon him after his death. Read Gay's verses to him on his supposed return from Greece, after his translation of Homer was finished, and say if you would not gladly join the bright procession that welcomed him home, or see it once more land at Whitehall stairs."—"Still," said [Mrs. Reynolds], "I would rather have seen him talking with Patty Blount, or riding by in a coronet-coach with Lady Mary Wortley Montagu!"

E[rasmus Phillips], who was deep in a game of piquet at the other end of the room, whispered to M[artin Burney] to ask if Junius would not be a fit person to invoke from the dead. "Yes," said Lamb, "provided he would agree to lay aside his mask."

We were now at a stand for a short time, when Fielding was mentioned as a candidate; only one, however, seconded the proposition. "Richardson?"—"By all means, but only to look at him through the glass-door of his back-shop, hard at work upon one of his novels (the most extraordinary contrast that ever was presented between an author and his works), but not to let him come behind his counter, lest he should want you to turn customer, nor to go upstairs with him, lest he should offer to read the first manuscript of Sir Charles Grandison, which was originally written in eight-and-twenty volumes octavo, or get out the letters of his female correspondents, to prove that Joseph Andrews was low."

There was but one statesman in the whole of English history that anyone expressed the least desire to see— Oliver Cromwell, with his fine, frank, rough, pimply face, and wily policy; and one enthusiast, John Bunyan, the immortal author of the *Pilgrim's Progress*. It seemed that

if he came into the room, dreams would follow him, and
that each person would nod under his golden cloud, "nigh-
sphered in heaven," a canopy as strange and stately as any
in Homer.

Of all persons near our own time, Garrick's name was
received with the greatest enthusiasm, who was proposed
by [Barron] F[ield]. He presently superseded both Hogarth
and Handel, who had been talked of, but then it was on
condition that he should act in tragedy and comedy, in
the play and the farce, *Lear* and *Wildair* and *Abel Drugger.*
What a *sight for sore eyes* that would be! Who would not
part with a year's income at least, almost with a year of
his natural life, to be present at it? Besides, as he could
not act alone, and recitations are unsatisfactory things,
what a troop he must bring with him—the silver-tongued
Barry, and Quin, and Shuter and Weston, and Mrs. Clive
and Mrs. Pritchard, of whom I have heard my father speak
as so great a favorite when he was young. This would
indeed be a revival of the dead, the restoring of art; and
so much the more desirable, as such is the lurking scepticism mingled with our overstrained admiration of past
excellence, that though we have the speeches of Burke,
the portraits of Reynolds, the writings of Goldsmith, and
the conversation of Johnson, to show what people could
do at that period, and to confirm the universal testimony
to the merits of Garrick; yet, as it was before our time,
we have our misgivings, as if he was probably, after all,
little better than a Bartlemy-fair actor, dressed out to play
Macbeth in a scarlet and laced cocked-hat. For one, I
should like to have seen and heard with my own eyes and
ears. Certainly, by all accounts, if any one was ever moved
by the true histrionic *œstus,* it was Garrick. When he followed the Ghost in *Hamlet,* he did not drop the sword, as
most actors do, behind the scenes, but kept the point raised
the whole way round, so fully was he possessed with the
idea, or so anxious not to lose sight of his part for a moment. Once at a splendid dinner-party at Lord ———'s,
they suddenly missed Garrick, and could not imagine what
was become of him, till they were drawn to the window by
the convulsive screams and peals of laughter of a young
negro boy, who was rolling on the ground in an ecstasy of
delight to see Garrick mimicking a turkey-cock in the court-
yard, with his coat-tail stuck out behind, and in a seeming
flutter of feathered rage and pride. Of our party only two

persons present had seen the British Roscius; and they seemed as willing as the rest to renew their acquaintance with their old favorite.

We were interrupted in the hey-day and mid-career of this fanciful speculation, by a grumbler in a corner, who declared it was a shame to make all this rout about a mere player and farce-writer, to the neglect and exclusion of the fine old dramatists, the contemporaries and rivals of Shakespeare. Lamb said he had anticipated this objection when he had named the author of *Mustapha* and *Alaham;* and, out of caprice, insisted upon keeping him to represent the set, in preference to the wild, hare-brained enthusiast, Kit Marlowe; to the sexton of St. Ann's, Webster, with his melancholy yew-trees and death's-heads; to Dekker, who was but a garrulous proser; to the voluminous Heywood; and even to Beaumont and Fletcher, whom we might offend by complimenting the wrong author on their joint productions. Lord Brooke, on the contrary, stood quite by himself, or, in Cowley's words, was "a vast species alone." Some one hinted at the circumstances of his being a lord, which rather startled Lamb, but he said a *ghost* would perhaps dispense with strict etiquette, on being regularly addressed by his title. Ben Jonson divided our suffrages pretty equally. Some were afraid he would begin to traduce Shakespeare, who was not present to defend himself. "If he grows disagreeable," it was whispered aloud, "there is G[odwin] can match him." At length, his romantic visit to Drummond of Hawthornden was mentioned, and turned the scale in his favor.

Lamb inquired if there was any one that was hanged that I would choose to mention? And I answered, Eugene Aram. The name of the "Admirable Crichton" was suddenly started as a splendid example of *waste* talents, so different from the generality of his countrymen. This choice was mightily approved by a North-Briton present, who declared himself descended from that prodigy of learning and accomplishment, and said he had family plate in his possession as vouchers for the fact, with the initials A.C. —*Admirable Crichton!* H———— laughed, or rather roared, as heartily at this as I should think he has done for many years.

The last-named Mitre-courtier then wished to know whether there were any metaphysicians to whom one might be tempted to apply the wizard spell? I replied, there were only six in modern times deserving the name—Hobbes, Berkeley, Butler, Hartley, Hume, Leibnitz; and perhaps Jonathan Edwards, a Massachusetts man. As to the French, who talked fluently of having *created* this science, there was not a title in any of their writings that was not to be found literally in the authors I had mentioned. (Horne Tooke, who might have a claim to come in under the head of Grammar, was still living.) None of these names seemed to excite much interest, and I did not plead for the re-appearance of those who might be thought best fitted by the abstracted nature of their studies for the present spiritual and disembodied state, and who, even while on this living stage, were nearly divested of common flesh and blood. As A[yrton], with an uneasy, fidgety face, was about to put some question about Mr. Locke and Dugald Stewart, he was prevented by M[artin Burney], who observed, "If J——— was here, he would undoubtedly be for having up those profound and redoubted scholiasts, Thomas Aquinas and Duns Scotus." I said this might be fair enough in him who had read, or fancied he had read, the original works, but I did not see how we could have any right to call up these authors to give an account of themselves in person, till we had looked into their writings.

By this time it should seem that some rumor of our whimsical deliberation had got wind, and had disturbed the *irritabile genus* in their shadowy abodes, for we received messages from several candidates that we had just been thinking of. Gray declined our invitation, though he had not yet been asked: Gay offered to come, and bring in his hand the Duchess of Bolton, the original Polly: Steele and Addison left their cards as Captain Sentry and Sir Roger de Coverley: Swift came in and sat down without speaking a word and quitted the room as abruptly: Otway and Chatterton were seen lingering on the opposite side of the Styx, but could not muster enough between them to pay Charon his fare: Thomson fell asleep in the boat, and was rowed back again—and Burns sent a low fellow, one John Barleycorn, an old companion of his, who had conducted him to the other world, to say that he had during his lifetime been drawn out of his retirement as a show, only to be made an excise-man of, and that he would rather remain where he was. He desired, however, to shake hands by his representative—the hand, thus held out, was in a burning fever, and shook prodigiously.

The room was hung round with several portraits of eminent painters. While we were debating whether we should demand speech with these masters of mute eloquence, whose features were so familiar to us, it seemed that all at once they glided from their frames, and seated themselves at some little distance from us. There was Leonardo, with his majestic beard and watchful eye, having a bust of Archimedes before him; next him was Raphael's graceful head turned round to the Fornarina; and on his other side was Lucretia Borgia, with calm, golden locks; Michael Angelo had placed the model of St. Peter's on the table before him; Correggio had an angel at his side; Titian was seated with his mistress between himself and Giorgione; Guido was accompanied by his own Aurora, who took a dice-box from him; Claude held a mirror in his hand; Rubens patted a beautiful panther (led in by a satyr) on the head; Vandyke appeared as his own Paris, and Rembrandt was hid under furs, gold chains, and jewels, which Sir Joshua eyed closely, holding his hand so as to shade his forehead. Not a word was spoken; and as we rose to do them homage, they still presented the same surface to the view. Not being *bonâfide* representations of living people, we got rid of the splendid apparitions by signs and dumb show. As soon as they had melted into thin air, there was a loud noise at the outer door, and we found it was Giotto, Cimabue, and Ghirlandaio, who had been raised from the dead by their earnest desire to see their illustrious successors—

> *"Whose names on earth*
> *In Fame's eternal records live for aye!"*

Finding them gone, they had no ambition to be seen after them, and mournfully withdrew. "Egad!" said Lamb, "these are the very fellows I should like to have had some talk with, to know how they could see to paint when all was dark around them."

"But shall we have nothing to say," interrogated G. J———, "to the *Legend of Good Women?*"—"Name, name, Mr. J———," cried H——— in a boisterous tone of friendly exultation, "name as many as you please, without reserve or fear of molestation!" J——— was perplexed between so many amiable recollections, that the name of the lady of his choice expired in a pensive whiff of his pipe; and Lamb impatiently declared for the Duchess of Newcastle. Mrs. Hutchinson was no sooner mentioned, than she carried the day from the Duchess. We were the less solicitous on this subject of filling up the posthumous lists of Good Women, as there was already one in the room as good, as sensible, and in all respects as exemplary, as the best of them could be for their lives! "I should like vastly to have seen Ninon de l'Enclos," said that incomparable person; and this immediately put us in mind that we had neglected to pay honor due to our friends on the other side of the Channel: Voltaire, the patriarch of levity, and Rousseau, the father of sentiment; Montaigne and Rabelais (great in wisdom and in wit); Molière and that illustrious group that are collected round him (in the print of that subject) to hear him read his comedy of the *Tartuffe* at the house of Ninon; Racine, La Fontaine, Rochefoucault, St. Evremont, etc.

"There is one person," said a shrill, querulous voice, "I would rather see than all these—Don Quixote!"

"Come, come!" said H———; "I thought we should have no heroes, real or fabulous. What say you, Mr. Lamb? Are you for eking out your shadowy list with such names as Alexander, Julius Cæsar, Tamerlane, or Ghengis Khan?" —"Excuse me," said Lamb, "on the subject of characters in active life, plotters and disturbers of the world, I have a crotchet of my own, which I beg leave to reserve."—"No, no! come, out with your worthies!"—"What do you think of Guy Fawkes and Judas Iscariot?" H——— turned an eye upon him like a wild Indian, but cordial and full of smothered glee. "Your most exquisite reason!" was echoed on all sides; and A[yrton] thought that Lamb had now fairly entangled himself. "Why I cannot but think," retorted he of the wistful countenance, "that Guy Fawkes, that poor, fluttering annual scare-crow of straw and rags, is an ill-used gentleman. I would give something to see him sitting pale and emaciated, surrounded by his matches and his barrels of gunpowder, and expecting the moment that was to transport him to Paradise for his heroic self-devotion; but if I say any more, there is that fellow G[odwin] will make something of it. And as to Judas Iscariot, my reason is different. I would fain see the face of him who, having dipped his hand in the same dish with the Son of Man, could afterwards betray him. I have no conception of such a thing; nor have I ever seen any picture (not even

Leonardo's very fine one) that gave me the least idea of it."—"You have said enough, Mr. Lamb, to justify your choice."

"Oh! ever right, Menenius—ever right!"

"There is only one other person I can ever think of after this," continued H———; but without mentioning a name that once put on a semblance of mortality. "If Shakespeare was to come into the room, we should all rise up to meet him; but if that person was to come into it, we should all fall down and try to kiss the hem of his garment!"

As a lady present seemed now to get uneasy at the turn the conversation had taken, we rose up to go. The morning broke with that dim, dubious light by which Giotto, Cimabue, and Ghirlandaio must have seen to paint their earliest works; and we parted to meet again and renew similar topics at night, the next night, and the night after that, till that night overspread Europe which saw no dawn. The same event, in truth, broke up our little Congress that broke up the great one. But that was to meet again: our deliberations have never been resumed.

On Swift

*The qualities that made Swift one of Hazlitt's favorite
authors—"earnestness of mind" and "exquisite tone
of irony"—are emphasized in this neglected criticism,
first published in 1818.*

Swift's reputation as a poet has been in a manner obscured by the greater splendor, by the natural force and
inventive genius of his prose writings; but if he had never
written either the *Tale of a Tub* or *Gulliver's Travels,* his
name merely as a poet would have come down to us, and
have gone down to posterity with well-earned honors. His
Imitations of Horace, and still more his *Verses on his own
Death,* place him on the first rank of agreeable moralists
in verse. There is not only a dry humor, an exquisite tone
of irony, in these productions of his pen: but there is a
touching, unpretending pathos, mixed up with the most
whimsical and eccentric strokes of pleasantry and satire.
His *Description of the Morning in London,* and of a *City
Shower,* which were first published in the *Tatler,* are among
the most delightful of the contents of that very delightful
work. Swift shone as one of the most sensible of the poets;
he is also distinguished as one of the most nonsensical of
them. No man has written so many lackadaisical, slip-shod,
tedious, trifling, foolish, fantastical verses as he, which are
so little an imputation on the wisdom of the writer; and
which, in fact, only show his readiness to oblige others, and
to forget himself. He has gone so far as to invent a new
stanza of fourteen and sixteen syllable lines for Mary the
cookmaid to vent her budget of nothings, and for Mrs.
Harris to gossip with the deaf old housekeeper. Oh, when
shall we have such another Rector of Laracor! The *Tale of
a Tub* is one of the most masterly compositions in the language whether for thought, wit, or style. It is so capital and
undeniable a proof of the author's talents, that Dr. Johnson,
who did not like Swift, would not allow that he wrote it.
It is hard that the same performance should stand in the
way of a man's promotion to a bishopric, as wanting gravity, and at the same time be denied to be his, as having too
much wit. It is a pity the Doctor did not find out some
graver author, for whom he felt a critical kindness, on

whom to father this splendid but unacknowledged production. Dr. Johnson could not deny that *Gulliver's Travels* were his; he therefore disputed their merits, and said that after the first idea of them was conceived, they were easy to execute; all the rest followed mechanically. I do not know how that may be; but the mechanism employed is something very different from any that the author of *Rasselas* was in the habit of bringing to bear on such occasions. There is nothing more futile as well as invidious than this mode of criticizing a work of original genius. Its greatest merit is supposed to be in the invention; and you say, very wisely, that it is not in the execution. You might as well take away the merit of the invention of the telescope by saying that after its uses were explained and understood any ordinary eyesight could look through it. Whether the excellence of *Gulliver's Travels* is in the conception or the execution is of little consequence; the power is somewhere and it is a power that has moved the world. The power is not that of big words and vaunting common places. Swift left these to those who wanted them; and has done what his acuteness and intensity of mind alone could enable anyone to conceive or to perform. His object was to strip empty pride and grandeur of the imposing air which external circumstances throw around them; and for this purpose he has cheated the imagination of the illusions which the prejudices of sense and of the world put upon it by reducing everything to the abstract predicament of size. He enlarges or diminishes the scale as he wishes to show the insignificance or the grossness of our overweening self-love. That he has done this with mathematical precision, with complete presence of mind and perfect keeping in a manner that comes equally home to the understanding of the man and of the child does not take away from the merit of the work or the genius of the author. He has taken a new view of human nature, such as a being of a higher sphere might take of it; he has torn the scales from off his moral vision; he has tried an experiment upon human life, and sifted its pretensions from the alloy of circumstances. He has measured it with a rule, has weighed it in a balance, and found it, for the most part, wanting and worthless—in substance and in show. Nothing solid, nothing valuable is left in his system but virtue and wisdom. What a libel is this upon mankind! What a convincing proof of misanthropy! What presumption and what *malice prepense,* to show men what they are, and to teach them what they ought to be! What a mortifying stroke aimed at national glory is that unlucky incident of Gulliver's wading across the channel and carrying off the whole fleet of Blefuscu! After that, we have only to consider which of the contending parties was in the right. What a shock to personal vanity is given in the account of Gulliver's nurse Glumdalclitch! Still, notwithstanding the disparagement to her personal charms, her good-nature remains the same amiable quality as before. I cannot see the harm, the misanthropy, the immoral and degrading tendency of this. The moral lesson is as fine as the intellectual exhibition is amusing. It is an attempt to tear off the mask of imposture from the world; and nothing but imposture has a right to complain of it. It is, indeed, the way with our quacks in morality to preach up the dignity of human nature, to pamper pride and hypocrisy with the idle mockeries of the virtues they pretend to, and which they have not: but it was not Swift's way to cant morality, or anything else; nor did his genius prompt him to write unmeaning panegyrics on mankind!

The determination with which Swift persisted in a preconcerted theory savored of the morbid affection of which he died. There is nothing more likely to drive a man mad than the being unable to get rid of the idea of the distinction between right and wrong, and an obstinate, constitutional preference of the true to the agreeable. Swift was not a Frenchman. In this respect he differed from Rabelais and Voltaire. They have been accounted the three greatest wits in modern times; but their wit was of a peculiar kind in each. They are little beholden to each other; there is some resemblance between Lord Peter in the *Tale of a Tub* and Rabelais' Friar John; but in general they are all three authors of a substantive character in themselves. Swift's wit (particularly in his chief prose works) was serious, saturnine, and practical; Rabelais' was fantastical and joyous; Voltaire's was light, sportive, and verbal. Swift's wit was the wit of sense; Rabelais', the wit of nonsense; Voltaire's, of indifference to both. The ludicrous in Swift arises out of his keen sense of impropriety, his soreness and impatience of the least absurdity. He separates, with a severe and caustic air, truth from falsehood, folly from wisdom, "shows vice her own image, scorn her own feature"; and it is the force, the precision, and the honest abruptness with which the separation is made that excites our surprise, our admiration, and laughter. He sets a mark of reprobation on that which offends good sense and good manners, which cannot be mistaken, and which holds it up to our ridicule and contempt ever after. His occasional disposition to trifling was a relaxation from the excessive earnestness of his mind. His better genius was his spleen. It was the biting acrimony of his temper that sharpened his other faculties. The truth of his perceptions produced the pointed coruscations of his wit; his playful irony was the result of inward bitterness of thought; his imagination was the product of the literal, dry, incorrigible tenaciousness of his understanding. He endeavored to escape from the persecution of realities into the regions of fancy, and invented his Lilliputians and Brobdingnagians, Yahoos, and Houynhyms as a diversion to the more painful knowledge of the world around him: *they* only made him laugh, while men and women made him angry. His feverish impatience made him view the infirmities of that great baby the world with the same scrutinizing glance and jealous irritability that a parent regards the failings of its offspring.

Whether Genius is Conscious
of Its Powers?

Two of Hazlitt's chief interests, literature and paint-ing, are combined in this essay, which appeared in The Plain Speaker *(1826).*

No really great man ever thought himself so. The idea of greatness in the mind answers but ill to our knowledge—or to our ignorance of ourselves. What living prose-writer for instance would think of comparing himself with Burke? Yet would it not have been equal presumption or egotism in him to fancy himself equal to those who had gone before him—Bolingbroke, or Johnson, or Sir William Temple? Because his rank in letters is become a settled point with us, we conclude that it must have been quite as self-evident to him, and that he must have been perfectly conscious of his vast superiority to the rest of the world. Alas! not so. No man is truly himself but in the idea which others entertain of him. The mind, as well as the eye, "sees not itself, but by reflection from some other thing." What parity can there be between the effect of habitual composition on the mind of the individual, and the surprise occasioned by first reading a fine passage in an admired author; between what we do with ease, and what we thought it next to impossible ever to be done; between the reverential awe we have for years encouraged, without seeing reason to alter it, for dis-tinguished genius, and the slow, reluctant, unwelcome con-viction that after infinite toil and repeated disappointments, and when it is too late and to little purpose, we have our-selves at length accomplished what we at first proposed; between the insignificance of our petty, personal preten-tions, and the vastness and splendor which the atmosphere of imagination lends to an illustrious name? He who comes up to his own idea of greatness, must always have had a very low standard of it in his mind. "What a pity," said some one, "that Milton had not the pleasure of reading *Paradise Lost!*" He could not read it, as we do, with the weight of impression that a hundred years of admiration have added to it—"a phœnix gazed by all"—with the sense of the number of editions it has passed through with still

99

increasing reputation, with the tone of solidity, time-proof, which it has received from the breath of cold, envious maligners, with the sound which the voice of Fame has lent to every line of it! The writer of an ephemeral production may be as much dazzled with it as the public: it may sparkle in his own eyes for a moment, and be soon forgotten by everyone else. But no one can anticipate the suffrages of posterity. Every man, in judging of himself, is his own contemporary. He may feel the gale of popularity, but he cannot tell how long it will last. His opinion of himself wants distance, wants time, wants numbers, to set it off and confirm it. He must be indifferent to his own merits before he can feel a confidence in them. Besides, everyone must be sensible of a thousand weaknesses and deficiencies in himself; whereas Genius only leaves behind it the monuments of its strength. A great name is an abstraction of some one excellence: but whoever fancies himself an abstraction of excellence, so far from being great, may be sure that he is a blockhead, equally ignorant of excellence or defect, of himself or others. Mr. Burke, besides being the author of the *Reflections,* and the *Letter to a Noble Lord,* had a wife and son; and had to think as much about them as we do about him. The imagination gains nothing by the minute details of personal knowledge.

On the other hand, it may be said that no man knows so well as the author of any performance what it has cost him, and the length of time and study devoted to it. This is one, among other reasons, why no man can pronounce an opinion upon himself. The happiness of the result bears no proportion to the difficulties overcome or the pains taken. *Materiam superabat opus,* is an old and fatal complaint. The definition of genius is that it acts unconsciously; and those who have produced immortal works have done so without knowing how or why. The greatest power operates unseen, and executes its appointed task with as little ostentation as difficulty. Whatever is done best, is done from the natural bent and disposition of the mind. It is only where our incapacity begins, that we begin to feel the obstacles, and to set an undue value on our triumph over them. Correggio, Michael Angelo, Rembrandt, did what they did without premeditation or effort—their works came from their minds as a natural birth—if you had asked them why they adopted this or that style, they would have answered, *because they could not help it,* and because they knew of no other. . . . Shakespeare himself was an example of his own rule, and appears to have owed almost everything to industry or design. His poetry flashes from him like the lightning from the summer-cloud, or the stroke from the sunflower. When we look at the admirable comic designs of Hogarth, they seem from the unfinished state in which they are left, and from the freedom of the penciling, to have cost him little trouble; whereas the "Sigismunda" is a very labored and comparatively feeble performance, and he accordingly set great store by it. He also thought highly of his portraits, and boasted that "he could paint equal to Vandyke, give him his time and let him choose his subject." This was the very reason why he could not. Vandyke's excellence consisted in this, that he could paint a fine portrait of anyone at sight: let him take ever so much pains or choose ever so bad a subject, he could not help making something of it. His eye, his mind, his hand was cast in the mold of grace and delicacy. Milton, again, is understood to have preferred *Paradise Regained* to his other works. This, if so, was either because he himself was conscious of having failed in it, or because others thought he had. We are willing to think well of that which we know wants our favorable opinion, and to prop the rickety bantling. Every step taken, *invitâ Minerva,* costs us something, and is set down to account; whereas we are borne on the full tide of genius and success into the very haven of our desires almost imperceptibly. The strength of the impulse by which we are carried along prevents the sense of difficulty or resistance: the true inspiration of the Muse is soft and balmy as the air we breathe; and indeed leaves us little to boast of, for the effect hardly seems to be our own.

There are two persons who always appear to me to have worked under this involuntary, silent impulse more than any others; I mean Rembrandt and Correggio. It is not known that Correggio ever saw a picture of any great master. He lived and died obscurely in an obscure village. We have few of his works, but they are all perfect. What truth, what grace, what angelic sweetness are there! Not one line or tone that is not divinely soft or exquisitely fair; the painter's mind rejecting, by a natural process, all that is discordant, coarse, or unpleasing. The whole is an emanation of pure thought. The work grew under his hand as if of itself, and came out without a flaw, like the diamond from the rock. He knew not what he did; and looked at each modest grace as it stole from the canvas with anxious delight and wonder. Ah! gracious God! not he alone; how many more in all time have looked at their works with the same feelings, not knowing but they too may have done something divine, immortal, and finding in that sole doubt ample amends for pining solitude, for want, neglect, and an untimely fate. Oh! for one hour of that uneasy rapture, when the mind first thinks that it has struck out something that may last forever; when the germ of excellence bursts from nothing on the startled sight! Take, take away the gaudy triumphs of the world, the long deathless shout of fame, and give back that heartfelt sigh with which the youthful enthusiast first weds immortality as his secret bride! And thou too, Rembrandt! Thou wert a man of genius, if ever painter was a man of genius!—did his dream hang over you as you painted that strange picture of "Jacob's Ladder"? Did your eye strain over those gradual dusky clouds into futurity, or did those white-vested, beaked figures babble to you of fame as they approached? Did you know what you were about, or did you not paint much as it happened? Oh! if you had thought once about yourself, or anything but the subject, it would have been all over with "the glory, the intuition, the amenity," the dream had fled, the spell had been broken. The hills would not have looked like those we see in sleep —that tatterdemalion figure of Jacob, thrown on one side, would not have slept as if the breath was fairly taken out of his body. So much do Rembrandt's pictures savor of the soul and body of reality, that the thoughts seem identical with the objects—if there had been the least question what he should have done, or how he should do it, or how far he had succeeded, it would have spoiled everything. Lumps of light hung upon his pencil and fell upon his canvas like dew-drops: the shadowy veil was drawn over his backgrounds by the dull, obtuse finger of night, making darkness visible by still greater darkness that could only be felt! Cervantes is another instance of a man of genius, whose work may be said to have sprung from his mind, like Minerva from the head of Jupiter. Don Quixote and Sancho were a kind of twins; and the jests of the latter, as he says, fell from him like drops of rain when he least thought of it. Shakespeare's creations were more multiform, but equally natural and unstudied. Raphael and

Milton seem partial exceptions to this rule. Their productions were of the *composite order;* and those of the latter sometimes even amount to centos. Accordingly, we find Milton quoted among those authors who have left proofs of their entertaining a high opinion of themselves, and of cherishing a strong aspiration after fame. Some of Shakespeare's *Sonnets* have been also cited to the same purpose; but they seem rather to convey wayward and dissatisfied complaints of his untoward fortune than anything like a triumphant and confident reliance on his future renown. He appears to have stood more alone and to have thought less about himself than any living being. One reason for this indifference may have been, that as a writer he was tolerably successful in his life-time, and no doubt produced his works with very great facility. . . .

On the English Novelists

The great English novelists' "profound knowledge of human nature" and the ability to mirror their age in literature are discussed in Lectures on the English Comic Writers.

There is very little to warrant the common idea that Fielding was an imitator of Cervantes, except his own declaration of such an intention in the title-page of *Joseph Andrews,* the romantic turn of the character of Parson Adams (the only romantic character in his works), and the proverbial humor of Partridge, which is kept up only for a few pages. Fielding's novels are, in general, thoroughly his own; and they are thoroughly English. What they are most remarkable for is neither sentiment nor imagination nor wit, nor even humor, though there is an immense deal of this last quality; but profound knowledge of human nature, at least of English nature; and masterly pictures of the characters of men as he saw them existing. This quality distinguishes all his works, and is shown almost equally in all of them. As a painter of real life, he was equal to Hogarth; as a mere observer of human nature, he was little inferior to Shakespeare, though without any of the genius and poetical qualities of his mind. His humor is less rich and laughable than Smollett's; his wit as often misses as hits; he has none of the fine pathos of Richardson or Sterne; but he has brought together a greater variety of characters in common life, marked with more distinct peculiarities, and without an atom of caricature, than any other novel writer whatever. The extreme subtlety of observation on the springs of human conduct in ordinary characters is only equalled by the ingenuity of contrivance in bringing those springs into play, in such a manner as to lay open their smallest irregularity. The detection is always complete, and made with the certainty and skill of a philosophical experiment, and the obviousness and familiarity of a casual observation. The truth of the imitation is indeed so great, that it has been argued that Fielding must have had his materials ready-made to his hands, and was merely a transcriber of local manners and individual habits. For this conjecture, however, there seems to be no foundation. His representations, it is true, are local and individual; but they are not the less profound and conclusive. The feeling of the general principles of human nature operating in particular circumstances is always intense and uppermost in his mind, and he makes use of incident and situation only to bring out character. It is scarcely necessary to give any illustrations. *Tom Jones* is full of them. There is the account, for example, of the gratitude of the elder Blifil to his brother, for assisting him to obtain the fortune of Miss Bridget Alworthy by marriage; and of the gratitude of the poor of his neighborhood to Alworthy himself, who had done so much good in the country that he had made every one in it his enemy. There is the account of the Latin dialogues between Partridge and his maid, of the assault made on him during one of these by Mrs. Partridge, and the severe bruises he patiently received on that occasion, after which the parish of Little Baddington rang with the story that the schoolmaster had killed his wife. There is the exquisite keeping in the character of Blifil, and the want of it in that of Jones. There is the gradation in the lovers of Molly Seagrim; the philosopher Square succeeding to Tom Jones, who again finds that he himself had succeeded to the accomplished Will Barnes, who had the first possession of her person, and had still possession of her heart, Jones being only the instrument of her vanity, as Square was of her interest. Then there is the discreet honesty of Black George, the learning of Thwackum and Square, and the profundity of Squire Western, who considered it as a physical impossibility that his daughter should fall in love with Tom Jones. We have also that gentleman's disputes with his sister, and the inimitable appeal of that lady to her niece: "I was never so handsome as you, Sophy: yet I had something of you formerly. I was called the cruel Parthenissa. Kingdoms and states, as Tully Cicero says, undergo alteration, and so must the human form!" The adventure of the same lady with the highwayman who robbed her of her jewels while he complimented her beauty ought not to be passed over, nor that of Sophia and her muff, nor the reserved coquetry of her cousin Fitzpatrick, nor the description of Lady Bellaston, nor the modest overtures of the pretty widow Hunt, nor the indiscreet babblings of Mrs. Honour. The moral of this book has been objected to without much reason; but a more serious objection has been made to the want of refinement and elegance in two principal characters. We never feel this objection, indeed, while we are reading the book: but at other times, we have something like a lurking suspicion that Jones was but an awkward fellow and Sophia a pretty simpleton. . . .

Smollett's first novel, *Roderick Random*, which is also his best, appeared about the same time as *Tom Jones*, and yet it has a much more modern air with it; but this may be accounted for from the circumstance that Smollett was quite a young man at the time whereas Fielding's manner must have been formed long before. The style of *Roderick Random* is more easy and flowing than that of *Tom Jones*; the incidents follow one another more rapidly; the humor is broader and as effectual; and there is very nearly, if not quite, an equal interest excited by the story. What then is it that gives the superiority to Fielding? It is the superior insight into the springs of human character and the constant development of that character through every change of circumstance. Smollett's humor often arises from the situation of the persons, or the peculiarity of their external appearance; as, from Roderick Random's carrotty locks, which hung down over his shoulders like a pound of candles, or Strap's ignorance of London and the blunders that follow from it. There is a tone of vulgarity about all his productions. The incidents frequently resemble detached anecdotes taken from a newspaper or magazine; and, like those in *Gil Blas*, might happen to a hundred other characters. He exhibits the ridiculous accidents and reverses to which human life is liable, not the stuff of which it is composed. He seldom probes to the quick or penetrates beyond the surface; and, therefore, he leaves no stings in the minds of his readers and in this respect is far less interesting than Fielding. His novels always enliven and never tire us: we take them up with pleasure and lay them down without any strong feeling of regret. We look on and laugh as spectators of a highly amusing scene without closing in with the combatants, or being made parties in the event. We read *Roderick Random* as an entertaining story; for the particular accidents and modes of life which it describes have ceased to exist, but we regard *Tom Jones* as a real history because the author never stops short of those essential principles which lie at the bottom of all our actions and in which we feel an immediate interest. . . . *Humphry Clinker* and *Count Fathom* are both equally admirable in their way. Perhaps the former is the most pleasing gossiping novel that ever was written, that which gives the most pleasure with the least effort to the reader. It is quite as amusing as going the journey could have been, and we have just as good an idea of what happened on the road as if we had been of the party. Humphry Clinker himself is exquisite; and his sweetheart, Winifred Jenkins, not much behind him. Matthew Bramble, though not altogether original, is excellently supported and seems to have been the prototype of Sir Anthony Absolute in the Rivals. But Lismahago is the flower of the flock. His tenaciousness in argument is not so delightful as the relaxation of his logical severity when he finds his fortune mellowing in the wintry smiles of Mrs. Tabitha Bramble. This is the best preserved and most severe of all Smollett's characters. . . .

Pamela is the first of Richardson's productions and the very child of his brain. Taking the general idea of the character of a modest and beautiful country girl and of the ordinary situation in which she is placed, he makes out all the rest, even to the smallest circumstance by the mere force of a reasoning imagination. It would seem as if a step lost would be as fatal here as in a mathematical demonstration. The development of the character is the most simple and comes the nearest to nature that it can do, without being the same thing. The interest of the story increases with the dawn of understanding and reflection in the heroine: her sentiments gradually expand themselves like opening flowers. She writes better every time and acquires a confidence in herself just as a girl would do, writing such letters in such circumstances; and yet it is certain that no girl would write such letters in such circumstances. What I mean is this: Richardson's nature is always the nature of sentiment and reflection, not of impulse or situation. He furnishes his characters on every occasion with the presence of mind of the author. He makes them act not as they would from the impulse of the moment, but as they might upon reflection and upon a careful review of every motive and circumstance in their situation. They regularly sit down to write letters and if the business of life consisted in letter-writing, and was carried on by the post, human nature would be what Richardson represents it.

It remains to speak of Sterne, and I shall do it in few words. There is more of mannerism and affectation in him and a more immediate reference to preceding authors; but his excellences, where he is excellent, are of the first order. His characters are intellectual and inventive, like Richardson's, but totally opposite in the execution. The one are made out by continuity and patient repetition of touches: the others, by glancing transitions and graceful apposition. His style is equally different from Richardson's; it is at times the most rapid, the most happy, the most idiomatic of any that is to be found. It is the pure essence of English conversational style. His works consist only of *morceaux*—of brilliant passages. I wonder that Goldsmith, who ought to have known better, should call him "a dull fellow." His wit is poignant, though artificial; and his characters (though the groundwork of some of them had been laid before) have yet invaluable original differences; and the spirit of the execution, the master-strokes constantly thrown into them, are not to be surpassed. It is sufficient to name them: Yorick, Dr. Slop, Mr. Shandy, My Uncle Toby, Trim, Susanna, and the Widow Wadman. In these he has contrived to oppose with equal felicity and originality two characters, one of pure intellect and the other of pure good nature, in My Father and My Uncle Toby. There appears to have been in Sterne a vein of dry, sarcastic humor and of extreme tenderness of feeling; the latter sometimes carried to affectation, as in the tale of Maria, and the apostrophe to the recording angel; but at other times pure and without blemish. The story of Le Fevre is perhaps the finest in the English language. My Father's restlessness, both of body and mind, is inimitable. It is the model from which all those despicable performances against modern philosophy ought to have been copied, if their authors had known anything of the subject they were writing about. My Uncle Toby is one of the finest compliments ever paid to human nature.

On Poetry in General

Aesthetically important, the next three essays contain the core of Hazlitt's literary and artistic theories. "On Poetry in General," from Lectures on the English Poets, *formulates an expressive concept of poetry as "the language of the imagination and the passions." "On Gusto" and "Why the Arts are not Progressive" from* The Round Table *(1817) attempt, respectively, to define "the internal character, the living principle" in great art and to re-establish a universal standard of judgment—nature—for the "improvement of taste."*

The best general notion which I can give of poetry is, that it is the natural impression of any object or event, by its vividness exciting an involuntary movement of imagination and passion, and producing, by sympathy, a certain modulation of the voice, or sounds, expressing it.

In treating of poetry, I shall speak first of the subject-matter of it, next of the forms of expression to which it gives birth, and afterwards of its connection with harmony of sound.

Poetry is the language of the imagination and the passions. It relates to whatever gives immediate pleasure or pain to the human mind. It comes home to the bosoms and businesses of men; for nothing but what so comes home to them in the most general and intelligible shape, can be a subject for poetry. Poetry is the universal language which the heart holds with nature and itself. He who has a contempt for poetry, cannot have much respect for himself, or for anything else. It is not a mere frivolous accomplishment (as some persons have been led to imagine), the trifling amusement of a few idle readers or leisure hours—it has been the study and delight of mankind in all ages. Many people suppose that poetry is something to be found only in books, contained in lines of ten syllables, with like endings: but wherever there is a sense of beauty, or power, or harmony, as in the motion of a wave of the sea, in the growth of a flower that "spreads its sweet leaves to the air, and dedicates its beauty to the sun,"—*there* is poetry, in its birth. If history is a grave study, poetry may be said to be a graver: its materials lie deeper, and are spread wider. History treats, for the most part, of the cumbrous and unwieldy masses of things, the empty cases in which the affairs of the world are packed, under the heads of intrigue or war, in different states, and from century to century: but there is no thought or feeling that can have entered into the mind of man, which he would be eager to communicate to others, or which they would listen to with delight, that is not a fit subject for poetry. It is not a branch of authorship: it is "the stuff of which our life is made." The rest is "mere oblivion," a dead letter: for all that is worth remembering in life is the poetry of it. Fear is poetry, hope is poetry, love is poetry, hatred is poetry; contempt, jealousy, remorse, admiration, wonder, pity, despair, or madness, are all poetry. Poetry is that fine particle within us, that expands, rarefies, refines, raises our whole being: without it "man's life is poor as beast's." Man is a poetical animal: and those of us who do not study the principles of poetry, act upon them all our lives, like Molière's *Bourgeois Gentilhomme,* who had always spoken prose without knowing it. . . .

We shape things according to our wishes and fancies, without poetry; but poetry is the most emphatical language that can be found for those creations of the mind "which ecstasy is very cunning in." Neither a mere description of natural objects, nor a mere delineation of natural feelings, however distinct or forcible, constitutes the ultimate end and aim of poetry, without the heightenings of the imagination. The light of poetry is not only a direct but also a reflected light, that while it shows us the object, throws a sparkling radiance on all around it: the flame of the passions, communicated to the imagination, reveals to us, as with a flash of lightning, the inmost recesses of thought, and penetrates our whole being. Poetry represents forms chiefly as they suggest other forms; feelings, as they suggest forms or other feelings. Poetry puts a spirit of life and motion into the universe. It describes the flowing, not the fixed. It does not define the limits of sense, or analyze the distinctions of understanding, but signifies the excess of the imagination beyond the actual or ordinary impression of any object or feeling. The poetical impression of any object is that uneasy, exquisite sense of beauty or power that cannot be contained within itself; that is impatient of all limit; that (as flame bends to flame) strives to link itself to some other image of kindred beauty or grandeur; to enshrine itself, as it were, in the highest forms of fancy, and to relieve the aching sense of pleasure by expressing it in the boldest manner, and by the most striking examples of the same quality in other instances. Poetry, according to Lord Bacon, for this reason, "has something divine in it, because it raises the mind and hurries it into sublimity, by conforming the shows of things to the desires of the soul, instead of subjecting the soul to external things, as reason and history do." It is strictly the language of the imagination; and the imagination is that faculty which represents objects, not as they are in themselves, but as they are molded by other thoughts and feelings, into an infinite variety of shapes and combinations of power. This language is not the less true to nature, because it is false in point of fact; but so much the more true and natural, if it conveys the impression which the object under the influence of passion makes on the mind. Let an object, for instance, be presented to the senses in a state of agitation or fear—and the imagination will distort or magnify the object, and convert it into the likeness of whatever is most proper to encourage the fear.

Poetry is the high-wrought enthusiasm of fancy and feeling. As in describing natural objects, it impregnates sensible impressions with the forms of fancy, so it describes the feelings of pleasure or pain, by blending them with the strongest movements of passion, and the most striking forms of nature. Tragic poetry, which is the most impassioned species of it, strives to carry on the feeling to the utmost point of sublimity or pathos, by all the force of comparison or contrast; loses the sense of present suffering in the imaginary exaggeration of it; exhausts the terror or pity by an unlimited indulgence of it; grapples with impossibilities in its desperate impatience of restraint; throws us back upon the past, forward into the future; brings every moment of our being or object of nature in startling review before us; and in the rapid whirl of events, lifts us from the depths of woe to the highest contemplations on human life. When Lear says of Edgar, "Nothing but his unkind daughters could have brought him to this;" what a bewildered amazement, what a wrench of the imagination, that cannot be brought to conceive of any other cause of misery than that which has bowed it down, and absorbs all other sorrow in its own! His sorrow, like a flood, supplies the sources of all other sorrow. Again, when he exclaims in the mad scene, "The little dogs and all, Tray,

Blanche, and Sweetheart, see, they bark at me!" it is passion lending occasion to imagination to make every creature in league against him, conjuring up ingratitude and insult in their least looked-for and most galling shapes, searching every thread and fibre of his heart, and finding out the last remaining image of respect or attachment in the bottom of his breast, only to torture and kill it! In like manner, the "So I am" of Cordelia gushes from her heart like a torrent of tears, relieving it of a weight of love and of supposed ingratitude, which had pressed upon it for years. What a fine return of the passion upon itself is that in Othello—with what a mingled agony of regret and despair he clings to the last traces of departed happiness—when he exclaims,

> ——"Oh now, for ever
> *Farewel the tranquil mind. Farewel content;*

Impassioned poetry is an emanation of the moral and intellectual part of our nature, as well as of the sensitive —of the desire to know, the will to act, and the power to feel; and ought to appeal to these different parts of our constitution, in order to be perfect. The domestic or prose tragedy, which is thought to be the most natural, is in this sense the least so, because it appeals almost exclusively to one of these faculties, our sensibility. The tragedies of Moore and Lillo, for this reason, however affecting at the time, oppress and lie like a dead weight upon the mind, a load of misery which it is unable to throw off; the tragedy of Shakespeare, which is true poetry, stirs our inmost affections; abstracts evil from itself by combining it with all the forms of imagination, and with the deepest workings of the heart, and rouses the whole man within us.

The pleasure, however, derived from tragic poetry, is not anything peculiar to it as poetry, as a fictitious and fanciful thing. It is not an anomaly of the imagination. It has its source and ground-work in the common love of strong excitement. As Mr. Burke observes, people flock to see a tragedy; but if there were a public execution in the next street, the theatre would very soon be empty. It is not then the difference between fiction and reality that solves the difficulty. Children are satisfied with the stories of ghosts and witches in plain prose: nor do the hawkers of full, true, and particular accounts of murders

and executions about the streets, find it necessary to have
them turned into penny ballads, before they can dispose
of these interesting and authentic documents. The grave
politician drives a thriving trade of abuse and calumnies
poured out against those whom he makes his enemies
for no other end than that he may live by them. The
popular preacher makes less frequent mention of heaven
than of hell. Oaths and nicknames are only a more vulgar
sort of poetry or rhetoric. We are as fond of indulging
our violent passions as of reading a description of those
of others. We are as prone to make a torment of our
fears, as to luxuriate in our hopes of good. . . . Poetry
is only the highest eloquence of passion, the most vivid
form of expression that can be given to our conception
of anything, whether pleasurable or painful, mean or
dignified, delightful or distressing. It is the perfect coincidence of the image and the words with the feeling we
have, and of which we cannot get rid in any other way,
that gives an instant "satisfaction to the thought." This
is equally the origin of wit and fancy, of comedy and
tragedy, of the sublime and pathetic. When Pope says
of the Lord Mayor's show,—

> *"Now night descending, the proud scene is o'er,*
> *But lives in Settle's numbers one day more!"*

—when Collins makes Danger, "with limbs of giant
mould,"

> ——*"Throw him on the steep*
> *Of some loose hanging rock asleep."*

when Lear calls out in extreme anguish,

> *"Ingratitude, thou marble-hearted fiend,*
> *How much more hideous shew'st in a child*
> *Than the sea-monster!"*

—the passion of contempt in the one case, of terror in
the other, and of indignation in the last, is perfectly satisfied. We see the thing ourselves, and show it to others
as we feel it to exist, and as, in spite of ourselves, we are
compelled to think of it. The imagination, by thus embodying and turning them to shape, gives an obvious
relief to the indistinct and importunate cravings of the will.

—We do not wish the thing to be so; but we wish it to appear such as it is. For knowledge is conscious power; and the mind is no longer, in this case, the dupe, though it may be the victim of vice or folly.

Poetry is in all its shapes the language of the imagination and the passions, of fancy and will. Nothing, therefore, can be more absurd than the outcry which has been sometimes raised by frigid and pedantic critics, for reducing the language of poetry to the standard of common sense and reason: for the end and use of poetry, "both at the first and now, was and is to hold the mirror up to nature," seen through the medium of passion and imagination, not divested of that medium by means of literal truth or abstract reason. The painter of history might as well be required to represent the face of a person who has just trod upon a serpent with the still-life expression of a common portrait, as the poet to describe the most striking and vivid impressions which things can be supposed to make upon the mind, in the language of common conversation. Let who will strip nature of the colors and the shapes of fancy, the poet is not bound to do so; the impressions of common sense and strong imagination, that is, of passion and indifference, cannot be the same, and they must have a separate language to do justice to either. Objects must strike differently upon the mind, independently of what they are in themselves, as long as we have a different interest in them, as we see them in a different point of view, nearer or at a greater distance (morally or physically speaking), from novelty, from old acquaintance, from our ignorance of them, from our fear of their consequences, from contrast, from unexpected likeness. We can no more take away the faculty of the imagination, than we can see all objects without light or shade. Some things must dazzle us by their preternatural light; others must hold us in suspense, and tempt our curiosity to explore their obscurity. Those who would dispel these various illusions, to give us their drab-colored creation in their stead, are not very wise. Let the naturalist, if he will, catch the glow-worm, carry it home with him in a box, and find it next morning nothing but a little grey worm; let the poet or the lover of poetry visit it at evening, when beneath the scented hawthorn and the crescent moon it has built itself a palace of emerald light. This is also one part of nature, one appearance which the glow-worm presents, and that not the least interesting; so poetry is one part of the history of the human mind, though it is neither science nor philosophy. It cannot be concealed, however, that the progress of knowledge and refinement has a tendency to circumscribe the limits of the imagination, and to clip the wings of poetry. The province of the imagination is principally visionary, the unknown and undefined: the understanding restores things to their natural boundaries, and strips them of their fanciful pretensions. Hence the history of religious and poetical enthusiasm is much the same; and both have received a sensible shock from the progress of experimental philosophy. It is the undefined and uncommon that gives birth and scope to the imagination; we can only fancy what we do not know. As in looking into the mazes of a tangled wood we fill them with what shapes we please, with ravenous beasts, with caverns vast, and drear enchantments, so in our ignorance of the world about us, we make gods or devils of the first object we see, and set no bounds to the wilful suggestions of our hopes and fears.

> *And visions, as poetic eyes avow,*
> *Hang on each leaf and cling to every bough.*

There can never be another Jacob's dream. Since that time, the heavens have gone farther off, and grown astronomical. They have become averse to the imagination, nor will they return to us on the squares of the distances, or on Doctor Chalmers's Discourses. Rembrandt's picture brings the matter nearer to us.—It is not only the progress of mechanical knowledge, but the necessary advances of civilization that are unfavorable to the spirit of poetry. We not only stand in less awe of the preternatural world, but we can calculate more surely, and look with more indifference, upon the regular routine of this. The heroes of the fabulous ages rid the world of monsters and giants. At present we are less exposed to the vicissitudes of good or evil, to the incursions of wild beasts or "bandit fierce," or to the unmitigated fury of the elements. The time has been that "our fell of hair would at a dismal treatise rouse and stir as life were in it." But the police spoils all; and we now hardly so much as dream of a midnight murder. *Macbeth* is only tolerated in this country for the sake of the music; and in the United States of America, where the philosophical principles of government are carried still farther in theory and practice, we find that the *Beggar's Opera* is hooted from the stage. Society, by degrees, is constructed into a machine that carries us safely and insipidly from one end of life to the other, in a very comfortable prose style.

> *Obscurity her curtain round them drew,*
> *And siren Sloth a dull quietus sung.*

The remarks which have been here made, would, in some measure, lead to a solution of the question of the comparative merits of painting and poetry. I do not mean to give any preference, but it should seem that the argument which has been sometimes set up, that painting must affect the imagination more strongly, because it represents the image more distinctly, is not well founded. We may assume without much temerity, that poetry is more poetical than painting. When artists or connoisseurs talk on stilts about the poetry of painting, they show that they know little about poetry, and have little love for the art. Painting gives the object itself; poetry what it implies. Painting embodies what a thing contains in itself: poetry suggests what exists out of it, in any manner connected with it. But this last is the proper province of the imagination. Again, as it relates to passion, painting gives the event, poetry the progress of events: but it is during the progress, in the interval of expectation and suspense, while our hopes and fears are strained to the highest pitch of breathless agony, that the pinch of the interest lies.

> *Between the acting of a dreadful thing*
> *And the first motion, all the interim is*
> *Like a phantasma or a hideous dream.*
> *The mortal instruments are then in council;*
> *And the state of man, like to a little kingdom,*
> *Suffers then the nature of an insurrection.*

But by the time that the picture is painted, all is over. Faces are the best part of a picture; but even faces are not what we chiefly remember in what interests us most. —But it may be asked then, Is there anything better than Claude Lorraine's landscapes, than Titian's portraits, than Raphael's cartoons, or the Greek statues? Of the two first I shall say nothing, as they are evidently picturesque, rather than imaginative. Raphael's cartoons are certainly the finest comments that ever were made on the Scriptures.

Would their effect be the same if we were not acquainted with the text? But the New Testament existed before the cartoons. There is one subject of which there is no cartoon, Christ washing the feet of the disciples the night before his death. But that chapter does not need a commentary! It is for want of some such resting place for the imagination that the Greek statues are little else than specious forms. They are marble to the touch and to the heart. They have not an informing principle within them. In their faultless excellence they appear sufficient to themselves. By their beauty they are raised above the frailties of passion or suffering. By their beauty they are deified. But they are not objects of religious faith to us, and their forms are a reproach to common humanity. They seem to have no sympathy with us, and not to want our admiration.

Poetry in its matter and form is natural imagery or feeling, combined with passion and fancy. In its mode of conveyance, it combines the ordinary use of language with musical expression. There is a question of long standing, in what the essence of poetry consists; or what it is that determines why one set of ideas should be expressed in prose, another in verse. Milton has told us his idea of poetry in a single line—

> *Thoughts that voluntary move*
> *Harmonious numbers.*

As there are certain sounds that excite certain movements, and the song and dance go together, so there are, no doubt, certain thoughts that lead to certain tones of voice, or modulations of sound, and change "the words of Mercury into the songs of Apollo." There is a striking instance of this adaptation of the movement of sound and rhythm to the subject, in Spenser's description of the Satyrs accompanying Una to the cave of Sylvanus.

> *So from the ground she fearless doth arise*
> *And walketh forth without suspect of crime.*
> *They, all as glad as birds of joyous prime,*
> *Thence lead her forth, about her dancing round,*
> *Shouting and singing all a shepherd's rhyme;*
> *And with green branches strewing all the ground,*
> *Do worship her as queen with olive garland crown'd.*

> *And all the way their merry pipes they sound,*
> *That all the woods and doubled echoes ring;*
> *And with their horned feet do wear the ground,*
> *Leaping like wanton kids in pleasant spring;*
> *So towards old Sylvanus they her bring,*
> *Who with the noise awaked, cometh out.*

On the contrary, there is nothing either musical or natural in the ordinary construction of language. It is a thing altogether arbitrary and conventional. Neither in the sounds themselves, which are the voluntary signs of certain ideas, nor in their grammatical arrangements in common speech, is there any principle of natural imitation, or correspondence to the individual ideas, or to the tone of feeling with which they are conveyed to others. The jerks, the breaks, the inequalities, and harshnesses of prose, are fatal to the flow of a poetical imagination, as a jolting road or a stumbling horse disturbs the reverie of an absent man. But poetry makes these odds all even. It is the music of language, answering to the music of the mind, untying as it were "the secret soul of harmony." Wherever any object takes such a hold of the mind as to make us dwell upon it, and brood over it, melting the heart in tenderness, or kindling it to a sentiment of enthusiasm;—wherever a movement of imagination or passion is impressed on the mind, by which it seeks to prolong and repeat the emotion, to bring all other objects into accord with it, and to give the same movement of harmony, sustained and continuous, or gradually varied according to the occasion, to the sounds that express it—this is poetry. The musical in sound is the sustained and continuous; the musical in thought is the sustained and continuous also. There is a near connection between music and deep-rooted passion. Mad people sing. As often as articulation passes naturally into intonation, there poetry begins. Where one idea gives a tone and color to others, where one feeling melts others into it, there can be no reason why the same principle should not be extended to the sounds by which the voice utters these emotions of the soul, and blends syllables and lines into each other. It is to supply the inherent defect of harmony in the customary mechanism of language, to make the sound an echo to the sense, when the sense becomes a sort of echo to itself—to mingle the tide of verse, "the golden cadences of poetry," with the tide of feeling, flowing and murmuring as it flows—in short, to take the language of the imagination from off the ground, and enable it to spread its wings where it may indulge its own impulses—

> *Sailing with supreme dominion*
> *Through the azure deep of air—*

without being stopped, or fretted, or diverted with the abruptness and petty obstacles, and discordant flats and sharps of prose, that poetry was invented. It is to common language, what springs are to a carriage, or wings to feet. In ordinary speech we arrive at a certain harmony by the modulations of the voice: in poetry the same thing is done systematically by a regular collocation of syllables. It has been well observed, that every one who declaims warmly, or grows intent upon a subject, rises into a sort of blank verse or measured prose. The merchant, as described in Chaucer, went on his way "sounding always the increase of his winning." Every prose-writer has more or less of rhythmical adaptation, except poets, who, when deprived of the regular mechanism of verse, seem to have no principle of modulation left in their writings.

An excuse might be made for rhyme in the same manner. It is but fair that the ear should linger on the sounds that delight it, or avail itself of the same brilliant coincidence and unexpected recurrence of syllables, that have been displayed in the invention and collocation of images. It is allowed that rhyme assists the memory; and that a man of wit and shrewdness has been heard to say, that the only four good lines of poetry are the well-known ones which tell the number of days in the months of the year.

> *"Thirty days hath September,"* etc.

But if the jingle of names assists the memory, may it not also quicken the fancy? and there are other things worth having at our fingers' ends, besides the contents of the almanac.—Pope's versification is tiresome, from its excessive sweetness and uniformity. Shakespeare's blank verse is the perfection of dramatic dialogue.

All is not poetry that passes for such: nor does verse make the whole difference between poetry and prose. The *Iliad* does not cease to be poetry in a literal translation; and Addison's *Campaign* has been very properly denominated a Gazette in rhyme. Common prose differs from poetry, as treating for the most part either of such trite, familiar, and irksome matters of fact, as convey no extraordinary impulse to the imagination, or else of such difficult and laborious processes of the understanding, as do not admit of the wayward or violent movements either of the imagination or the passions. . . .

On Gusto

Gusto in art is power or passion defining any object.— It is not so difficult to explain this term in what relates to expression (of which it may be said to be the highest degree) as in what relates to things without expression, to the natural appearances of objects, as mere color or form. In one sense, however, there is hardly any object entirely devoid of expression, without some character of power belonging to it, some precise association with pleasure or pain: and it is in giving this truth of character from the truth of feeling, whether in the highest or the lowest degree, but always in the highest degree of which the subject is capable, that gusto consists.

There is a gusto in the coloring of Titian. Not only do his heads seem to think—his bodies seem to feel. This is what the Italians mean by the *morbidezza* of his flesh-color. It seems sensitive and alive all over; not merely to have the look and texture of flesh, but the feeling in itself. For example, the limbs of his female figures have a luxurious softness and delicacy, which appears conscious of the pleasure of the beholder. As the objects themselves in nature would produce an impression on the sense, distinct from every other object, and having something divine in it, which the heart owns and the imagination consecrates, the objects in the picture preserve the same impression, absolute, unimpaired, stamped with all the truth of passion, the pride of the eye, and the charm of beauty. Rubens makes his flesh-color like flowers; Albano's is like ivory; Titian's is like flesh, and like nothing else. It is as different from that of other painters, as the skin is from a piece of white or red drapery thrown over it. The blood circulates here and there, the blue veins just appear, the rest is distinguished throughout only by that sort of tingling sensation to the eye, which the body feels within itself. This is gusto.—Vandyke's flesh-color, though it has great truth and purity, wants gusto. It has not the internal character, the living principle in it. It is a smooth surface, not a warm, moving mass. It is painted without passion, with indifference. The hand only has been concerned. The impression slides off from the eye, and does not, like the tones of Titian's pencil, leave a sting behind it in the mind of the spectator. The eye does not acquire a taste or appetite for what it sees. In a word, gusto in painting is where the impression made on one sense excites by affinity those of another.

Michael Angelo's forms are full of gusto. They everywhere obtrude the sense of power upon the eye. His limbs convey an idea of muscular strength, of moral grandeur, and even of intellectual dignity: they are firm, commanding, broad, and massy, capable of executing with ease the determined purposes of the will. His faces have no other expression than his figures, conscious power and capacity. They appear only to think what they shall do, and to know that they can do it. This is what is meant by saying that his style is hard and masculine. It is the reverse of Correggio's, which is effeminate. That is, the gusto of Michael Angelo consists in expressing energy of will without proportionable sensibility, Correggio's in expressing exquisite sensibility without energy of will. In Correggio's faces as well as figures we see neither bones nor muscles, but then what a soul is there, full of sweetness and of grace—pure, playful, soft, angelical! There is sentiment enough in a hand painted by Correggio to set up a school of history painters. Whenever we look at the hands of Correggio's women or of Raphael's, we always wish to touch them.

Again, Titian's landscapes have a prodigious gusto, both in the coloring and forms. We shall never forget one that we saw many years ago in the Orleans Gallery of Acteon hunting. It had a brown, mellow, autumnal look. The sky was of the color of stone. The winds seemed to sing through the rustling branches of the trees, and already you might hear the twanging of bows resound through the tangled mazes of the wood. Mr. West, we understand, has this landscape. He will know if this description of it is just. The landscape background of the St. Peter Martyr is another well-known instance of the power of this great painter to give a romantic interest and an appropriate character to the objects of his pencil, where every circumstance adds to the effect of the scene,—the bold trunks of the tall forest trees, the trailing ground plants, with that cold convent spire rising in the distance, amidst the blue sapphire mountains and the golden sky.

Rubens has a great deal of gusto in his Fauns and Satyrs, and in all that expresses motion, but in nothing else. Rembrandt has it in everything; everything in his pictures has a tangible character. If he puts a diamond in the ear of a Burgomaster's wife, it is of the first water; and his furs and stuffs are proof against a Russian winter. Raphael's gusto was only in expression; he had no idea of the character of anything but the human form. The dryness and poverty of his style in other respects is a phenomenon in the art. His trees are like sprigs of grass stuck in a book of botanical specimens. Was it that Raphael never had time to go beyond the walls of Rome? That he was always in the streets, at church, or in the bath? He was not one of the Society of Arcadians.

Claude's landscapes, perfect as they are, want gusto. This is not easy to explain. They are perfect abstractions of the visible images of things; they speak the visible language of nature truly. They resemble a mirror or microscope. To the eye only they are more perfect than any other landscapes that ever were or will be painted; they give more of nature, as cognizable by one sense alone; but they lay an equal stress on all visible impressions; they do not interpret one sense by another; they do not distinguish the character of different objects as we are taught, and can only be taught, to distinguish them by their effect on the different senses. That is, his eye wanted imagination: it did not strongly sympathize with his other faculties. He saw the atmosphere, but he did not feel it. He painted the trunk of a tree or a rock in the foreground as smooth—with as complete an abstraction of the gross, tangible impression, as any other part of the picture; his trees are perfectly beautiful, but quite immovable; they have a look of enchantment. In short, his landscapes are unequalled imitations of nature, released from its subjection to the elements, —as if all objects were become a delightful fairy vision, and the eye had rarefied and refined away the other senses.

The gusto in the Greek statues is of a very singular kind. The sense of perfect form nearly occupies the whole mind, and hardly suffers it to dwell on any other feeling. It seems enough for them *to be,* without acting or suffering. Their forms are ideal, spiritual. Their beauty is power. By their beauty they are raised above the frailties of pain or passion; by their beauty they are deified.

The infinite quantity of dramatic invention in Shakespeare takes from his gusto. The power he delights to show is not intense, but discursive. He never insists on any thing as much as he might, except a quibble. Milton has great gusto. He repeats his blow twice; grapples with and exhausts his subject. His imagination has a double relish of its objects, an inveterate attachment to the things he describes, and to the words describing them.

> ———*Or where Chineses drive*
> *With sails and wind their cany waggons light.*
>
> . . . .
>
> *Wild above rule or art,* enormous *bliss.*

There is a gusto in Pope's compliments, in Dryden's satires, and Prior's tales; and among prose-writers, Boccaccio and Rabelais had the most of it. We will only mention one other work which appears to us to be full of gusto, and that is the *Beggar's Opera.* If it is not, we are altogether mistaken in our notions on this delicate subject.

Why the Arts are not Progressive

It is often made a subject of complaint and surprise, that the arts in this country, and in modern times, have not kept pace with the general progress of society and civilization in other respects, and it has been proposed to remedy the deficiency by more carefully availing ourselves of the advantages which time and circumstances have placed within our reach, but which we have hitherto neglected, the study of the antique, the formation of academies, and the distribution of prizes.

First, the complaint itself, that the arts do not attain that progressive degree of perfection which might reasonably be expected from them, proceeds on a false notion, for the analogy appealed to in support of the regular advances of art to higher degrees of excellence, totally fails; it applies to science, not to art.—Secondly, the expedients proposed to remedy the evil by adventitious means are only calculated to confirm it. The arts hold immediate communication with nature, and are only derived from that source. When that original impulse no longer exists, when the inspiration of genius is fled, all the attempts to recall it are no better than the tricks of galvanism to restore the dead to life. The arts may be said to resemble Antæus in his struggle with Hercules, who was strangled when he was raised above the ground, and only revived and recovered his strength when he touched his mother earth.

Nothing is more contrary to the fact than the supposition that in what we understand by the *fine arts,* as painting and poetry, relative perfection is only the result of repeated efforts, and that what has been once well done constantly leads to something better. What is mechanical, reducible to rule, or capable of demonstration, is progressive, and admits of gradual improvement: what is not mechanical or definite, but depends on genius, taste, and feeling, very soon becomes stationary, or retrograde, and loses more than it gains by transfusion. The contrary opinion is, indeed, a common error, which has grown up, like many others, from transferring an analogy of one kind to something quite distinct, without thinking of the difference in the nature of the things, or attending to the difference of the results. For most persons, finding what wonderful advances have been made in biblical criticism, in chemistry, in mechanics, in geometry, astronomy, &c., i.e. in things depending on mere inquiry and experiment, or on absolute demonstration, have been led hastily to conclude, that there was a general tendency in the efforts of the human intellect to improve by repetition, and in all other arts and institutions to grow perfect and mature by time. We look back upon the theological creed of our ancestors, and their discoveries in natural philosophy, with a smile of pity; science, and the arts connected with it, have all had their infancy, their youth, and manhood, and seem to have in them no principle of limitation or decay; and, inquiring no farther about the matter, we infer, in the height of our self-congratulation, and in the intoxication of our pride, that the same progress has been, and will continue to be, made in all other things which are the work of man. The fact, however, stares us so plainly in the face, that one would think the smallest reflection must suggest the truth, and overturn our sanguine theories. The greatest poets, the ablest orators, the best painters, and the finest sculptors that the world ever saw, appeared soon after the birth of these arts, and lived in a state of society, which was, in other respects, comparatively barbarous. Those arts, which depend on individual genius and incommunicable power, have always leaped at once from infancy to manhood, from the first rude dawn of invention to their meridian height and dazzling lustre, and have in general declined ever after. This is the peculiar distinction and privilege of each, of science and of art; of the one, never to attain its utmost summit of perfection, and of the other, to arrive at it almost at once. Homer, Chaucer, Spenser, Shakespeare, Dante, and Ariosto (Milton alone was of a later age, and not the worse for it), Raphael, Titian, Michael Angelo, Correggio, Cervantes, and Boccaccio—all lived near the beginning of their arts— perfected, and all but created them. These giant sons of genius stand, indeed, upon the earth, but they tower above their fellows, and the long line of their successors does not interpose anything to obstruct their view, or lessen their brightness. In strength and stature they are unrivaled, in grace and beauty they have never been surpassed. In afterages, and more refined periods, (as they are called) great men have arisen one by one, as it were by throes and at intervals: though in general the best of these cultivated and artificial minds were of an inferior order, as Tasso and Pope among poets, Guido and Vandyke among paint-ers. But in the earliest stages of the arts, when the first mechanical difficulties had been got over, and the language as it were acquired, they rose by clusters and in constella-tions, never to rise again.

The arts of painting and poetry are conversant with the world of thought within us, and with the world of sense without us—with what we know, and see, and feel inti-mately. They flow from the sacred shrine of our own breasts, and are kindled at the living lamp of nature. The pulse of the passions assuredly beats as high, the depths and soundings of the human heart were as well understood three thousand years ago, as they are at present; the face of nature, and "the human face divine," shone as bright then as they have ever done. It is this light, reflected by true genius on art, that marks out its path before it, and sheds a glory round the Muses' feet, like that which "circled Una's angel face,

And made a sunshine in the shady place."

Nature is the soul of art. There is a strength in the imagi-nation that reposes entirely on nature, which nothing else can supply. There is in the old poets and painters a vigor and grasp of mind, a full possession of their subject, a con-fidence and firm faith, a sublime simplicity, an elevation of thought, proportioned to their depth of feeling, an in-creasing force and impetus, which moves, penetrates, and kindles all that come in contact with it, which seems not theirs, but given to them. It is this reliance on the power of nature which has produced those masterpieces by the Prince of Painters, in which expression is all in all, where one spirit—that of truth—pervades every part, brings down heaven to earth, mingles cardinals and popes with angels and apostles, and yet blends and harmonizes the whole by the true touches and intense feeling of what is beautiful and grand in nature. It was the same trust in nature that enabled Chaucer to describe the patient sorrow of Griselda; or the delight of that young beauty, in the *Flower and the Leaf,* shrouded in her bower, and listening, in the morning of the year, to the singing of the nightingale, while her joy rises with the rising song, and gushes out afresh at every pause, and is borne along with the full tide of pleasure, and still

increases and repeats and prolongs itself, and knows no
ebb. It is thus that Boccaccio, in the divine story of the
Hawk, has represented Frederigo Alberigi steadily con-
templating his favorite Falcon (the wreck and remnant of
his fortune), and glad to see how fat and fair a bird she is,
thinking what a dainty repast she would make for his Mistress, who had deigned to visit him in his low cell. So Isabel-
la mourns over her pot of Basil, and never asks for
anything but that. So Lear calls out for his poor fool, and
invokes the heavens, for they are old like him. So Titian impressed on the countenance of that young Neapolitan
nobleman in the Louvre, a look that never passed away.
So Nicolas Poussin describes some shepherds wandering
out in a morning of the spring, and coming to a tomb with
this inscription, "I ALSO WAS AN ARCADIAN."

In general, it must happen in the first stages of the Arts,
that as none but those who had a natural genius for them
would attempt to practice them, so none but those who had
a natural taste for them would pretend to judge of or criticize them. This must be an incalculable advantage to the
man of true genius, for it is no other than the privilege of
being tried by his peers. In an age when connoisseurship
had not become a fashion; when religion, war, and intrigue,
occupied the time and thoughts of the great, only those
minds of superior refinement would be led to notice the
works of art, who had a real sense of their excellence; and
in giving way to the powerful bent of his own genius, the
painter was most likely to consult the taste of his judges.
He had not to deal with pretenders to taste, through vanity,
affectation, and idleness. He had to appeal to the higher
faculties of the soul; to that deep and innate sensibility to
truth and beauty, which required only a proper object to
have its enthusiasm excited; and to that independent
strength of mind, which, in the midst of ignorance and
barbarism, hailed and fostered genius, wherever it met with
it. Titian was patronized by Charles V. Count Castiglione
was the friend of Raphael. These were true patrons, and
true critics; and as there were no others, (for the world, in
general, merely looked on and wondered) there can be
little doubt, that such a period of dearth of factitious patronage would be the most favorable to the full development of the greatest talents, and the attainment of the
highest excellence.

The diffusion of taste is not the same thing as the improvement of taste; but it is only the former of these objects that is promoted by public institutions and other artificial means. The number of candidates for fame, and of pretenders to criticism, is thus increased beyond all proportion, while the quantity of genius and feeling remains the same; with this difference, that the man of genius is lost in the crowd of competitors, who would never have become such but from encouragement and example; and that the opinion of those few persons whom nature intended for judges, is drowned in the noisy suffrages of shallow smatterers in taste. The principle of universal suffrage, however applicable to matters of government, which concern the common feelings and common interests of society, is by no means applicable to matters of taste, which can only be decided upon by the most refined understandings. The highest efforts of genius, in every walk of art, can never be properly understood by the generality of mankind: There are numberless beauties and truths which lie far beyond their comprehension. It is only as refinement and sublimity are blended with other qualities of a more obvious and grosser nature, that they pass current with the world. Taste is the highest degree of sensibility, or the impression made on the most cultivated and sensible minds, as genius is the result of the highest powers both of feeling and invention. It may be objected, that the public taste is capable of gradual improvement, because, in the end, the public do justice to works of the greatest merit. This is a mistake. The reputation ultimately, and often slowly affixed to works of genius, is stamped upon them by authority, not by popular consent or the common sense of the world. We imagine that the admiration of the works of celebrated men has become common, because the admiration of their names has become so. But does not every ignorant connoisseur pretend the same veneration, and talk with the same vapid assurance of Michael Angelo, though he has never seen even a copy of any of his pictures, as if he had studied them accurately,—merely because Sir Joshua Reynolds has praised him? Is Milton more popular now than when the *Paradise Lost* was first published? Or does he not rather owe his reputation to the judgment of a few persons in every successive period, accumulating in his favor, and overpowering by its weight the public indifference? Why is Shakespeare popular? Not from his refinement of character or sentiment, so much as from his power of telling a story, the variety and invention, the tragic catastrophe and broad farce of his plays. Spenser is not yet understood. Does not Boccaccio pass to this day for a writer of ribaldry, because his jests and lascivious tales were all that caught the vulgar ear, while the story of the Falcon is forgotten!

On Wordsworth and Coleridge

As critic and interpreter of the writers of his age, Hazlitt is unsurpassed. Although sensitive to faults that were more glaring to a contemporary than they are to later readers, he judged Wordsworth "the most original poet now living" and considered Coleridge, a "mind reflecting ages past," as the foremost intellect of the Romantic period. Passages from reviews of their works and from The Spirit of the Age *(1825) follow.*

Wordsworth is the most original poet now living. His poetry is not external but internal; it does not depend on tradition, or story, or old song; he furnishes it from his own mind, and is his own subject. Of many of the *Lyrical Ballads,* it is not possible to speak in terms of too high praise, such as *Hart-leap Well,* the *Banks of the Wye, Poor Susan,* parts of the *Leech-gatherer,* the lines *to a Cuckoo, to a Daisy,* the *Complaint,* several of the *Sonnets,* and a hundred others of inconceivable beauty, of perfect originality and pathos. They open a finer and deeper vein of thought and feeling than any poet in modern times has done or attempted. He has produced a deeper impression, and on a smaller circle, than any other of his contemporaries. His powers have been mistaken by the age, nor does he exactly understand them himself. He cannot form a whole. He has not the constructive faculty. He can give only the fine tones of thought, drawn from his mind by accident or nature, like the sounds drawn from the Aeolian harp by the wandering gale. . . . Wordsworth's genius is a pure emanation of the Spirit of the Age. Had he lived in any other period of the world, he would never have been heard of. As it is, he has some difficulty to contend with the hebetude of his intellect and the meanness of his subject. With him "lowliness is young ambition's ladder"; but he finds it a toil to climb in his way the steep of Fame. His homely Muse can hardly raise her wing from the ground, nor spread her hidden glories to the sun. He has "no figures nor no fantasies, which busy *passion* draws in the brains of men": neither the gorgeous machinery of mythologic lore, nor the splendid colors of poetic diction. His style is vernacular: he delivers household truths. He sees nothing loftier than human hopes, nothing deeper than the human heart. This he probes, this he tampers with, this he poises, with all its incalculable weight of thought and feeling, in his hands, and at the same time calms the throbbing pulses of his own heart by keeping his eye ever fixed on the face of nature. If he can make the life-blood flow from the wounded breast, this is the living coloring with which he paints his verse: if he can assuage the pain or close up the wound with the balm of solitary musing, or the healing power of plants and herbs and "skyey influences," this is the sole triumph of his art. He takes the simplest elements of nature and of the human mind, the mere abstract conditions inseparable from our being, and tries to compound a new system of poetry from them; and has perhaps succeeded as well as any one could. *"Nihil humani a me alienum puto"* is the motto of his works. He thinks nothing low or indifferent of which this can be affirmed: everything that professes to be more than this, that is not an absolute essence of truth and feeling, he holds to be vitiated, false, and spurious. In a word, his poetry is founded on setting up an opposition (and pushing it to the utmost length) between the natural and the artificial, between the spirit of humanity and the spirit of fashion and of the world!

It is one of the innovations of the time. It partakes of, and is carried along with, the revolutionary movement of our age: the political changes of the day were the model on which he formed and conducted his poetical experiments. His Muse (it cannot be denied, and without this we cannot explain its character at all) is a levelling one. It proceeds on a principle of equality, and strives to reduce all things to the same standard. It is distinguished by a proud humility. It relies upon its own resources, and disdains external show and relief. It takes the commonest events and objects, as a test to prove that nature is always interesting from its inherent truth and beauty, without any of the ornaments of dress or pomp of circumstances to set it off. Hence the unaccountable mixture of seeming simplicity and real abstruseness in the *Lyrical Ballads*. Fools have laughed at, wise men scarcely understand, them. He takes a subject or a story merely as pegs or loops to hang thought and feeling on; the incidents are trifling, in proportion to his contempt for imposing appearances; the reflections are profound, according to the gravity and aspiring pretensions of his mind.

His popular, inartificial style gets rid (at a blow) of all the trappings of verse, of all the high places of poetry: "the cloud-capt towers, the solemn temples, the gorgeous palaces," are swept to the ground, and "like the baseless fabric of a vision, leave not a rack behind." All the traditions of learning, all the superstitions of age, are obliterated and effaced. We begin *de novo* on a *tabula rasa* of poetry. The purple pall, the nodding plume of tragedy are exploded as mere pantomime and trick, to return to the simplicity of truth and nature. Kings, queens, priests, nobles, the altar and the throne, the distinctions of rank, birth, wealth, power, "the judge's robe, the marshal's truncheon, the ceremony that to great ones 'longs," are not to be found here. The author tramples on the pride of art with greater pride. The Ode and Epode, the Strophe and the Antistrophe, he laughs to scorn. The harp of Homer, the trump of Pindar and of Alcæus, are still. The decencies of costume, the decorations of vanity are stripped off without mercy as barbarous, idle, and Gothic. The jewels in the crisped hair, the diadem on the polished brow, are thought meretricious, theatrical, vulgar; and nothing contents his fastidious taste beyond a simple garland of flowers. Neither does he avail himself of the advantages which nature or accident holds out to him. He chooses to have his subject a foil to his invention, to owe nothing but to himself. He gathers manna in the wilderness, he strikes the barren rock for the gushing moisture. He elevates the mean by the strength of his own aspirations; he clothes the naked with beauty and grandeur from the stores of his own recollections. No cypress grove loads his verse with funeral pomp: but his imagination lends 'a sense of joy

> *To the bare trees and mountains bare,*
> *And grass in the green field.'*

No storm, no shipwreck startles us by its horrors: but the rainbow lifts its head in the cloud, and the breeze sighs through the withered fern. No sad vicissitude of fate, no overwhelming catastrophe in nature deforms his page: but the dew-drop glitters on the bending flower, the tear collects in the glistening eye.

As the lark ascends from its low bed on fluttering wing,

and salutes the morning skies, so Mr. Wordsworth's unpretending Muse, in russet guise, scales the summits of reflection, while it makes the round earth its footstool and its
home!

Possibly a good deal of this may be regarded as the effect of disappointed views and an inverted ambition. Prevented by native pride and indolence from climbing the
ascent of learning or greatness, taught by political opinions
to say to the vain pomp and glory of the world, "I hate ye,"
seeing the path of classical and artificial poetry blocked
up by the cumbrous ornaments of style and turgid *common-places,* so that nothing more could be achieved in that
direction but by the most ridiculous bombast or the tamest
servility, he has turned back, partly from the bias of his
mind, partly perhaps from a judicious policy—has struck
into the sequestered vale of humble life, sought out the
Muse among sheep-cotes and hamlets, and the peasant's
mountain-haunts, has discarded all the tinsel pageantry of
verse, and endeavored (not in vain) to aggrandize the
trivial, and add the charm of novelty to the familiar. No
one has shown the same imagination in raising trifles into
importance: no one has displayed the same pathos in treating of the simplest feelings of the heart. Reserved, yet
haughty, having no unruly or violent passions (or those
passions having been early suppressed), Mr. Wordsworth
has passed his life in solitary musing or in daily converse
with the face of nature. He exemplifies in an eminent degree the power of *association;* for his poetry has no other
source or character. He has dwelt among pastoral scenes,
till each object has become connected with a thousand
feelings, a link in the chain of thought, a fibre of his own
heart. Everyone is by habit and familiarity strongly at-
tached to the place of his birth, or to objects that recall the
most pleasing and eventful circumstances of his life. But to
the author of the *Lyrical Ballads* nature is a kind of home;
and he may be said to take a personal interest in the universe. There is no image so insignificant that it has not in
some mood or other found the way into his heart: no sound
that does not awaken the memory of other years.—

> *To him the meanest flower that blows can give*
> *Thoughts that do often lie too deep for tears.*

The daisy looks up to him with sparkling eye as an old

acquaintance: the cuckoo haunts him with sounds of early youth not to be expressed: a linnet's nest startles him with boyish delight: an old withered thorn is weighed down with a heap of recollections: a grey cloak, seen on some wild moor, torn by the wind, or drenched in the rain, afterwards becomes an object of imagination to him: even the lichens on the rock have a life and being in his thoughts. He has described all these objects in a way and with an intensity of feeling that no one else had done before him, and has given a new view or aspect of nature. He is in this sense the most original poet now living, and the one whose writings could the least be spared: for they have no substitute elsewhere. The vulgar do not read them; the learned, who see all things through books, do not understand them, the great despise, the fashionable may ridicule them: but the author has created himself an interest in the heart of the retired and lonely student of nature, which can never die. Persons of this class will still continue to feel what he has felt: he has expressed what they might in vain wish to express, except with glistening eye and faltering tongue! There is a lofty philosophic tone, a thoughtful humanity, infused into his pastoral vein. Remote from the passions and events of the great world, he has communicated interest and dignity to the primal movèments of the heart of man, and ingrafted his own conscious reflections on the casual thoughts of hinds and shepherds. Nursed amidst the grandeur of mountain scenery, he has stooped to have a nearer view of the daisy under his feet, or plucked a branch of white-thorn from the spray: but, in describing it, his mind seems imbued with the majesty and solemnity of the objects around him—the tall rock lifts its head in the erectness of his spirit; the cataract roars in the sound of his verse; and in its dim and mysterious meaning the mists seem to gather in the hollows of Helvellyn, and the forked Skiddaw hovers in the distance. There is little mention of mountainous scenery in Mr. Wordsworth's poetry; but by internal evidence one might be almost sure that it was written in a mountainous country, from its bareness, its simplicity, its loftiness and its depth!

His later philosophic productions have a somewhat different character. They are a departure from, a dereliction of, his first principles. They are classical and courtly. They are polished in style, without being gaudy; dignified in subject, without affectation. They seem to have been composed not in a cottage at Grasmere, but among the half-inspired groves and stately recollections of Cole-Orton. We might allude in particular, for examples of what we mean, to the lines on a Picture by Claude Lorraine, and to the exquisite poem, entitled *Laodamia*. The last of these breathes the pure spirit of the finest fragments of antiquity —the sweetness, the gravity, the strength, the beauty and the languor of death—

Calm contemplation and majestic pains.

Its glossy brilliancy arises from the perfection of the finishing, like that of a careful sculpture, not from gaudy coloring—the texture of the thoughts has the smoothness and solidity of marble. It is a poem that might be read aloud in Elysium, and the spirits of departed heroes and sages would gather round to listen to it!

Mr. Wordsworth's philosophic poetry, with a less glowing aspect and less tumult in the veins than Lord Byron's on similar occasions, bends a calmer and keener eye on mortality; the impression, if less vivid, is more pleasing and permanent; and we confess it (perhaps it is a want of taste and proper feeling) that there are lines and poems of our author's, that we think of ten times for once that we recur to any of Lord Byron's. Or if there are any of the latter's writings, that we can dwell upon in the same way, that is, as lasting and heart-felt sentiments, it is when laying aside his usual pomp and pretension, he descends with Mr. Wordsworth to the common ground of a disinterested humanity. It may be considered as characteristic of our poet's writings, that they either make no impression on the mind at all, seem mere *nonsense-verses,* or that they leave a mark behind them that never wears out. They either

Fall blunted from the indurated breast—

without any perceptible result, or they absorb it like a passion. To one class of readers he appears sublime, to another (and we fear the largest) ridiculous. He has probably realized Milton's wish,—"and fit audience found, though few": but we suspect he is not reconciled to the alternative. . . .

The present is an age of talkers, and not of doers; and the reason is, that the world is growing old. We are so far

advanced in the Arts and Sciences, that we live in retrospect, and dote on past achievements. The accumulation
of knowledge has been so great, that we are lost in wonder
at the height it has reached, instead of attempting to climb
or add to it; while the variety of objects distracts and
dazzles the looker-on. What *niche* remains unoccupied?
What path untried? What is the use of doing anything, unless we could do better than all those who have gone before us? What hope is there of this? We are like those who
have been to see some noble monument of art, who are
content to admire without thinking of rivaling it; or like
guests after a feast, who praise the hospitality of the donor
"and thank the bounteous Pan"—perhaps carrying away
some trifling fragments; or like the spectators of a mighty
battle, who still hear its sound afar off, and the clashing of
armor and the neighing of the war-horse and the shout of
victory is in their ears, like the rushing of innumerable
waters!

Mr. Coleridge has "a mind reflecting ages past": his
voice is like the echo of the congregated roar of the "dark
rearward and abyss" of thought. He who has seen a moldering tower by the side of a crystal lake, hid by the mist,
but glittering in the wave below, may conceive the dim,
gleaming, uncertain intelligence of his eye: he who has
marked the evening clouds uprolled (a world of vapors)
has seen the picture of his mind, unearthly, unsubstantial,
with gorgeous tints and ever-varying forms—

That which was now a horse, even with a thought
The rack dislimns, and makes it indistinct
As water is in water.

Our author's mind is (as he himself might express it)
tangential. There is no subject on which he has not touched,
none on which he has rested. With an understanding,
fertile, subtle, expansive, "quick, forgetive, apprehensive,"
beyond all living precedent, few traces of it will perhaps
remain. He lends himself to all impressions alike; he gives
up his mind and liberty of thought to none. He is a general
lover of art and science, and wedded to no one in particular. He pursues knowledge as a mistress, with outstretched
hands and winged speed; but as he is about to embrace her,
his Daphne turns—alas! not to a laurel! Hardly a speculation has been left on record from the earliest time, but it is

loosely folded up in Mr. Coleridge's memory, like a rich, but somewhat tattered piece of tapestry: we might add (with more seeming than real extravagance) that scarce a thought can pass through the mind of man, but its sound has at some time or other passed over his head with rustling pinions.

On whatever question or author you speak, he is prepared to take up the theme with advantage—from Peter Abelard down to Thomas Moore, from the subtlest metaphysics to the politics of the *Courier*. There is no man of genius, in whose praise he descants, but the critic seems to stand above the author, and "what in him is weak, to strengthen, what is low, to raise and support": nor is there any work of genius that does not come out of his hands like an illuminated Missal, sparkling even in its defects. If Mr. Coleridge had not been the most impressive talker of his age, he would probably have been the finest writer; but he lays down his pen to make sure of an auditor, and mortgages the admiration of posterity for the stare of an idler. If he had not been a poet, he would have been a powerful logician; if he had not dipped his wing in the Unitarian controversy, he might have soared to the very summit of fancy. But, in writing verse, he is trying to subject the Muse to *transcendental* theories: in his abstract reasoning, he misses his way by strewing it with flowers.

All that he has done of moment, he had done twenty years ago: since then, he may be said to have lived on the sound of his own voice. Mr. Coleridge is too rich in intellectual wealth, to need to task himself to any drudgery: he has only to draw the sliders of his imagination, and a thousand subjects expand before him, startling him with their brilliancy, or losing themselves in endless obscurity—

And by the force of blear illusion,
They draw him on to his confusion.

What is the little he could add to the stock, compared with the countless stores that lie about him, that he should stoop to pick up a name, or to polish an idle fancy? He walks abroad in the majesty of an universal understanding, eyeing the "rich strond" or golden sky above him, and "goes sounding on his way" in eloquent accents, uncompelled and free!

Persons of the greatest capacity are often those, who for

this reason do the least; for surveying themselves from the highest point of view, amidst the infinite variety of the universe, their own share in it seems trifling, and scarce worth a thought; and they prefer the contemplation of all that is, or has been, or can be, to the making a coil about doing what, when done, is no better than vanity. It is hard to concentrate all our attention and efforts on one pursuit, except from ignorance of others; and without this concentration of our faculties no great progress can be made in any one thing. It is not merely that the mind is not capable of the effort; it does not think the effort worth making. Action is one; but thought is manifold. He whose restless eye glances through the wide compass of nature and art, will not consent to have "his own nothings monstered"; but he must do this before he can give his whole soul to them. The mind, after "letting contemplation have its fill," or

> Sailing with supreme dominion
> Through the azure deep of air,

sinks down on the ground, breathless, exhausted, powerless, inactive; or if it must have some vent to its feelings, seeks the most easy and obvious; is soothed by friendly flattery, lulled by the murmur of immediate applause: thinks, as it were, aloud, and babbles in its dreams!

A scholar (so to speak) is a more disinterested and abstracted character than a mere author. The first looks at the numberless volumes of a library, and says, "All these are mine": the other points to a single volume (perhaps it may be an immortal one) and says, "My name is written on the back of it." This is a puny and groveling ambition, beneath the lofty amplitude of Mr. Coleridge's mind. No, he revolves in his wayward soul, or utters to the passing wind, or discourses to his own shadow, things mightier and more various!—Let us draw the curtain, and unlock the shrine.

Learning rocked him in his cradle, and while yet a child,

> He lisped in numbers, for the numbers came.

At sixteen he wrote his *Ode on Chatterton,* and he still reverts to that period with delight, not so much as it relates to himself (for that string of his own early promise of fame rather jars than otherwise) but as exemplifying the youth of a poet. Mr. Coleridge talks of himself without being an egotist; for in him the individual is always merged in the abstract and general. He distinguished himself at school and at the University by his knowledge of the classics, and gained several prizes for Greek epigrams. How many men are there (great scholars, celebrated names in literature) who, having done the same thing in their youth, have no other idea all the rest of their lives but of this achievement, of a fellowship and dinner, and who, installed in academic honors, would look down on our author as a mere strolling bard! At Christ's Hospital, where he was brought up, he was the idol of those among his schoolfellows who mingled with their bookish studies the music of thought and of humanity; and he was usually attended round the cloisters by a group of these (inspiring and inspired) whose hearts, even then, burnt within them as he talked, and where the sounds yet linger to mock ELIA on his way, still turning pensive to the past!

One of the finest and rarest parts of Mr. Coleridge's conversation is, when he expatiates on the Greek tragedians (not that he is not well acquainted, when he pleases, with the epic poets, or the philosophers, or orators, or historians of antiquity)—on the subtle reasonings and melting pathos of Euripides, on the harmonious gracefulness of Sophocles, tuning his love-labored song, like sweetest warblings from a sacred grove; on the high-wrought, trumpet-tongued eloquence of Æschylus, whose *Prometheus,* above all, is like an Ode to Fate and a pleading with Providence, his thoughts being let loose as his body is chained on his solitary rock, and his afflicted will (the emblem of mortality)

Struggling in vain with ruthless destiny.

As the impassioned critic speaks and rises in his theme, you would think you heard the voice of the Man hated by the Gods, contending with the wild winds as they roar; and his eye glitters with the spirit of Antiquity!

Next, he was engaged with Hartley's tribes of mind, "etherial braid, thought-woven,"—and he busied himself for a year or two with vibrations and vibratiuncles, and the great law of association that binds all things in its mystic chain, and the doctrine of Necessity (the mild teacher of Charity) and the Millennium, anticipative of a life to come; and he plunged deep into the controversy

on Matter and Spirit, and, as an escape from Dr. Priestley's Materialism, where he felt himself imprisoned by
the logician's spell, like Ariel in the cloven pine-tree, he
became suddenly enamored of Bishop Berkeley's fairy-
world, and used in all companies to build the universe,
like a brave poetical fiction, of fine words. And he was
deep-read in Malebranche, and in Cudworth's Intellectual
System (a huge pile of learning, unwieldy, enormous)
and in Lord Brook's hieroglyphic theories, and in Bishop
Butler's Sermons and in the Duchess of Newcastle's fantastic folios, and in Clarke and South, and Tillotson, and
all the fine thinkers and masculine reasoners of that age;
and Leibnitz's *Pre-established Harmony* reared its arch
above his head, like the rainbow in the cloud, covenanting
with the hopes of man—and then he fell plump, ten
thousand fathoms down (but his wings saved him harmless) into the *hortus siccus* of Dissent, where he pared
religion down to the standard of reason, and stripped faith
of mystery, and preached Christ crucified and the Unity
of the Godhead, and so dwelt for a while in the spirit with
John Huss and Jerome of Prague and Socinus and old
John Zisca, and ran through Neal's *History of the Puritans*
and Calamy's *Non-Conformists' Memorial,* having like
thoughts and passions with them—but then Spinoza became
his God, and he took up the vast chain of being in his hand,
and the round world became the centre and the soul of
all things in some shadowy sense, forlorn of meaning, and
around him he beheld the living traces and the sky-pointing
proportions of the mighty Pan—but poetry redeemed him
from this spectral philosophy, and he bathed his heart in
beauty, and gazed at the golden light of heaven, and drank
of the spirit of the universe, and wandered at eve by fairy-
stream or fountain,

> —*When he saw nought but beauty,*
> *When he heard the voice of that Almighty One*
> *In every breeze that blew, or wave that murmured*—

and wedded with truth in Plato's shade, and in the writings
of Proclus and Plotinus saw the ideas of things in the
eternal mind, and unfolded all mysteries with the Schoolmen and fathomed the depths of Duns Scotus and Thomas
Aquinas, and entered the third heaven with Jacob Behmen,
and walked hand in hand with Swedenborg through the

pavilions of the New Jerusalem, and sung his faith in the promise and in the word in his *Religious Musings*—and lowering himself from that dizzy height poised himself on Milton's wings, and spread out his thoughts in charity with the glad prose of Jeremy Taylor, and wept over Bowles's *Sonnets,* and studied Cowper's blank verse, and betook himself to Thomson's *Castle of Indolence,* and sported with the wits of Charles the Second's days and of Queen Anne, and relished Swift's style and that of the John Bull (Arbuthnot's we mean, not Mr. Croker's), and dallied with the British Essayists and Novelists, and knew all qualities of more modern writers with a learned spirit: Johnson, and Goldsmith, and Junius, and Burke, and Godwin, and the *Sorrows of Werter,* and Jean Jacques Rousseau, and Voltaire, and Marivaux, and Crebillon, and thousands more—now "laughed with Rabelais in his easy chair" or pointed to Hogarth, or afterwards dwelt on Claude's classic scenes, or spoke with rapture of Raphael, and compared the women at Rome to figures that had walked out of his pictures, or visited the Oratory of Pisa, and described the works of Giotto and Ghirlandaio and Massaccio, and gave the moral of the picture of the Triumph of Death, where the beggars and the wretched invoke his dreadful dart, but the rich and mighty of the earth quail and shrink before it; and in that land of siren sights and sounds, saw a dance of peasant girls, and was charmed with lutes and gondolas,—or wandered into Germany and lost himself in the labyrinths of the Hartz Forest and of the Kantean philosophy, and amongst the cabalistic names of Fichtè and Schelling and Lessing, and God knows who—this was long after, but all the former while, he had nerved his heart and filled his eyes with tears, as he hailed the rising orb of liberty, since quenched in darkness and in blood, and had kindled his affections at the blaze of the French Revolution, and sang for joy, when the towers of the Bastille and the proud places of the insolent and the oppressor fell, and would have floated his bark, freighted with fondest fancies, across the Atlantic wave with Southey and others to seek for peace and freedom—

In Philarmonia's undivided dale!

Alas! "Frailty, thy name is *Genius!*"—What is become of all this mighty heap of hope, of thought, of learning and humanity? It has ended in swallowing doses of oblivion and in writing paragraphs in the *Courier*.—Such and so little is the mind of man!

Of all Mr. Coleridge's productions, the *Ancient Mariner* is the only one that we could with confidence put into any person's hands, on whom we wished to impress a favorable idea of his extraordinary powers. Let whatever other objections be made to it, it is unquestionably a work of genius —of wild, irregular, overwhelming imagination, and has that rich, varied movement in the verse, which gives a distant idea of the lofty or changeful tones of Mr. Coleridge's voice. In the *Christabel*, there is one splendid passage on divided friendship. The Translation of Schiller's *Wallenstein* is also a masterly production in its kind, faithful and spirited. Among his smaller pieces there are occasional bursts of pathos and fancy, equal to what we might expect from him; but these form the exception, and not the rule. Such, for instance, is his affecting Sonnet to the author of the *Robbers.* . . .

Remembrance of Things Past

*"My First Acquaintance with Poets," originally pub-
lished in* The Liberal *(1823), "Liber Amoris," from
Hazlitt's famous confession of love (1823), "On the
Feeling of Immortality in Youth" (Monthly Magazine, 1827), "On Living to One's-Self," (Table-Talk),
"On the Pleasure of Painting," (London Magazine,
1820), and "On Going a Journey" (New Monthly
Magazine, 1822), are grouped here as a remembrance
of things past. The first, Hazlitt's famous account of
his meeting Coleridge and Wordsworth in "the golden
light of other years," is acclaimed for its vivid prose
and descriptive power.*

My First Acquaintance with Poets

My father was a Dissenting Minister, at Wem, in Shropshire; and in the year 1798 (the figures that compose the
date are to me like the "dreaded name of Demogorgon")
Mr. Coleridge came to Shrewsbury, to succeed Mr. Rowe
in the spiritual charge of a Unitarian Congregation there.
He did not come till late on the Saturday afternoon before
he was to preach; and Mr. Rowe, who himself went down
to the coach, in a state of anxiety and expectation, to look
for the arrival of his successor, could find no one at all
answering the descrip on but a round-faced man, in a
short black coat (like a shooting-jacket) which hardly
seemed to have been made for him, but who seemed to be
talking at a great rate to his fellow-passengers. Mr. Rowe
had scarce returned to give an account of his disappointment when the round-faced man in black entered, and
dissipated all doubts on the subject by beginning to talk.
He did not cease while he stayed; nor has he since, that
I know of. He held the good town of Shrewsbury in delightful suspense for three weeks that he remained there,
"fluttering the *proud Salopians,* like an eagle in a dove-
cote"; and the Welsh mountains that skirt the horizon with
their tempestuous confusion, agree to have heard no such
mystic sounds since the days of

High-born Hoel's harp or soft Llewellyn's lay.

As we passed along between Wem and Shrewsbury, and
I eyed their blue tops seen through the wintry branches,
or the red rustling leaves of the sturdy oak-trees by the
road-side, a sound was in my ears as of a Siren's song;
I was stunned, startled with it, as from deep sleep; but
I had no notion then that I should ever be able to express
my admiration to others in motley imagery of quaint
allusion, till the light of his genius shone into my soul,
like the sun's rays glittering in the puddles of the road.
I was at that time dumb, inarticulate, helpless, like a worm
by the way-side, crushed, bleeding, lifeless; but now, bursting from the deadly bands that "bound them,

With Styx nine times round them,"

my ideas float on winged words, and as they expand their
plumes, catch the golden light of other years. My soul
has indeed remained in its original bondage, dark, obscure,
with longings infinite and unsatisfied; my heart, shut up
in the prison-house of this rude clay, has never found,
nor will it ever find, a heart to speak to; but that my
understanding also did not remain dumb and brutish, or
at length found a language to express itself, I owe to
Coleridge. But this is not to my purpose.

My father lived ten miles from Shrewsbury, and was in
the habit of exchanging visits with Mr. Rowe, and with
Mr. Jenkins of Whitchurch (nine miles farther on), according to the custom of Dissenting Ministers in each other's
neighborhood. A line of communication is thus established,
by which the flame of civil and religious liberty is kept
alive, and nourishes its smoldering fire unquenchable, like
the fires in the *Agamemnon* of Æschylus, placed at different stations, that waited for ten long years to announce
with their blazing pyramids the destruction of Troy. Coleridge had agreed to come over and see my father, according
to the courtesy of the country, as Mr. Rowe's probable
successor; but in the meantime, I had gone to hear him
preach the Sunday after his arrival. A poet and a philosopher getting up into a Unitarian pulpit to preach the
gospel, was a romance in these degenerate days, a sort
of revival of the primitive spirit of Christianity, which was
not to be resisted.

It was in January of 1798, that I rose one morning
before daylight, to walk ten miles in the mud, to hear

this celebrated person preach. Never, the longest day I have to live, shall I have such another walk as this cold, raw, comfortless one, in the winter of the year 1798. *Il y a des impressions que ni le tems ni les circonstances peuvent effacer. Dussé-je vivre des siecles entiers, le doux tems de ma jeunesse ne peut renaître pour moi, ni s'effacer jamais dans ma mémoire.* When I got there, the organ was playing the 100th Psalm, and when it was done, Mr. Coleridge rose and gave out his text, "And he went up into the mountain to pray, HIMSELF, ALONE." As he gave out this text, his voice "rose like a steam of rich distilled perfumes," and when he came to the two last words, which he pronounced loud, deep, and distinct, it seemed to me, who was then young, as if the sounds had echoed from the bottom of the human heart, and as if that prayer might have floated in solemn silence through the universe. The idea of St. John came into my mind, "of one crying in the wilderness, who had his loins girt about, and whose food was locusts and wild honey." The preacher then launched into his subject, like an eagle dallying with the wind. The sermon was upon peace and war; upon church and state—not their alliance, but their separation—on the spirit of the world and the spirit of Christianity, not as the same, but as opposed to one another. He talked of those who had "inscribed the cross of Christ on banners dripping with human gore." He made a poetical and pastoral excursion—and to show the fatal effects of war, drew a striking contrast between the simple shepherd-boy, driving his team afield, or sitting under the hawthorn, piping to his flock, "as though he should never be old," and the same poor country-lad, crimped, kidnapped, brought into town, made drunk at an alehouse, turned into a wretched drummer-boy, with his hair sticking on end with powder and pomatum, a long cue at his back, and tricked out in the loathsome finery of the profession of blood:

Such were the notes our once-loved poet sung.

And for myself, I could not have been more delighted if I had heard the music of the spheres. Poetry and Philosophy had met together. Truth and Genius had embraced, under the eye and with the sanction of Religion. This was even beyond my hopes. I returned home well satisfied. The sun that was still laboring pale and wan

through the sky, obscured by thick mists, seemed an emblem of the *good cause;* and the cold dank drops of dew,
that hung half melted on the beard of the thistle, had
something genial and refreshing in them; for there was
a spirit of hope and youth in all nature, that turned everything into good. The face of nature had not then the
brand of JUS DIVINUM on it:

Like to that sanguine flower inscrib'd with woe.

On the Tuesday following, the half-inspired speaker
came. I was called down into the room where he was,
and went half-hoping, half-afraid. He received me very
graciously, and I listened for a long time without uttering
a word. I did not suffer in his opinion by my silence. "For
those two hours," he afterwards was pleased to say, "he
was conversing with William Hazlitt's forehead!" His appearance was different from what I had anticipated from
seeing him before. At a distance, and in the dim light of
the chapel, there was to me a strange wildness in his
aspect, a dusky obscurity, and I thought him pitted with
the smallpox. His complexion was at that time clear, and
even bright—

As are the children of yon azure sheen.

His forehead was broad and high, light as if built of ivory,
with large projecting eyebrows, and his eyes rolling beneath them, like a sea with darkened lustre. "A certain
tender bloom his face o'erspread," a purple tinge as we
see it in the pale thoughtful complexions of the Spanish
portrait-painters, Murillo and Velasquez. His mouth was
gross, voluptuous, open, eloquent; his chin good-humored
and round; but his nose, the rudder of the face, the index
of the will, was small, feeble, nothing—like what he has
done. It might seem that the genius of his face as from a
height surveyed and projected him (with sufficient capacity and huge aspiration) into the world unknown of
thought and imagination, with nothing to support or guide
his veering purpose, as if Columbus had launched his
adventurous course for the New World in a scallop, without oars or compass. So, at least, I comment on it after
the event. Coleridge, in his person, was rather above the
common size, inclining to the corpulent, or like Lord

Hamlet, "somewhat fat and pursy." His hair (now, alas! grey) was then black and glossy as the raven's and fell in smooth masses over his forehead. This long pendulous hair is peculiar to enthusiasts, to those whose minds tend heavenward; and is traditionally inseparable (though of a different color) from the pictures of Christ. It ought to belong, as a character, to all who preach *Christ crucified*, and Coleridge was at that time one of those!

It was curious to observe the contrast between him and my father, who was a veteran in the cause, and then declining into the vale of years. He had been a poor Irish lad, carefully brought up by his parents, and sent to the University of Glasgow (where he studied under Adam Smith) to prepare him for his future destination. It was his mother's proudest wish to see her son a Dissenting Minister. So, if we look back to past generations (as far as eye can reach), we see the same hopes, fears, wishes, followed by the same disappointments, throbbing in the human heart; and so we may see them (if we look forward) rising up forever, and disappearing, like vaporish bubbles, in the human breast! After being tossed about from congregation to congregation in the heats of the Unitarian controversy, and squabbles about the American war, he had been relegated to an obscure village, where he was to spend the last thirty years of his life, far from the only converse that he loved, the talk about disputed texts of Scripture, and the cause of civil and religious liberty. Here he passed his days, repining, but resigned, in the study of the Bible, and the perusal of the Commentators— huge folios, not easily got through, one of which would outlast a winter! Why did he pore on these from morn to night (with the exception of a walk in the fields or a turn in the garden to gather broccoli-plants or kidney beans of his own rearing, with no small degree of pride and pleasure)? Here were "no figures nor no fantasies"— neither poetry nor philosophy—nothing to dazzle, nothing to excite modern curiosity; but to his lack-lustre eyes there appeared within the pages of the ponderous, unwieldy, neglected tomes, the sacred name of JEHOVAH in Hebrew capitals: pressed down by the weight of the style, worn to the last fading thinness of the understanding, there were glimpses, glimmering notions of the patriarchal wanderings, with palm-trees hovering in the horizon, and processions of camels at the distance of three thousand years;

there was Moses with the Burning Bush, the number of the Twelve Tribes, types, shadows, glosses on the law and the prophets; there were discussions (dull enough) on the age of Methuselah, a mightly speculation! there were outlines, rude guesses at the shape of Noah's Ark and of the riches of Solomon's Temple; questions as to the date of the creation, predictions of the end of all things; the great lapses of time, the strange mutations of the globe were unfolded with the voluminous leaf, as it turned over; and though the soul might slumber with an hiero-glyphic veil of inscrutable mysteries drawn over it, yet it was in a slumber ill-exchanged for all the sharpened real-ities of sense, wit, fancy, or reason. My father's life was comparatively a dream; but it was a dream of infinity and eternity, of death, the resurrection, and a judgment to come!

No two individuals were ever more unlike than were the host and his guest. A poet was to my father a sort of nondescript; yet whatever added grace to the Unitarian cause was to him welcome. He could hardly have been more surprised or pleased, if our visitor had worn wings. Indeed, his thoughts had wings: and as the silken sounds rustled round our little wainscoted parlor, my father threw back his spectacles over his forehead, his white hairs mixing with its sanguine hue; and a smile of delight beamed across his rugged, cordial face, to think that Truth had found a new ally in Fancy! Besides, Coleridge seemed to take considerable notice of me, and that of itself was enough. He talked very familiarly, but agreeably, and glanced over a variety of subjects. At dinner-time he grew more animated, and dilated in a very edifying manner on Mary Wolstonecraft and Mackintosh. The last, he said, he considered (on my father's speaking of his *Vindiciæ Gallicæ* as a capital performance) as a clever, scholastic man—a master of the topics—or, as the ready warehouse-man of letters, who knew exactly where to lay his hand on what he wanted, though the goods were not his own. He thought him no match for Burke, either in style or matter. Burke was a metaphysician, Mackintosh a mere logician. Burke was an orator (almost a poet) who rea-soned in figures, because he had an eye for nature: Mack-intosh, on the other hand, was a rhetorician, who had only an eye to common-places. On this I ventured to say that I had always entertained a great opinion of Burke, and that (as far as I could find) the speaking of him with contempt might be made the test of a vulgar, democratical mind. This was the first observation I ever made to Coleridge, and he said it was a very just and striking one. I remember the leg of Welsh mutton and the turnips on the table that day had the finest flavor imaginable. Coleridge added that Mackintosh and Tom Wedgwood (of whom, however, he spoke highly) had expressed a very indifferent opinion of his friend Mr. Wordsworth, on which he remarked to them—"He strides on so far before you, that he dwindles in the distance!" Godwin had once boasted to him of having carried on an argument with Mackintosh for three hours with dubious success; Coleridge told him —"If there had been a man of genius in the room, he would have settled the question in five minutes." He asked me if I had ever seen Mary Wolstonecraft, and I said, I had once for a few moments, and that she seemed to me to turn off Godwin's objections to something she advanced with quite a playful, easy air. He replied, that "this was only one instance of the ascendancy which people of imagination exercised over those of mere intellect." He did not rate Godwin very high (this was caprice or prejudice, real or affected), but he had a great idea of Mrs. Wolstonecraft's powers of conversation; none at all of her talent for book-making. We talked a little about Holcroft. He had been asked if he was not much struck *with* him, and he said, he thought himself in more danger of being struck *by* him. I complained that he would not let me get on at all, for he required a definition of even the commonest word, exclaiming, "What do you mean by a *sensation,* Sir? What do you mean by an *idea?*" This, Coleridge said, was barricadoing the road to truth; it was setting up a turnpike-gate at every step we took. I forget a great number of things, many more than I remember; but the day passed off pleasantly, and the next morning Mr. Coleridge was to return to Shrewsbury. When I came down to breakfast, I found that he had just received a letter from his friend, T. Wedgwood, making him an offer of 150£. a-year if he chose to waive his present pursuit, and devote himself entirely to the study of poetry and philosophy. Coleridge seemed to make up his mind to close with this proposal in the act of tying on one of his shoes. It threw an additional damp on his departure. It took the wayward enthusiast quite from us to cast him into Deva's winding vales, or by the shores of old romance. Instead of living at ten miles' distance, of being the pastor of a Dissenting congregation at Shrewsbury, he was henceforth to inhabit the Hill of Parnassus, to be a Shepherd on the Delectable Mountains. Alas! I knew not the way thither, and felt very little gratitude for Mr. Wedgwood's bounty. I was presently relieved from this dilemma; for Mr. Coleridge, asking for a pen and ink, and going to a table to write something on a bit of card, advanced towards me with undulating step, and giving me the precious document, said that that was his address, *Mr. Coleridge, Nether-Stowey, Somersetshire;* and that he should be glad to see me there in a few weeks' time, and, if I chose, would come half-way to meet me. I was not less surprised than the shepherd-boy (this simile is to be found in *Cassandra*), when he sees a thunder-bolt fall close at his feet. I stammered out my acknowledgments and acceptance of this offer (I thought Mr. Wedgwood's annuity a trifle to it) as well as I could; and this mighty business being settled, the poet-preacher took leave, and I accompanied him six miles on the road. It was a fine morning in the middle of winter, and he talked the whole way. The scholar in Chaucer is described as going

—Sounding on his way.

So Coleridge went on his. In digressing, in dilating, in passing from subject to subject, he appeared to me to float in air, to slide on ice. He told me in confidence (going along) that he should have preached two sermons before he accepted the situation at Shrewsbury, one on Infant Baptism, the other on the Lord's Supper, showing that he could not administer either, which would have effectually disqualified him for the object in view. I observed that he continually crossed me on the way by shifting from one side of the foot-path to the other. This struck me as an odd movement; but I did not at that time connect it with any instability of purpose or involuntary change of principle, as I have done since. He seemed unable to keep on in a straight line. He spoke slightingly of Hume (whose *Essay on Miracles* he said was stolen from an objection started in one of South's sermons—*Credat Judæus Apella!*). I was not very much pleased at this account of Hume, for I had just been reading, with infinite relish, that completest of all metaphysical *choke-pears,* his *Treatise on Human Nature,* to which the *Essays,* in point of scholastic subtility and close reasoning, are mere elegant trifling, light summer reading. Coleridge even denied the excellence of Hume's general style, which I think betrayed a want of taste or candor. He however made me amends by the manner in which he spoke of Berkeley. He dwelt particularly on his *Essay on Vision* as a masterpiece of analytical reasoning. So it undoubtedly is. He was exceedingly angry with Dr. Johnson for striking the stone with his foot, in allusion to this author's *Theory of Matter and Spirit,* and saying, "Thus I confute him, Sir." Coleridge drew a parallel (I don't know how he brought about the connection) between Bishop Berkeley and Tom Paine. He said the one was an instance of a subtle, the other of an acute mind, than which no two things could be more distinct. The one was a shop-boy's quality, the other the characteristic of a philosopher. He considered Bishop Butler as a true philosopher, a profound and conscientious thinker, a genuine reader of nature and his own mind. He did not speak of his *Analogy,* but of his *Sermons at the Rolls' Chapel,* of which I had never heard. Coleridge somehow always contrived to prefer the *unknown* to the *known.* In this instance, he was right. The *Analogy* is a tissue of sophistry, of wire-drawn, theological special-pleading; the *Sermons* (with the preface to them) are in a fine vein of deep, matured reflection, a candid appeal to our observation of human nature, without pedantry and without bias. I told Coleridge I had written a few remarks, and was sometimes foolish enough to believe that I had made a discovery on the same subject (the *Natural Disinterestedness of the Human Mind*)—and I tried to explain my view of it to Coleridge, who listened with great willingness, but I did not succeed in making myself understood. I sat down to the task shortly afterwards for the twentieth time, got new pens and paper, determined to make clear work of it, wrote a few meagre sentences in the skeleton-style of a mathematical demonstration, stopped half-way down the second page; and, after trying in vain to pump up any words, images, notions, apprehensions, facts, or observations, from that gulf of abstraction in which I had plunged myself for four or five years preceding, gave up the attempt as labor in vain, and shed tears of helpless despondency on the blank, unfinished paper. I can write fast enough now. Am I better than I was then? Oh no! One truth discovered, one pang of regret at not being able to express it, is better than all the fluency and flippancy in the world. Would that I could go back to what I then was! Why can we not revive past times as we can revisit old places? If I had the quaint Muse of Sir Philip Sidney to assist me, I would write a *Sonnet to the Road between Wem and Shrewsbury,* and immortalize every step of it by some fond enigmatical conceit. I would swear that the very milestones had ears, and that Harmer-hill stooped with all its pines, to listen to a poet, as he passed! I remember but one other topic of discourse in this walk. He mentioned Paley, praised the naturalness and clearness of his style, but condemned his sentiments, thought him a mere time-serving casuist, and said that "the fact of his work on Moral and Political Philosophy being made a textbook in our Universities was a disgrace to the national character." We parted at the six-mile stone; and I returned homeward, pensive, but much pleased. I had met with unexpected notice from a person whom I believed to have been prejudiced against me. "Kind and affable to me had been his condescension, and should be honored ever with suitable regard." He was the first poet I had known, and he certainly answered to that inspired name. I had heard a great deal of his powers of conversation, and was not disappointed. In fact, I never met with anything at all like them, either before or since. I could easily credit the accounts which were circulated of his holding forth to a large party of ladies and gentlemen, an evening or two before, on the Berkeleian Theory, when he made the whole material universe look like a transparency of fine words; and another story (which I believe he has somewhere told himself) of his being asked to a party at Birmingham, of his smoking tobacco and going to sleep after dinner on a sofa, where the company found him, to their no small surprise, which was increased to wonder when he started up of a sudden, and rubbing his eyes, looked about him, and launched into a three hours' description of the third heaven, of which he had had a dream, very different from Mr. Southey's *Vision of Judgment,* and also from that other *Vision of Judgment,* which Mr. Murray, the Secretary of the Bridge-street Junto, took into his especial keeping!

On my way back, I had a sound in my ears—it was the

voice of Fancy; I had a light before me—it was the face of Poetry. The one still lingers there, the other has not quitted my side! Coleridge, in truth, met me half-way on the ground of philosophy, or I should not have been won over to his imaginative creed. I had an uneasy, pleasurable sensation all the time, till I was to visit him. During those months the chill breath of winter gave me a welcoming; the vernal air was balm and inspiration to me. The golden sun-sets, the silver star of evening, lighted me on my way to new hopes and prospects. *I was to visit Coleridge in the Spring.* This circumstance was never absent from my thoughts, and mingled with all my feelings. I wrote to him at the time proposed, and received an answer postponing my intended visit for a week or two, but very cordially urging me to complete my promise then. This delay did not damp, but rather increased my ardor. In the meantime, I went to Llangollen Vale, by way of initiating myself in the mysteries of natural scenery; and I must say I was enchanted with it. I had been reading Coleridge's description of England in his fine *Ode on the Departing Year,* and I applied it, *con amore,* to the objects before me. That valley was to me (in a manner) the cradle of a new existence: in the river that winds through it, my spirit was baptized in the waters of Helicon!

I returned home, and soon after set out on my journey with unworn heart, and untried feet. My way lay through Worcester and Gloucester, and by Upton, where I thought of Tom Jones and the adventure of the muff. I remember getting completely wet through one day, and stopping at an inn (I think it was Tewkesbury) where I sat up all night to read *Paul and Virginia.* Sweet were the showers in early youth that drenched my body, and sweet the drops of pity that fell upon the books I read! I recollect a remark of Coleridge's upon this very book—that nothing could show the gross indelicacy of French manners and the entire corruption of their imagination more strongly than the behavior of the heroine in the last fatal scene, who turns away from a person on board the sinking vessel, that offers to save her life, because he has thrown off his clothes to assist him in swimming. Was this a time to think of such a circumstance? I once hinted to Wordsworth, as we were sailing in his boat on Grasmere lake, that I thought he had borrowed the idea of his *Poems on the Naming of Places* from the local inscriptions of the same kind in *Paul and Virginia.* He did not own the obligation, and stated some distinction without a difference, in defense of his claim to originality. Any the slightest variation would be sufficient for this purpose in his mind; for whatever *he* added or altered would inevitably be worth all that any one else had done, and contain the marrow of the sentiment.—I was still two days before the time fixed for my arrival, for I had taken care to set out early enough. I stopped these two days at Bridgewater; and when I was tired of sauntering on the banks of its muddy river, returned to the inn and read *Camilla*. So have I loitered my life away, reading books, looking at pictures, going to plays, hearing, thinking, writing on what pleased me best. I have wanted only one thing to make me happy; but wanting that, have wanted everything!

I arrived, and was well received. The country about Nether-Stowey is beautiful, green and hilly, and near the sea-shore. I saw it but the other day, after an interval of twenty years, from a hill near Taunton. How was the map of my life spread out before me, as the map of the country lay at my feet! In the afternoon, Coleridge took me over to All-Foxden, a romantic old family mansion of the St. Aubins, where Wordsworth lived. It was then in the possession of a friend of the poet's, who gave him the free use of it. Somehow, that period (the time just after the French Revolution) was not a time when *nothing was given for nothing*. The mind opened and a softness might be perceived coming over the heart of individuals, beneath "the scales that fence" our self-interest. Wordsworth himself was from home, but his sister kept house, and set before us a frugal repast; and we had free access to her brother's poems, the *Lyrical Ballads*, which were still in manuscript, or in the form of *Sybilline Leaves*. I dipped into a few of these with great satisfaction, and with the faith of a novice. I slept that night in an old room with blue hangings, and covered with the round-faced family-portraits of the age of George I and II, and from the wooded declivity of the adjoining park that overlooked my window, at the dawn of day, could

—hear the loud stag speak.

In the outset of life (and particularly at this time I felt it so) our imagination has a body to it. We are in a state between sleeping and waking, and have indistinct but glorious glimpses of strange shapes, and there is always some-

thing to come better than what we see. As in our dreams the
fulness of the blood gives warmth and reality to the coinage
of the brain, so in youth our ideas are clothed, and fed, and
pampered with our good spirits; we breathe thick with
thoughtless happiness, the weight of future years presses on
the strong pulses of the heart, and we repose with undisturbed faith in truth and good. As we advance, we exhaust
our fund of enjoyment and of hope. We are no longer
wrapped in *lamb's-wool*, lulled in Elysium. As we taste the
pleasures of life, their spirit evaporates, the sense palls; and
nothing is left but the phantoms, the lifeless shadows of
what *has been!*

That morning, as soon as breakfast was over, we strolled
out into the park, and seating ourselves on the trunk of
an old ash-tree that stretched along the ground, Coleridge
read aloud with a sonorous and musical voice, the ballad
of *Betty Foy.* I was not critically or sceptically inclined. I
saw touches of truth and nature, and took the rest for
granted. But in the *Thorn*, the *Mad Mother*, and the *Complaint of a Poor Indian Woman*, I felt that deeper power
and pathos which have been since acknowledged,

> *In spite of pride, in erring reason's spite,*

as the characteristics of this author; and the sense of a new
style and a new spirit in poetry came over me. It had to me
something of the effect that arises from the turning up of
the fresh soil, or of the first welcome breath of Spring:

> *While yet the trembling year is unconfirmed.*

Coleridge and myself walked back to Stowey that evening,
and his voice sounded high

> *Of Providence, foreknowledge, will, and fate,*
> *Fix'd fate, free-will, foreknowledge absolute,*

as we passed through echoing grove, by fairy stream or
waterfall, gleaming in the summer moonlight! He lamented
that Wordsworth was not prone enough to believe in the
traditional superstitions of the place, and that there was a
something corporeal, a *matter-of-fact-ness*, a clinging to the
palpable, or often to the petty, in his poetry, in consequence.
His genius was not a spirit that descended to him through

the air; it sprung out of the ground like a flower, or unfolded itself from a green spray, on which the goldfinch sang. He said, however (if I remember right), that this objection must be confined to his descriptive pieces, that his philosophic poetry had a grand and comprehensive spirit in it, so that his soul seemed to inhabit the universe like a palace, and to discover truth by intuition, rather than by deduction. The next day Wordsworth arrived from Bristol at Coleridge's cottage. I think I see him now. He answered in some degree to his friend's description of him, but was more gaunt and Don Quixote-like. He was quaintly dressed (according to the *costume* of that unconstrained period) in a brown fustian jacket and striped pantaloons. There was something of a roll, a lounge in his gait, not unlike his own *Peter Bell.* There was a severe, worn pressure of thought about his temples, a fire in his eye (as if he saw something in objects more than the outward appearance), an intense, high, narrow forehead, a Roman nose, cheeks furrowed by strong purpose and feeling, and a convulsive inclination to laughter about the mouth, a good deal at variance with the solemn, stately expression of the rest of his face. Chantrey's bust wants the marking traits; but he was teased into making it regular and heavy: Haydon's head of him, introduced into the *Entrance of Christ into Jerusalem,* is the most like his drooping weight of thought and expression. He sat down and talked very naturally and freely, with a mixture of clear, gushing accents in his voice, a deep guttural intonation, and a strong tincture of the northern *burr,* like the crust on wine. He instantly began to make havoc of the half of a Cheshire cheese on the table, and said, triumphantly, that "his marriage with experience had not been so productive as Mr. Southey's in teaching him a knowledge of the good things of this life." He had been to see the *Castle Spectre* by Monk Lewis, while at Bristol, and described it very well. He said "it fitted the taste of the audience like a glove." This *ad captandum* merit was however by no means a recommendation of it, according to the severe principles of the new school, which reject rather than court popular effect. Wordsworth, looking out of the low, latticed window, said, "How beautifully the sun sets on that yellow bank!" I thought within myself, "With what eyes these poets see nature!" and ever after, when I saw the sun-set stream upon the objects facing it, conceived I had made a discovery, or thanked Mr. Wordsworth for having made one for me! We

went over to All-Foxden again the day following, and
Wordsworth read us the story of *Peter Bell* in the open air;
and the comment made upon it by his face and voice was
very different from that of some later critics! Whatever
might be thought of the poem, "his face was as a book where
men might read strange matters," and he announced the
fate of his hero in prophetic tones. There is a *chaunt* in the
recitation both of Coleridge and Wordsworth, which acts as
a spell upon the hearer, and disarms the judgment. Perhaps
they have deceived themselves by making habitual use of
this ambiguous accompaniment. Coleridge's manner is more
full, animated, and varied; Wordsworth's more equable,
sustained, and internal. The one might be termed more
dramatic, the other more *lyrical.* Coleridge has told me that
he himself liked to compose in walking over uneven ground,
or breaking through the straggling branches of a copse-
wood; whereas Wordsworth always wrote (if he could)
walking up and down a straight gravel-walk, or in some spot
where the continuity of his verse met with no collateral
interruption. Returning that same evening, I got into a metaphysical argument with Wordsworth, while Coleridge was
explaining the different notes of the nightingale to his sister,
in which we neither of us succeeded in making ourselves
perfectly clear and intelligible. Thus I passed three weeks at
Nether-Stowey and in the neighborhood, generally devoting
the afternoons to a delightful chat in an arbor made of bark
by the poet's friend Tom Poole, sitting under two fine elm-
trees, and listening to the bees humming round us, while we
quaffed our *flip.* It was agreed, among other things, that we
should make a jaunt down the Bristol Channel, as far as
Linton. We set off together on foot, Coleridge, John Chester,
and I. This Chester was a native of Nether-Stowey, one of
those who were attracted to Coleridge's discourse as flies
are to honey, or bees in swarming-time to the sound of a
brass pan. He "followed in the chace like a dog who hunts,
not like one that made up the cry." He had on a brown cloth
coat, boots, and corduroy breeches, was low in stature,
bow-legged, had a drag in his walk like a drover, which he
assisted by a hazel switch, and kept on a sort of trot by the
side of Coleridge, like a running footman by a state coach,
that he might not lose a syllable or sound that fell from
Coleridge's lips. He told me his private opinion, that Coleridge was a wonderful man. He scarcely opened his lips,
much less offered an opinion the whole way: yet of the

three, had I to choose during that journey, I would be John
Chester. He afterwards followed Coleridge into Germany,
where the Kantean philosophers were puzzled how to bring
him under any of their categories. When he sat down at
table with his idol, John's felicity was complete; Sir Walter
Scott's, or Mr. Blackwood's, when they sat down at the same
table with the King, was not more so. We passed Dunster
on our right, a small town between the brow of a hill and the
sea. I remember eyeing it wistfully as it lay below us: contrasted with the woody scene around, it looked as clear, as
pure, as *embrowned* and ideal as any landscape I have seen
since, of Gaspar Poussin's or Domenichino's. We had a long
day's march—(our feet kept time to the echoes of Coleridge's tongue)—through Minehead and by the Blue Anchor, and on to Linton, which we did not reach till near
midnight, and where we had some difficulty in making a
lodgment. We, however, knocked the people of the house up
at last, and we were repaid for our apprehensions and fatigue
by some excellent rashers of fried bacon and eggs. The view
in coming along had been splendid. We walked for miles and
miles on dark brown heaths overlooking the Channel, with
the Welsh hills beyond, and at times descended into little
sheltered valleys close by the sea-side, with a smuggler's face
scowling by us, and then had to ascend conical hills with a
path winding up through a coppice to a barren top, like a
monk's shaven crown, from one of which I pointed out to
Coleridge's notice the bare masts of a vessel on the very edge
of the horizon, and within the red-orbed disk of the setting
sun, like his own spectre-ship in the *Ancient Mariner*. At
Linton the character of the sea-coast becomes more marked
and rugged. There is a place called the *Valley of Rocks* (I
suspect this was only the poetical name for it), bedded
among precipices overhanging the sea, with rocky caverns
beneath, into which the waves dash, and where the sea-gull
forever wheels its screaming flight. On the tops of these are
huge stones thrown transverse, as if an earthquake had
tossed them there, and behind these is a fretwork of perpen-
dicular rocks, something like the *Giant's Causeway*. A
thunderstorm came on while we were at the inn, and Coleridge was running out bare-headed to enjoy the commotion
of the elements in the *Valley of Rocks,* but as if in spite,
the clouds only muttered a few angry sounds, and let fall a
few refreshing drops. Coleridge told me that he and Wordsworth were to have made this place the scene of a prose-tale,

which was to have been in the manner of, but far superior to, the *Death of Abel,* but they had relinquished the design. In the morning of the second day, we breakfasted luxuriously in an old-fashioned parlor on tea, toast, eggs, and honey, in the very sight of the bee-hives from which it had been taken, and a garden full of thyme and wild flowers that had produced it. On this occasion Coleridge spoke of Virgil's *Georgics,* but not well. I do not think he had much feeling for the classical or elegant. It was in this room that we found a little worn-out copy of the *Seasons,* lying in a window-seat, on which Coleridge exclaimed, *"That* is true fame!" He said Thomson was a great poet, rather than a good one; his style was as meretricious as his thoughts were natural. He spoke of Cowper as the best modern poet. He said the *Lyrical Ballads* were an experiment about to be tried by him and Wordsworth, to see how far the public taste would endure poetry written in a more natural and simple style than had hitherto been attempted; totally discarding the artifices of poetical diction, and making use only of such words as had probably been common in the most ordinary language since the days of Henry II. Some comparison was introduced between Shakespeare and Milton. He said "he hardly knew which to prefer. Shakespeare appeared to him a mere stripling in the art; he was as tall and as strong, with infinitely more activity than Milton, but he never appeared to have come to man's estate; or if he had, he would not have been a man, but a monster." He spoke with contempt of Gray, and with intolerance of Pope. He did not like the versification of the latter. He observed that "the ears of these couplet-writers might be charged with having short memories, that could not retain the harmony of whole passages." He thought little of Junius as a writer; he had a dislike of Dr. Johnson; and a much higher opinion of Burke as an orator and politician, than of Fox or Pitt. He, however, thought him very inferior in richness of style and imagery to some of our elder prose-writers, particularly Jeremy Taylor. He liked Richardson, but not Fielding; nor could I get him to enter into the merits of *Caleb Williams.* In short, he was profound and discriminating with respect to those authors whom he liked, and where he gave his judgment fair play; capricious, perverse, and prejudiced in his antipathies and distastes. We loitered on the "ribbed sea-sands," in such talk as this a whole morning, and, I recollect, met with a curious sea-weed, of which

John Chester told us the country name! A fisherman gave Coleridge an account of a boy that had been drowned the day before, and that they had tried to save him at the risk of their own lives. He said "he did not know how it was that they ventured, but, Sir, we have a *nature* towards one another." This expression, Coleridge remarked to me, was a fine illustration of that theory of disinterestedness which I (in common with Butler) had adopted. I broached to him an argument of mine to prove that *likeness* was not mere association of ideas. I said that the mark in the sand put one in mind of a man's foot, not because it was part of a former impression of a man's foot (for it was quite new), but because it was like the shape of a man's foot. He assented to the justness of this distinction (which I have explained at length elsewhere, for the benefit of the curious) and John Chester listened; not from any interest in the subject, but because he was astonished that I should be able to suggest anything to Coleridge that he did not already know. We returned on the third morning, and Coleridge remarked the silent cottage-smoke curling up the valleys where, a few evenings before, we had seen the lights gleaming through the dark.

In a day or two after we arrived at Stowey, we set out, I on my return home, and he for Germany. It was a Sunday morning, and he was to preach that day for Dr. Toulmin of Taunton. I asked him if he had prepared anything for the occasion? He said he had not even thought of the text, but should as soon as we parted. I did not go to hear him—this was a fault—but we met in the evening at Bridgewater. The next day we had a long day's walk to Bristol, and sat down, I recollect, by a well-side on the road, to cool ourselves and satisfy our thirst, when Coleridge repeated to me some descriptive lines of his tragedy of *Remorse;* which I must say became his mouth and that occasion better than they, some years after, did Mr. Elliston's and the Drury-lane boards—

Oh, memory! shield me from the world's poor strife,
And give those scenes thine everlasting life.

I saw no more of him for a year or two, during which period he had been wandering in the Hartz Forest, in Germany; and his return was cometary, meteorous, unlike his setting out. It was not till some time after that I knew his friends Lamb and Southey. The last always appears to me (as I first saw him) with a commonplace book under his arm, and the first with a *bon-mot* in his mouth. It was at Godwin's that I met him with Holcroft and Coleridge, where they were disputing fiercely which was the best— *Man as he was, or man as he is to be.* "Give me," says Lamb, "man as he is *not* to be." This saying was the beginning of a friendship between us, which I believe still continues.—Enough of this for the present.

But there is matter for another rhyme,
And I to this may add a second tale.

Liber Amoris

UNALTERED LOVE

Love is not love that alteration finds:
Oh no! it is an ever-fixed mark,
That looks on tempests and is never shaken.

Shall I not love her for herself alone, in spite of fickleness and folly? To love her for her regard to me, is not to love her, but myself. She has robbed me of herself: shall she also rob me of my love for her? Did I not live on her smile? Is it less sweet because it is withdrawn from me? Did I not adore her every grace? Does she bend less enchantingly, because she has turned from me to another? Is my love then in the power of fortune, or of her caprice? No, I will have it lasting as it is pure; and I will make a Goddess of her, and build a temple to her in my heart, and worship her on indestructible altars, and raise statues to her: and my homage shall be unblemished as her unrivalled symmetry of form; and when that fails, the memory of it shall survive; and my bosom shall be proof to scorn, as hers has been to pity; and I will pursue her with an unrelenting love, and sue to be her slave, and tend her steps without notice and without reward; and serve her living, and mourn for her when dead. And thus my love will have shown itself superior to her hate; and I shall triumph and then die. This is my idea of the only true and heroic love! Such is mine for her.

PERFECT LOVE

Perfect love has this advantage in it, that it leaves the possessor of it nothing farther to desire. There is one object (at least) in which the soul finds absolute content, for which it seeks to live, or dares to die. The heart has as it were filled up the molds of the imagination. The truth of passion keeps pace with and outvies the extravagance of mere language. There are no words so fine, no flattery so soft, that there is not a sentiment beyond them, that it is impossible to express, at the bottom of the heart where true love is. What

163

idle sounds the common phrases, *adorable creature, angel, divinity*, are! What a proud reflection it is to have a feeling answering to all these, rooted in the breast, unalterable, unutterable, to which all other feelings are light and vain! Perfect love reposes on the object of its choice, like the halcyon on the wave; and the air of heaven is around it.

On the Feeling of Immortality in Youth

No young man believes he shall ever die. It was a saying of my brother's, and a fine one. There is a feeling of Eternity in youth which makes us amends for everything. To be young is to be as one of the Immortals. One half of time indeed is spent—the other half remains in store for use with all its countless treasures, for there is no line drawn, and we see no limit to our hopes and wishes. We make the coming age our own—

The vast, the unbounded prospect lies before us.

Death, old age, are words without a meaning, a dream, a fiction, with which we have nothing to do. Others may have undergone, or may still undergo them—we "bear a charmed life," which laughs to scorn all such idle fancies. As, in setting out on a delightful journey, we strain our eager sight forward,

Bidding the lovely scenes at distance hail,

and see no end to prospect after prospect, new objects presenting themselves as we advance, so in the outset of life we see no end to our desires nor to the opportunities of gratifying them. We have as yet found no obstacle, no disposition to flag, and it seems that we can go on so forever. We look round in a new world, full of life and motion, and ceaseless progress, and feel in ourselves all the vigor and spirit to keep pace with it, and do not foresee from any present signs how we shall be left behind in the race, decline into old age, and drop into the grave. It is the simplicity and, as it were, abstractedness of our feelings in youth that (so to speak) identifies us with Nature and (our experience being weak and our passions strong) makes us fancy ourselves immortal like it. Our short-lived connection with being, we fondly flatter ourselves, is an indissoluble and lasting union. As infants smile and sleep, we are rocked in the cradle of our desires, and hushed into fancied security by the roar of the universe around us—we quaff the cup of life with eager thirst without draining it, and joy and hope seem ever mantling to the brim—objects press around us, filling the mind with their magnitude and with the throng of desires that wait upon them, so that there is no room for the thoughts of death. We are too much dazzled by the gorgeousness and novelty of the bright waking dream about us to discern the dim

165

shadow lingering for us in the distance. Nor would the hold that life has taken of us permit us to detach our thoughts that way, even if we could. We are too much absorbed in present objects and pursuits. While the spirit of youth remains unimpaired, ere "the wine of life is drunk," we are like people intoxicated or in a fever, who are hurried away by the violence of their own sensations: it is only as present objects begin to pall upon the sense, as we have been disappointed in our favorite pursuits, cut off from our closest ties, that we by degrees become weaned from the world, that passion loosens its hold upon futurity, and that we begin to contemplate as in a glass darkly the possibility of parting with it for good. Till then, the example of others has no effect upon us. Casualties we avoid; the slow approaches of age we play at *hide and seek* with. Like the foolish fat scullion in Sterne, who hears that Master Bobby is dead, our only reflection is, "So am not I!" The idea of death, instead of staggering our confidence, only seems to strengthen and enhance our sense of the possession and enjoyment of life. Others may fall around us like leaves, or be mowed down by the scythe of Time like grass: these are but metaphors to the unreflecting, buoyant ears and overweening presumption of youth. It is not till we see the flowers of Love, Hope, and Joy withering around us, that we give up the flattering delusions that before led us on, and that the emptiness and dreariness of the prospect before us reconciles us hypothetically to the silence of the grave.

Life is indeed a strange gift, and its privileges are most mysterious. No wonder when it is first granted to us, that our gratitude, our admiration, and our delight should prevent us from reflecting on our own nothingness, or from thinking it will ever be recalled. Our first and strongest impressions are borrowed from the mighty scene that is opened to us, and we unconsciously transfer its durability as well as its splendor to ourselves. So newly found, we cannot think of parting with it yet, or at least put off that consideration *sine die*. Like a rustic at a fair, we are full of amazement and rapture, and have no thought of going home, or that it will soon be night. We know our existence only by ourselves, and confound our knowledge with the objects of it. We and Nature are therefore one. Otherwise the illusion, the "feast of reason and the flow of soul," to which we are invited, is a mockery and a cruel insult. We do not go from a play till the last act is ended, and the lights are about to be extinguished. But the fairy face of Nature still shines on: shall we be called away before the curtain falls, or ere we have scarce had a glimpse of what is going on? Like children, our step-mother Nature holds us up to see the raree-show of the universe, and then, as if we were a burden to her to support, lets us fall down again. Yet what brave sublunary things does not this pageant present, like a ball or fête of the universe!

To see the golden sun, the azure sky, the outstretched ocean; to walk upon the green earth, and be lord of a thousand creatures; to look down yawning precipices or over distant sunny vales; to see the world spread out under one's feet on a map; to bring the stars near; to view the smallest insects through a microscope; to read history, and consider the revolutions of empire and the successions of generations; to hear of the glory of Tyre, of Sidon, of Babylon, and of Susa, and to say all these were before me and are now nothing; to say I exist in such a point of time, and in such a point of space; to be a spectator and a part of its ever-moving scene; to witness the change of season, of spring and autumn, of winter and summer; to feel hot and cold, pleasure and pain, beauty and deformity, right and wrong; to be sensible to the accidents of Nature; to consider the mighty world of eye and ear; to listen to the stock-dove's notes amid the forest deep; to journey over moor and mountain; to hear the midnight sainted choir; to visit lighted halls, or the cathedral's gloom, or sit in crowded theatres and see life itself mocked; to study the works of art and refine the sense of beauty to agony; to worship fame, and to dream of immortality; to look upon the Vatican, and to read Shakespeare; to gather up the wisdom of the ancients, and to pry into the future; to listen to the trump of war, the shout of victory; to question history as to the movements of the human heart; to seek for truth; to plead the cause of humanity; to overlook the world as if time and Nature poured their treasures at our feet—to be and to do all this, and then in a moment to be nothing—to have it all snatched from us as by a juggler's trick, or a phantasmagoria! There is something in this transition from all to nothing that shocks us and damps the enthusiasm of youth new flushed with hope and pleasure, and we cast the comfortless thought as far from us as we can. In the first enjoyment of the estate of

life we discard the fear of debts and duns, and never think
of the final payment of our great debt to Nature. Art we
know is long; life, we flatter ourselves, should be so too. We
see no end of the difficulties and delays we have to encounter: perfection is slow of attainment, and we must have
time to accomplish it in. The fame of the great names we
look up to is immortal: and shall not we who contemplate it
imbibe a portion of ethereal fire, the *divinae particula aurae,*
which nothing can extinguish? A wrinkle in Rembrandt or
in Nature takes whole days to resolve itself into its com-
ponent parts, its softenings and its sharpnesses; we refine
upon our perfections, and unfold the intricacies of Nature.
What a prospect for the future! What a task have we not
begun! And shall we be arrested in the middle of it? We
do not count our time thus employed lost, or our pains
thrown away; we do not flag or grow tired, but gain new
vigor at our endless task. Shall Time, then, grudge us to
finish what we have begun, and have formed a compact
with Nature to do? Why not fill up the blank that is left us
in this manner? I have looked for hours at a Rembrandt
without being conscious of the flight of time, but with ever
new wonder and delight, have thought that not only my
own but another existence I could pass in the same manner.
This rarefied, refined existence seemed to have no end, nor
stint, nor principle of decay in it. The print would remain
long after I who looked on it had become the prey of
worms. The thing seems in itself out of all reason: health,
strength, appetite are opposed to the idea of death, and we
are not ready to credit it till we have found our illusions
vanished, and our hopes grown cold. Objects in youth, from
novelty, etc., are stamped upon the brain with such force
and integrity that one thinks nothing can remove or oblit-
erate them. They are riveted there, and appear to us as an
element of our nature. It must be a mere violence that
destroys them, not a natural decay. In the very strength of
this persuasion we seem to enjoy an age by anticipation.
We melt down years into a single moment of intense sympathy, and by anticipating the fruits defy the ravages of
time. If, then, a single moment of our lives is worth years,
shall we set any limits to its total value and extent? Again,
does it not happen that so secure do we think ourselves of
an indefinite period of existence, that at times, when left to
ourselves, and impatient of novelty, we feel annoyed at
what seems to us the slow and creeping progress of time,

and argue that if it always moves at this tedious snail's pace it will never come to an end? How ready are we to sacrifice any space of time which separates us from a favorite object. little thinking that before long we shall find it move too fast.

For my part, I started in life with the French Revolution, and I have lived, alas! to see the end of it. But I did not foresee this result. My sun arose with the first dawn of liberty, and I did not think how soon both must set. The new impulse to ardor given to men's minds imparted a congenial warmth and glow to mine; we were strong to run a race together, and I little dreamed that long before mine was set, the sun of liberty would turn to blood, or set once more in the night of despotism. Since then, I confess, I have no longer felt myself young, for with that my hopes fell.

I have since turned my thoughts to gathering up some of the fragments of my early recollections, and putting them into a form to which I might occasionally revert. The future was barred to my progress, and I turned for consolation and encouragement to the past. It is thus that, while we find our personal and substantial identity vanishing from us, we strive to gain a reflected and vicarious one in our thoughts: we do not like to perish wholly, and wish to bequeath our names, at least, to posterity. As long as we can make our cherished thoughts and nearest interests live in the minds of others, we do not appear to have retired altogether from the stage. We still occupy the breasts of others, and exert an influence and power over them, and it is only our bodies that are reduced to dust and powder. Our favorite speculations still find encouragement, and we make as great a figure in the eye of the world, or perhaps a greater than in our lifetime. The demands of our self-love are thus satisfied, and these are the most imperious and unremitting. Besides, if by our intellectual superiority we survive ourselves in this world, by our virtues and faith we may attain an interest in another, and a higher state of being, and may thus be recipients at the same time of men and of angels.

> *E'en from the tomb the voice of Nature cries,*
> *E'en in our ashes live their wonted fires.*

As we grow old, our sense of the value of time becomes vivid. Nothing else, indeed, seems of any consequence. We can never cease wondering that that which has ever been should cease to be. We find many things remain the same:

why then should there be change in us. This adds a convulsive grasp of whatever is, a sense of fallacious hollowness in all we see. Instead of the full, pulpy feeling of youth tasting existence and every object in it, all is flat and vapid, —a whited sepulchre, fair without but full of ravening and all uncleanness within. The world is a witch that puts us off with false shows and appearances. The simplicity of youth, the confiding expectation, the boundless raptures, are gone: we only think of getting out of it as well as we can, and without any great mischance or annoyance. The flush of illusion, even the complacent retrospect of past joys and hopes, is over: if we can slip out of life without indignity, can escape with little bodily infirmity, and frame our minds to the calm and respectable composure of *still-life* before we return to absolute nothingness, it is as much as we can expect. We do not die wholly at our deaths: we have moldered away gradually long before. Faculty after faculty, interest after interest, attachment after attachment disappear: we are torn from ourselves while living, year after year sees us no longer the same, and death only consigns the last fragment of what we were to the grave. That we should wear out by slow stages, and dwindle at last into nothing, is not wonderful, when even in our prime our strongest impressions leave little trace but for the moment, and we are the creatures of petty circumstance. How little effect is made on us in our best days by the books we have read, the scenes we have witnessed, the sensations we have gone through! Think only of the feelings we experience in reading a fine romance (one of Sir Walter's, for instance); what beauty, what sublimity, what interest, what heart-rending emotions! You would suppose the feelings you then experienced would last forever, or subdue the mind to their own harmony and tone: while we are reading it seems as if nothing could ever put us out of our way, or trouble us:—the first splash of mud that we get on entering the street, the first twopence we are cheated out of, the feeling vanishes clean out of our minds, and we become the prey of petty and annoying circumstance. The mind soars to the lofty: it is at home in the groveling, the disagreeable, and the little. And yet we wonder that age should be feeble and querulous,—that the freshness of youth should fade away. Both worlds would hardly satisfy the extravagance of our desires and of our presumption.

On Living to One's-Self

I never was in a better place or humor than I am at present for writing on this subject. I have a partridge getting ready for my supper, my fire is blazing on the hearth, the air is mild for the season of the year, I have had but a slight fit of indigestion to-day (the only thing that makes me abhor myself), I have three hours good before me, and therefore I will attempt it. It is as well to do it at once as to have it to do for a week to come.

If the writing on this subject is no easy task, the thing itself is a harder one. It asks a troublesome effort to ensure the admiration of others: it is a still greater one to be satisfied with one's own thoughts. As I look from the window at the wide bare heath before me, and through the misty moonlight air see the woods that wave over the top of Winterslow,

While Heav'n's chancel-vault is blind with sleet,

my mind takes its flight through too long a series of years, supported only by the patience of thought and secret yearnings after truth and good, for me to be at a loss to understand the feeling I intend to write about; but I do not know that this will enable me to convey it more agreeably to the reader.

Lady G[randison], in a letter to Miss Harriet Byron, assures her that "her brother Sir Charles lived to himself"; and Lady L. soon after (for Richardson was never tired of a good thing) repeats the same observation; to which Miss Byron frequently returns in her answers to both sisters, "For you know Sir Charles lives to himself," till at length it passes into a proverb among the fair correspondents. This is not, however, an example of what I understand by *living to one's-self*, for Sir Charles Grandison was indeed always thinking of himself; but by this phrase I mean never thinking at all about one's-self, any more than if there was no such person in existence. The character I speak of is as little of an egotist as possible: Richardson's great favorite was as much of one as possible. Some satirical critic has represented him in Elysium "bowing over the *faded* hand of Lady Grandison" (Miss Byron that was)—he ought to have been represented bowing over his own hand, for he never admired any one but himself, and was the God of his own idolatry.—Neither do I call it living to one's-self to retire into a desert (like the saints and martyrs of old) to be devoured by wild beasts, nor to descend into a cave to be considered as a hermit, nor to get to the top of a pillar or rock to do fanatic penance and be seen of all men. What I mean by living to one's-self is living in the world, as in it, not of it: it is as if no one knew there was such a person, and you wished no one to know it: it is to be a silent spectator of the mighty scene of things, not an object of attention or curiosity in it; to take a thoughtful, anxious interest in what is passing in the world, but not to feel the slightest inclination to make or meddle with it. It is such a life as a pure spirit might be supposed to lead, and such an interest as it might take in the affairs of men: calm, contemplative, passive, distant, touched with pity for their sorrows, smiling at their follies without bitterness, sharing their affections, but not troubled by their passions, not seeking their notice, nor once dreamt of by them. He who lives wisely to himself and to his own heart looks at the busy world through the loop-holes of retreat, and does not want to mingle in the fray. "He hears the tumult, and is still." He is not able to mend it, nor willing to mar it. He sees enough in the universe to interest him without putting himself forward to try what he can do to fix the eyes of the universe upon him. Vain the attempt! He reads the clouds, he looks at the stars, he watches the return of the seasons, the falling leaves of autumn, the perfumed breath of spring, starts with delight at the note of a thrush in a copse near him, sits by the fire, listens to the moaning of the wind, pores upon a book, or discourses the freezing hours away, or melts down hours to minutes in pleasing thought. All this while he is taken up with other things, forgetting himself. He relishes an author's style without thinking of turning author. He is fond of looking at a print from an old picture in the room, without teasing himself to copy it. He does not fret himself to death with trying to be what he is not, or to do what he cannot. He hardly knows what he is capable of, and is not in the least concerned whether he shall ever make a figure in the world. . . . He looks out of himself at the wide, extended prospect of nature, and takes an interest beyond his narrow pretensions in general humanity. He is free as air and independent as the wind. Woe be to him when he first begins

to think what others say of him. While a man is contented
with himself and his own resources, all is well. When he
undertakes to play a part on the stage, and to persuade
the world to think more about him than they do about
themselves, he is got into a track where he will find nothing
but briars and thorns, vexation and disappointment. I can
speak a little to this point. For many years of my life I did
nothing but think. I had nothing else to do but solve some
knotty point, or dip in some abstruse author, or look at the
sky, or wander by the pebbled sea-side—

> *To see the children sporting on the shore,*
> *And hear the mighty waters rolling evermore*

I cared for nothing, I wanted nothing. I took my time
to consider whatever occurred to me, and was in no hurry
to give a sophistical answer to a question—there was no
printer's devil waiting for me. I used to write a page or two
perhaps in half a year; and remember laughing heartily at
the celebrated experimentalist Nicholson, who told me that
in twenty years he had written as much as would make
three hundred octavo volumes. If I was not a great author,
I could read with ever fresh delight, "never ending, still beginning," and had no occasion to write a criticism when
I had done. If I could not paint like Claude, I could admire
"the witchery of the soft blue sky" as I walked out, and was
satisfied with the pleasure it gave me. If I was dull, it gave
me little concern: if I was lively, I indulged my spirits. I
wished well to the world, and believed as favorably of it as
I could. I was like a stranger in a foreign land, at which
I looked with wonder, curiosity, and delight, without expecting to be an object of attention in return. I had no
relations to the state, no duty to perform, no ties to bind
me to others: I had neither friend nor mistress, wife nor
child. I lived in a world of contemplation, and not of
action.

This sort of dreaming existence is the best. He who quits
it to go in search of realities generally barters repose for
repeated disappointments and vain regrets. His time,
thoughts, and feelings are no longer at his own disposal.
From that instant he does not survey the objects of nature
as they are in themselves, but looks asquint at them to see
whether he cannot make them the instruments of his ambition, interest, or pleasure; for a candid, undesigning, un-

disguised simplicity of character, his views become jaundiced, sinister, and double: he takes no farther interest in the great changes of the world but as he has a paltry share in producing them: instead of opening his senses, his understanding, and his heart to the resplendent fabric of the universe, he holds a crooked mirror before his face, in which he may admire his own person and pretensions, and just glance his eye aside to see whether others are not admiring him too. He no more exists in the impression which "the fair variety of things" makes upon him, softened and subdued by habitual contemplation, but in the feverish sense of his own upstart self-importance. By aiming to fix, he is become the slave of opinion. He is a tool, a part of a machine that never stands still, and is sick and giddy with the ceaseless motion. He has no satisfaction but in the reflection of his own image in the public gaze—but in the repetition of his own name in the public ear. He himself is mixed up with and spoils everything. I wonder Buonaparte was not tired of the N. N.'s stuck all over the Louvre and throughout France. Goldsmith (as we all know), when in Holland, went out into a balcony with some handsome Englishwomen, and on their being applauded by the spectators, turned round and said peevishly, "There are places where I also am admired." He could not give the craving appetite of an author's vanity one day's respite. I have seen a celebrated talker of our own time turn pale and go out of the room when a showy-looking girl has come into it, who for a moment divided the attention of his hearers.—Infinite are the mortifications of the bare attempt to emerge from obscurity; numberless the failures; and greater and more galling still the vicissitudes and tormenting accompaniments of success—

> *Whose top to climb*
> *Is certain falling, or so slippery, that*
> *The fear's as bad as falling.*

"Would to God," exclaimed Oliver Cromwell, when he was at any time thwarted by the Parliament, "that I had remained by my woodside to tend a flock of sheep, rather than have been thrust on such a government as this!" When Buonaparte got into his carriage to proceed on his Russian expedition, carelessly twirling his glove, and singing the air, "Malbrook to the wars is going," he did not think of the tumble he has got since, the shock of which no one could have stood but himself. We see and hear chiefly of the favorites of Fortune and the Muse, of great generals, of first-rate actors, of celebrated poets. These are at the head; we are struck with the glittering eminence on which they stand, and long to set out on the same tempting career,— not thinking how many discontented half-pay lieutenants are in vain seeking promotion all their lives, and obliged to put up with "the insolence of office, and the spurns which patient merit of the unworthy takes"; how many half-starved strolling players are doomed to penury and tattered robes in country places, dreaming to the last of a London engagement; how many wretched daubers shiver and shake in the ague-fit of alternate hopes and fears, waste and pine away in the atrophy of genius, or else turn drawing-masters, picture-cleaners, or newspaper-critics; how many hapless poets have sighed out their souls to the Muse in vain, without ever getting their effusions farther known than the Poet's Corner of a country newspaper, and looked and looked with grudging, wistful eyes at the envious horizon that bounded their provincial fame!—Suppose an actor, for instance, "after the heart-aches and the thousand natural pangs that flesh is heir to," *does* get at the top of his profession, he can no longer bear a rival near the throne; to be second or only equal to another is to be nothing: he starts at the prospect of a successor, and retains the mimic sceptre with a convulsive grasp: perhaps as he is about to seize the first place which he has long had in his eye, an unsuspected competitor steps in before him, and carries off the prize, leaving him to commence his irksome toil again. He is in a state of alarm at every appearance or rumor of the appearance of a new actor: "a mouse that takes up its lodging in a cat's ear" has a mansion of peace to him: he dreads every hint of an objection, and least of all can forgive praise mingled with censure: to doubt is to insult; to discriminate is to degrade: he dare hardly look into a criticism unless some one has *tasted* it for him, to see that there is no offense in it: if he does not draw crowded houses every night, he can neither eat nor sleep; or if all these terrible inflictions are removed, and he can "eat his meal in peace," he then becomes surfeited with applause and dissatisfied with his profession: he wants to be something else, to be distinguished as an author, a collector, a classical scholar, a man of sense and information, and weighs every word he utters, and half retracts it before he utters it, lest if he were to make the smallest slip of the tongue it should get buzzed abroad that *Mr. —— was only clever as an actor!* If ever there was a man who did not derive more pain than pleasure from his vanity, that man, says Rousseau, was no other than a fool. A country gentleman near Taunton spent his whole life in making some hundreds of wretched copies of second-rate pictures, which were bought up at his death by a neighboring baronet, to whom

> *Some Demon whisper'd, L——, have a taste!*

A little Wilson in an obscure corner escaped the man of *virtù,* and was carried off by a Bristol picture-dealer for three guineas, while the muddled copies of the owner of the mansion (with the frames) fetched thirty, forty, sixty, a hundred ducats a piece. A friend of mine found a very fine Canaletti in a state of strange disfigurement, with the upper part of the sky smeared over and fantastically variegated with English clouds; and on inquiring of the person to whom it belonged whether something had not been done to it, received for answer "that a gentleman, a great artist in the neighborhood, had retouched some parts of it." What infatuation! Yet this candidate for the honors of the pencil might probably have made a jovial fox-hunter or respectable justice of the peace if he could only have stuck to what nature and fortune intended him for. Miss —— can by no means be persuaded to quit the boards of the theatre at ——, a little country town in the West of England. Her salary has been abridged, her person ridiculed, her acting laughed at; nothing will serve—she is determined to be an actress, and scorns to return to her former business as a milliner. Shall I go on? An actor in the same company was visited by the apothecary of the place in an ague-fit, who, on asking his landlady as to his way of life, was told that the poor gentleman was very quiet and gave little trouble, that he generally had a plate of mashed potatoes for his dinner, and lay in bed most of his time, repeating his part. A young couple, every way amiable and deserving, were to have been married, and a benefit-play was bespoke by the officers of the regiment quartered there, to defray the expense of a license and of the wedding-ring, but the profits of the night did not amount to the necessary sum, and they have, I fear, "virgined it e'er since"! Oh for the pencil of Hogarth or Wilkie to give a view of the comic strength of the company at ———, drawn up in battle-array in the *Clandestine Marriage,* with a *coup d'œil* of the pit, boxes, and gallery, to cure forever the love of the *ideal,* and the desire to shine and make holiday in the eyes of others, instead of retiring within ourselves and keeping our wishes and our thoughts at home!—Even in the common affairs of life, in love, friendship, and marriage, how little security have we when we trust our happiness in the hands of others! Most of the friends I have seen have turned out the bitterest enemies, or cold, uncomfortable acquaintance. Old companions are like meats served up too often, that lose their relish and their wholesomeness. He who looks at beauty to admire, to adore it, who reads of its wondrous power in novels, in poems, or in plays, is not unwise; but let no man fall in love, for from that moment he is "the baby of a girl." . . .

On the Pleasure of Painting

There is a pleasure in painting which none but painters know. In writing, you have to contend with the world; in painting, you have only to carry on a friendly strife with Nature. You sit down to your task and are happy. From the moment that you take up the pencil and look Nature in the face, you are at peace with your own heart. No angry passions rise to disturb the silent progress of the work, to shake the hand, or dim the brow: no irritable humors are set afloat; you have no absurd opinions to combat, no point to strain, no adversary to crush, no fool to annoy—you are actuated by fear or favor to no man. There is "no juggling here," no sophistry, no intrigue, no tampering with the evidence, no attempt to make black white, or white black: but you resign yourself into the hands of a greater power, that of Nature, with the simplicity of a child, and the devotion of an enthusiast—"study with joy her manner, and with rapture taste her style." The mind is calm and full at the same time. The hand and eye are equally employed. In tracing the commonest object, a plant or the stump of a tree, you learn something every moment. You perceive unexpected differences, and discover likenesses where you looked for no such thing. You try to set down what you see —find out your error and correct it. You need not play tricks, or purposely mistake: with all your pains, you are still far short of the mark. Patience grows out of the endless pursuit and turns it into a luxury. A streak in a flower, a wrinkle in a leaf, a tinge in a cloud, a stain in an old wall or ruin grey, are seized with avidity as the *spolia opima* of this sort of mental warfare, and furnish out labor for another half day. The hours pass away untold, without chagrin, and without weariness; nor would you ever wish to pass them otherwise. Innocence is joined with industry, pleasure with business; and the mind is satisfied, though it is not engaged in thinking or in doing any mischief.

I have not much pleasure in writing these Essays, or in reading them afterwards; though I own I now and then meet with a phrase that I like, or a thought that strikes me as a true one. But after I begin them, I am only anxious to get to the end of them, which I am not sure I shall do, for I seldom see my way a page or even a sentence beforehand; and when I have as by a miracle escaped, I trouble myself little more about them. I sometimes have to write them twice over: then it is necessary to read the *proof,* to prevent mistakes by the printer; so that by the time they appear in a tangible shape, and one can con them over with a conscious, sidelong glance to the public approbation, they have lost their gloss and relish, and become "more tedious than a twice-told tale." For a person to read his own works over with any great delight, he ought first to forget that he ever wrote them. Familiarity naturally breeds contempt. It is, in fact, like poring fondly over a piece of blank paper; from repetition, the words convey no distinct meaning to the mind, are mere idle sounds, except that our vanity claims an interest and property in them. I have more satisfaction in my own thoughts than in dictating them to others: words are necessary to explain the impression of certain things upon me to the reader, but they rather weaken and draw a veil over than strengthen it to myself. However, I might say with the poet, "My mind to me a kingdom is," yet I have little ambition "to set a throne or chair of state in the understandings of other men." The ideas we cherish most exist best in a kind of shadowy abstraction,

Pure in the last recesses of the mind;

and derive neither force nor interest from being exposed to public view. They are old familiar acquaintance, and any change in them, arising from the adventitious ornaments of style or dress, is little to their advantage. After I have once written on a subject, it goes out of my mind: my feelings about it have been melted down into words, and *them* I forget. I have, as it were, discharged my memory of its old habitual reckoning, and rubbed out the score of real sentiment. For the future, it exists only for the sake of others.—But I cannot say, from my own experience, that the same process takes place in transferring our ideas to canvas; they gain more than they lose in the mechanical transformation. One is never tired of painting, because you have to set down not what you knew already, but what you have just discovered. In the former case, you translate feelings into words; in the latter, names into things. There is a continual creation out of nothing going on. With every stroke of the brush, a new field of inquiry is laid open; new difficulties arise, and new triumphs are prepared over them. By comparing the imitation with the original, you see what

you have done, and how much you have still to do. The test
of the senses is severer than that of fancy, and an over-
match even for the delusions of our self-love. One part of a
picture shames another, and you determine to paint up to
yourself, if you cannot come up to Nature. Every object
becomes lustrous from the light thrown back upon it by the
mirror of art: and by the aid of the pencil we may be said
to touch and handle the objects of sight. The air-drawn
visions that hover on the verge of existence have a bodily
presence given them on the canvas: the form of beauty is
changed into a substance: the dream and the glory of the
universe is made "palpable to feeling as to sight."—And
see! a rainbow starts from the canvas, with all its humid
train of glory, as if it were drawn from its cloudy arch in
heaven. The spangled landscape glitters with drops of dew
after the shower. The "fleecy fools" show their coats in the
gleams of the setting sun. The shepherds pipe their farewell
notes in the fresh evening air. And is this bright vision
made from a dead dull blank, like a bubble reflecting the
mighty fabric of the universe? Who would think this miracle of Rubens' pencil possible to be performed? Who, having seen it, would not spend his life to do the like? See how
the rich fallows, the bare stubble-field, the scanty harvest-
home, drag in Rembrandt's landscapes! How often have I
looked at them and Nature, and tried to do the same, till
the very "light thickened," and there was an earthiness in
the feeling of the air! There is no end of the refinements of
art and Nature in this respect. One may look at the
misty glimmering horizon till the eye dazzles and the imagination is lost, in hopes to transfer the whole interminable
expanse at one blow upon canvas. Wilson said, he used to
try to paint the effect of the motes dancing in the setting
sun. At another time, a friend coming into his painting-
room when he was sitting on the ground in a melancholy
posture, observed that his picture looked like a landscape
after a shower: he started up with the greatest delight, and
said, "That is the effect I intended to produce, but thought
I had failed." Wilson was neglected; and, by degrees, neglected his art to apply himself to brandy. His hand became
unsteady, so that it was only by repeated attempts that he
could reach the place, or produce the effect he aimed at;
and when he had done a little to a picture, he would say to
any acquaintance who chanced to drop in, "I have painted
enough for one day: come, let us go somewhere." It was

not so Claude left his pictures, or his studies on the banks
of the Tiber, to go in search of other enjoyments, or ceased
to gaze upon the glittering sunny vales and distant hills; and
while his eye drank in the clear sparkling hues and lovely
forms of Nature, his hand stamped them on the lucid canvas to last there forever!—One of the most delightful parts
of my life was one fine summer, when I used to walk out
of an evening to catch the last light of the sun, gemming the
green slopes or russet lawns, and gilding tower or tree,
while the blue sky gradually turning to purple and gold, or
skirted with dusky grey, hung its broad marble pavement
over all, as we see it in the great master of Italian landscape. But to come to a more particular explanation of the
subject.

The first head I ever tried to paint was an old woman
with the upper part of the face shaded by her bonnet, and
I certainly labored it with great perseverance. It took me
numberless sittings to do it. I have it by me still, and sometimes look at it with surprise, to think how much pains
were thrown away to little purpose,—yet not altogether in
vain if it taught me to see good in everything, and to know
that there is nothing vulgar in Nature seen with the eye of
science or of true art. Refinement creates beauty everywhere: it is the grossness of the spectator that discovers
nothing but grossness in the object. Be this as it may, I
spared no pains to do my best. If art was long, I thought
that life was so too at that moment. I got in the general
effect the first day; and pleased and surprised enough I
was at my success. The rest was a work of time—of weeks
and months (if need were) of patient toil and careful finishing. I had seen an old head by Rembrandt at Burleigh
House, and if I could produce a head at all like Rembrandt
in a year, in my life-time, it would be glory and felicity,
and wealth and fame enough for me! The head I had seen
at Burleigh was an exact and wonderful facsimile of Nature,
and I resolved to make mine (as nearly as I could) an exact
facsimile of Nature. I did not then, nor do I now believe,
with Sir Joshua, that the perfection of art consists in giving
general appearances without individual details, but in giving general appearances with individual details. Otherwise,
I had done my work the first day. But I saw something
more in Nature than general effect, and I thought it worth
my while to give it in the picture. There was a gorgeous

effect of light and shade: but there was a delicacy as well as depth in the *chiaro scuro,* which I was bound to follow into all its dim and scarce perceptible variety of tone and shadow. Then I had to make the transition from a strong light to as dark a shade, preserving the masses, but gradually softening off the intermediate parts. It was so in Nature: the difficulty was to make it so in the copy. I tried, and failed again and again; I strove harder, and succeeded as I thought. The wrinkles in Rembrandt were not hard lines; but broken and irregular. I saw the same appearance in Nature, and strained every nerve to give it. If I could hit off this edgy appearance, and insert the reflected light in the furrows of old age in half a morning, I did not think I had lost a day. Beneath the shrivelled yellow parchment look of the skin, there was here and there a streak of the blood color tinging the face; this I made a point of conveying, and did not cease to compare what I saw with what I did (with jealous lynx-eyed watchfulness) till I succeeded to the best of my ability and judgment. How many revisions were there! How many attempts to catch an expression which I had seen the day before! How often did we try to get the old position, and wait for the return of the same light! There was a puckering up of the lips, a cautious introversion of the eye under the shadow of the bonnet, indicative of the feebleness and suspicion of old age, which at last we managed, after many trials and some quarrels, to a tolerable nicety. The picture was never finished, and I might have gone on with it to the present hour. I used to set it on the ground when my day's work was done, and saw revealed to me with swimming eyes the birth of new hopes, and of a new world of objects. The painter thus learns to look at Nature with different eyes. He before saw her "as in a glass darkly, but now face to face." He understands the texture and meaning of the visible universe, and "sees into the life of things," not by the help of mechanical instruments, but of the improved exercise of his faculties, and an intimate sympathy with Nature. The meanest thing is not lost upon him, for he looks at it with an eye to itself, not merely to his own vanity or interest, or the opinion of the world. Even where there is neither beauty nor use—if that ever were—still there is truth, and a sufficient source of gratification in the indulgence of curiosity and activity of mind. The humblest painter is a true scholar, and the best of scholars—the scholar of Nature. For my-

self, and for the real comfort and satisfaction of the thing,
I had rather have been Jan Steen, or Gerard Dow, than
the greatest casuist or philologer that ever lived. The painter
does not view things in clouds or "mist, the common gloss
of theologians," but applies the same standard of truth and
disinterested spirit of inquiry, that influence his daily practice, to other subjects. He perceives form, he distinguishes
character. He reads men and books with an intuitive eye.
He is a critic as well as a connoisseur. The conclusions he
draws are clear and convincing, because they are taken
from the things themselves. He is not a fanatic, a dupe, or
a slave: for the habit of seeing for himself also disposes him
to judge for himself. The most sensible men I know (taken
as a class) are painters; that is, they are the most lively
observers of what passes in the world about them, and the
closest observers of what passes in their own minds. From
their profession they in general mix more with the world
than authors; and if they have not the same fund of acquired
knowledge, are obliged to rely more on individual sagacity.
I might mention the names of Opie, Fuseli, Northcote, as
persons distinguished for striking description and acquaintance with the subtle traits of character. Painters in ordinary
society, or in obscure situations where their value is not
known, and they are treated with neglect and indifference,
have sometimes a forward self-sufficiency of manner: but
this is not so much their fault as that of others. Perhaps
their want of regular education may also be in fault in such
cases. Richardson, who is very tenacious of the respect in
which the profession ought to be held, tells a story of
Michael Angelo, that after a quarrel between him and Pope
Julius II, "upon account of a slight the artist conceived the
pontiff had put upon him, Michael Angelo was introduced
by a bishop, who, thinking to serve the artist by it, made
it an argument that the Pope should be reconciled to him,
because men of his profession were commonly ignorant,
and of no consequence otherwise: his holiness, enraged
at the bishop, struck him with his staff, and told him, it
was he that was the blockhead, and affronted the man
himself would not offend; the prelate was driven out of
the chamber, and Michael Angelo had the Pope's benedic-
tion accompanied with presents. This bishop had fallen
into the vulgar error, and was rebuked accordingly."

Besides the exercise of the mind, painting exercises the
body. It is a mechanical as well as a liberal art. To do any-

thing, to dig a hole in the ground, to plant a cabbage, to hit a mark, to move a shuttle, to work a pattern,—in a word, to attempt to produce any effect, and to *succeed*, has something in it that gratifies the love of power, and carries off the restless activity of the mind of man. Indolence is a delightful but distressing state: we must be doing something to be happy. Action is no less necessary than thought to the instinctive tendencies of the human frame; and painting combines them both incessantly. The hand furnishes a practical test of the correctness of the eye; and the eye thus admonished, imposes fresh tasks of skill and industry upon the hand. Every stroke tells, as the verifying of a new truth; and every new observation, the instant it is made, passes into an act and emanation of the will. Every step is nearer what we wish, and yet there is always more to do. In spite of the facility, the fluttering grace, the evanescent hues, that play round the pencil of Rubens and Vandyke, however I may admire, I do not envy them this power so much as I do the slow, patient, laborious execution of Correggio, Leonardo da Vinci, and Andrea del Sarto, where every touch appears conscious of its charge, emulous of truth, and where the painful artist has so distinctly wrought,

that you might almost say his picture thought!

In the one case, the colors seem breathed on the canvas as by magic, the work and the wonder of a moment; in the other, they seem inlaid in the body of the work, and as if it took the artist years of unremitting labor, and of delightful never-ending progress to perfection. Who would wish ever to come to the close of such works,—not to dwell on them, to return to them, to be wedded to them to the last? Rubens, with his florid, rapid style, complained that when he had just learned his art, he should be forced to die. Leonardo, in the slow advances of his, had lived long enough!

Painting is not, like writing, what is properly understood by a sedentary employment. It requires not indeed a strong, but a continued and steady exertion of muscular power. The precision and delicacy of the manual operation makes up for the want of vehemence,—as to balance himself for any time in the same position the rope-dancer must strain every nerve. Painting for a whole morning gives one as excellent an appetite for one's dinner, as old Abraham Tucker acquired for his by riding over Banstead Downs. It is related of Sir Joshua Reynolds, that "he took no other exercise than what he used in his painting-room,"—the writer means, in walking backwards and forwards to look at his picture; but the act of painting itself, of laying on the colors in the proper place, and proper quantity, was a much harder exercise than this alternate receding from and returning to the picture. This last would be rather a relaxation and relief than an effort. It is not to be wondered at, that an artist like Sir Joshua, who delighted so much in the sensual and practical part of his art, should have found himself at a considerable loss when the decay of his sight precluded him, for the last year or two of his life, from the following up of his profession,—"the source," according to his own remark, "of thirty years' uninterrupted enjoyment and prosperity to him." It is only those who never think at all, or else who have accustomed themselves to brood incessantly on abstract ideas, that never feel *ennui*.

To give one instance more, and then I will have done with this rambling discourse. One of my first attempts was a picture of my father, who was then in a green old age, with strong-marked features, and scarred with the small-pox. I drew it with a broad light crossing the face, looking down, with spectacles on, reading. The book was Shaftesbury's *Characteristics,* in a fine old binding, with Gribelin's etchings. My father would as lieve it had been any other book; but for him to read was to be content, was "riches fineless." The sketch promised well; and I set to work to finish it, determined to spare no time nor pains. My father was willing to sit as long as I pleased; for there is a natural desire in the mind of man to sit for one's picture, to be the object of continued attention, to have one's likeness multiplied; and besides his satisfaction in the picture, he had some pride in the artist, though he would rather I should have written a sermon than painted like Rembrandt or like Raphael. Those winter days, with the gleams of sunshine coming through the chapel-windows, and cheered by the notes of the robin-redbreast in our garden (that "ever in the haunch of winter sings")—as my afternoon's work drew to a close,—were among the happiest of my life. When I gave the effect I intended to any part of the picture for which I had prepared my colors, when I imitated the roughness of the skin by a lucky stroke of the pencil, when I hit the clear pearly tone of a vein, when I gave the ruddy complexion of health, the blood circulating under the broad shadows of one side of the face, I thought my fortune made; or rather it was already more than made, in my fancying that I might one day be able to say with Correggio, *"I also am a painter!"* It was an idle thought, a boy's conceit; but it did not make me less happy at the time. I used regularly to set my work in the chair to look at it through the long evenings; and many a time did I return to take leave of it before I could go to bed at night. I remember sending it with a throbbing heart to the Exhibition and seeing it hung up there by the side of one of the Honorable Mr. Skeffington (now Sir George). There was nothing in common between them, but that they were the portraits of two very good-natured men. I think, but I am not sure, that I finished this portrait (or another afterwards) on the same day that the news of the battle of Austerlitz came; I walked out in the afternoon, and, as I returned, saw the evening star set over a poor man's cottage with other thoughts and feelings than I shall ever have again. Oh for the revolution of the great Platonic year, that those times might come over again! I could sleep out the three hundred and sixty-five thousand intervening years very contentedly!—The picture is left: the table, the chair, the window where I learned to construe Livy, the chapel where my father preached, remain where they were; but he himself is gone to rest, full of years, of faith, of hope, and charity!

On Going a Journey

One of the pleasantest things in the world is going a journey; but I like to go by myself. I can enjoy society in a room; but out of doors, nature is company enough for me. I am then never less alone than when alone.

The fields his study, nature was his book.

I cannot see the wit of walking and talking at the same time. When I am in the country I wish to vegetate like the country. I am not for criticizing hedge-rows and black cattle. I go out of town in order to forget the town and all that is in it. There are those who for this purpose go to watering-places, and carry the metropolis with them. I like more elbow-room and fewer incumbrances. I like solitude, when I give myself up to it, for the sake of solitude; nor do I ask for

> *a friend in my retreat,*
> *Whom I may whisper solitude is sweet.*

The soul of a journey is liberty, perfect liberty, to think, feel, do, just as one pleases. We go a journey chiefly to be free of all impediments and of all inconveniences; to leave ourselves behind, much more to get rid of others. It is because I want a little breathing-space to muse on indifferent matters, where Contemplation

> *May plume her feathers and let grow her wings,*
> *That in the various bustle of resort*
> *Were all too ruffled, and sometimes impair'd,*

that I absent myself from the town for a while, without feeling at a loss the moment I am left by myself. Instead of a friend in a post-chaise or in a Tilbury, to exchange good things with, and vary the same stale topics over again, for once let me have a truce with impertinence. Give me the clear blue sky over my head, and the green turf beneath my feet, a winding road before me, and a three hours' march to dinner—and then to thinking! It is hard if I cannot start some game on these lone heaths. I laugh, I run, I leap, I sing for joy. From the point of yonder rolling cloud I plunge into my past being, and revel there, as the

187

sun-burnt Indian plunges headlong into the wave that wafts
him to his native shore. Then long-forgotten things, like
"sunken wrack and sumless treasuries," burst upon my
eager sight, and I begin to feel, think, and be myself again.
Instead of an awkward silence, broken by attempts at wit or
dull common-places, mine is that undisturbed silence of the
heart which alone is perfect eloquence. No one likes puns,
alliterations, antitheses, argument, and analysis better than
I do; but I sometimes had rather be without them. "Leave,
oh, leave me to my repose!" I have just now other business
in hand, which would seem idle to you, but is with me "very
stuff of the conscience." Is not this wild rose sweet without
a comment? Does not this daisy leap to my heart set in its
coat of emerald? Yet if I were to explain to you the circumstance that has so endeared it to me, you would only
smile. Had I not better then keep it to myself, and let it
serve me to brood over, from here to yonder craggy point,
and from thence onward to the far-distant horizon? I
should be but bad company all that way, and therefore
prefer being alone. I have heard it said that you may, when
the moody fit comes on, walk or ride on by yourself, and
indulge your reveries. But this looks like a breach of manners, a neglect of others, and you are thinking all the time
that you ought to rejoin your party. "Out upon such half-
faced fellowship," say I. I like to be either entirely to myself, or entirely at the disposal of others; to talk or be
silent, to walk or sit still, to be sociable or solitary. I was
pleased with an observation of Mr. Cobbett's, that "he
thought it a bad French custom to drink our wine with our
meals, and that an Englishman ought to do only one thing
at a time." So I cannot talk and think, or indulge in melancholy musing and lively conversation by fits and starts. "Let
me have a companion of my way," says Sterne, "were it
but to remark how the shadows lengthen as the sun declines." It is beautifully said; but, in my opinion, this continual comparing of notes interferes with the involuntary
impression of things upon the mind, and hurts the sentiment. If you only hint what you feel in a kind of dumb
show, it is insipid: if you have to explain it, it is making
a toil of a pleasure. You cannot read the book of nature
without being perpetually put to the trouble of translating
it for the benefit of others. I am for this synthetical method
on a journey in preference to the analytical. I am content
to lay in a stock of ideas then, and to examine and anato-

mize them afterwards. I want to see my vague notions float like the down of the thistle before the breeze, and not to have them entangled in the briars and thorns of controversy. For once, I like to have it all my own way; and this is impossible unless you are alone, or in such company as I do not covet. I have no objection to argue a point with any one for twenty miles of measured road, but not for pleasure. If you remark the scent of a bean-field crossing the road, perhaps your fellow-traveller has no smell. If you point to a distant object, perhaps he is short-sighted, and has to take out his glass to look at it. There is a feeling in the air, a tone in the color of a cloud, which hits your fancy, but the effect of which you are unable to account for. There is then no sympathy, but an uneasy craving after it, and a dissatisfaction which pursues you on the way, and in the end probably produces ill-humor. Now I never quarrel with myself, and take all my own conclusions for granted till I find it necessary to defend them against objections. It is not merely that you may not be of accord on the objects and circumstances that present themselves before you—these may recall a number of objects, and lead to associations too delicate and refined to be possibly communicated to others. Yet these I love to cherish, and sometimes still fondly clutch them, when I can escape from the throng to do so. To give way to our feelings before company seems extravagance or affectation; and, on the other hand, to have to unravel this mystery of our being at every turn, and to make others take an equal interest in it (otherwise the end is not answered), is a task to which few are competent. We must "give it an understanding, but no tongue." My old friend C[oleridge], however, could do both. He could go on in the most delightful explanatory way over hill and dale a summer's day, and convert a landscape into a didactic poem or a Pindaric ode. "He talked far above singing." If I could so clothe my ideas in sounding and flowing words, I might perhaps wish to have someone with me to admire the swelling theme; or I could be more content, were it possible for me still to hear his echoing voice in the woods of All-Foxden. . . .

In general, a good thing spoils out-of-door prospects: it should be reserved for Table-talk. L[amb] is for this reason, I take it, the worst company in the world out of doors; because he is the best within. I grant, there is one subject on which it is pleasant to talk on a journey; and that is, what one shall have for supper when we get to our inn at night. The open air improves this sort of conversation or friendly altercation, by setting a keener edge on appetite. Every mile of the road heightens the flavor of the viands we expect at the end of it. How fine it is to enter some old town, walled and turreted, just at approach of night-fall, or to come to some straggling village, with the lights streaming through the surrounding gloom; and then, after inquiring for the best entertainment that the place affords, to "take one's ease at one's inn"! These eventful moments in our lives' history are too precious, too full of solid, heart-felt happiness to be frittered and dribbled away in imperfect sympathy. I would have them all to myself, and drain them to the last drop: they will do to talk of or to write about afterwards. What a delicate speculation it is, after drinking whole goblets of tea—

The cups that cheer, but not inebriate,

and letting the fumes ascend into the brain, to sit considering what we shall have for supper—eggs and a rasher, a rabbit smothered in onions, or an excellent veal-cutlet! Sancho in such a situation once fixed upon cow-heel; and his choice, though he could not help it, is not to be disparaged. Then, in the intervals of pictured scenery and Shandean contemplation, to catch the preparation and the stir in the kitchen. . . . These hours are sacred to silence and to musing, to be treasured up in the memory, and to feed the source of smiling thoughts hereafter. I would not waste them in idle talk; or if I must have the integrity of fancy broken in upon, I would rather it were by a stranger than a friend. A stranger takes his hue and character from the time and place; he is a part of the furniture and costume of an inn. If he is a Quaker, or from the West Riding of Yorkshire, so much the better. I do not even try to sympathize with him, and he breaks no squares. How I love to see the camps of the gypsies, and to sigh my soul into that sort of life. If I express this feeling to another, he may qualify and spoil it with some objection. I associate nothing with my traveling companion but present objects and passing events. In his ignorance of me and my affairs, I in a manner forget myself. But a friend reminds one of other things, rips up old grievances, and destroys the abstraction of the scene. He comes in ungraciously between

us and our imaginary character. Something is dropped in
the course of conversation that gives a hint of your profession and pursuits; or from having some one with you that
knows the less sublime portions of your history, it seems
that other people do. You are no longer a citizen of the
world; but your "unhoused free condition is put into cir-
cumscription and confine." The *incognito* of an inn is one
of its striking privileges—"lord of one's self, uncumber'd
with a name." Oh! it is great to shake off the trammels of
the world and of public opinion—to lose our importunate,
tormenting, everlasting personal identity in the elements of
nature, and become the creature of the moment, clear of
all ties—to hold to the universe only by a dish of sweet-
breads, and to owe nothing but the score of the evening—
and no longer seeking for applause and meeting with contempt, to be known by no other title than *the Gentleman in
the parlor!* One may take one's choice of all characters in
this romantic state of uncertainty as to one's real pretensions, and become indefinitely respectable and negatively
right-worshipful. We baffle prejudice and disappoint conjecture; and from being so to others, begin to be objects of
curiosity and wonder even to ourselves. We are no more
those hackneyed common-places that we appear in the
world; an inn restores us to the level of nature, and quits
scores with society! I have certainly spent some enviable
hours at inns—sometimes when I have been left entirely to
myself, and have tried to solve some metaphysical problem,
as once at Witham-common, where I found out the proof
that likeness is not a case of the association of ideas—at
other times, when there have been pictures in the room, as
at St. Neot's (I think it was), where I first met with Gribelin's engravings of the Cartoons, into which I entered at
once, and at a little inn on the borders of Wales, where there
happened to be hanging some of Westall's drawings, which
I compared triumphantly (for a theory that I had, not for
the admired artist) with the figure of a girl who had ferried
me over the Severn, standing up in the boat between me
and the twilight—at other times I might mention luxuriat-
ing in books, with a peculiar interest in this way, as I remember sitting up half the night to read *Paul and Virginia,*
which I picked up at an inn at Bridgewater, after being
drenched in the rain all day; and at the same place I got
through two volumes of Madame D'Arblay's *Camilla.* It
was on the tenth of April, 1798, that I sat down to a volume

of the *New Eloise,* at the inn at Llangollen, over a bottle of sherry and a cold chicken. The letter I chose was that in which St. Preux describes his feelings as he first caught a glimpse from the heights of the Jura of the Pays de Vaud, which I had brought with me as a *bon bouche* to crown the evening with. It was my birthday, and I had for the first time come from a place in the neighborhood to visit this delightful spot. The road to Llangollen turns off between Chirk and Wrexham; and on passing a certain point you come all at once upon the valley, which opens like an amphitheatre, broad, barren hills rising in majestic state on either side, with "green upland swells that echo to the bleat of flocks" below, and the river Dee babbling over its stony bed in the midst of them. The valley at this time "glittered green·with sunny showers," and a budding ash-tree dipped its tender branches in the chiding stream. How proud, how glad I was to walk along the high road that overlooks the delicious prospect, repeating the lines which I have just quoted from Mr. Coleridge's poems! But besides the prospect which opened beneath my feet, another also opened to my inward sight, a heavenly vision, on which were written, in letters large as Hope could make them, these four words, LIBERTY, GENIUS, LOVE, VIRTUE; which have since faded into the light of common day, or mock my idle gaze.

> *The beautiful is vanished, and returns not.*

Still I would return some time or other to this enchanted spot; but I would return to it alone. What other self could I find to share that influx of thoughts, of regret, and delight, the fragments of which I could hardly conjure up to myself, so much have they been broken and defaced. I could stand on some tall rock, and overlook the precipice of years that separates me from what I then was. I was at that time going shortly to visit the poet whom I have above named. Where is he now? Not only I myself have changed; the world which was then new to me, has become old and incorrigible. Yet will I turn to thee in thought, O sylvan Dee, in joy, in youth and gladness as thou then wert; and thou shalt always be to me the river of Paradise, where I will drink of the waters of life freely!

There is hardly anything that shows the short-sightedness or capriciousness of the imagination more than traveling does. With change of place we change our ideas; nay, our opinions and feelings. We can by an effort indeed transport ourselves to old and long-forgotten scenes, and then the picture of the mind revives again; but we forget those that we have just left. It seems that we can think but of one place at a time. The canvas of the fancy is but of a certain extent, and if we paint one set of objects upon it, they immediately efface every other. We cannot enlarge our conceptions, we only shift our point of view. The landscape bares its bosom to the enraptured eye, we take our fill of it, and seem as if we could form no other image of beauty or grandeur. We pass on, and think no more of it: the horizon that shuts it from our sight, also blots it from our memory like a dream. In traveling through a wild barren country I can form no idea of a woody and cultivated one. It appears to me that all the world must be barren, like what I see of it. In the country we forget the town, and in town we despise the country. "Beyond Hyde Park," says Sir Fopling Flutter, "all is a desert." All that part of the map that we do not see before us is a blank. The world in our conceit of it is not much bigger than a nutshell. It is not one prospect expanded into another, county joined to county, kingdom to kingdom, lands to seas, making an image voluminous and vast; —the mind can form no larger idea of space than the eye can take in at a single glance. The rest is a name written in a map, a calculation of arithmetic. For instance, what is the true signification of that immense mass of territory and population known by the name of China to us? An inch of pasteboard on a wooden globe, of no more account than a China orange! Things near us are seen of the size of life: things at a distance are diminished to the size of the understanding. We measure the universe by ourselves, and even comprehend the texture of our being only piecemeal. In this way, however, we remember an infinity of things and places. The mind is like a mechanical instrument that plays a great variety of tunes, but it must play them in succession. One idea recalls another, but it at the same time excludes all others. In trying to renew old recollections, we cannot as it were unfold the whole web of our existence; we must pick out the single threads. So in coming to a place where we have formerly lived, and with which we have intimate associations, every one must have found that the feeling grows more vivid the nearer we approach the spot, from the mere anticipation of the actual impression: we remember circumstances, feelings, persons, faces, names that we had not thought of for years; but for the time all the rest of the world is forgotten!—To return to the question I have quitted above:

I have no objection to go to see ruins, aqueducts, pictures, in company with a friend or a party, but rather the contrary, for the former reason reversed. They are intelligible matters, and will bear talking about. The sentiment here is not tacit, but communicable and overt. Salisbury Plain is barren of criticism, but Stonehenge will bear a discussion antiquarian, picturesque, and philosophical. In setting out on a party of pleasure, the first consideration always is where we shall go to: in taking a solitary ramble, the question is what we shall meet with by the way. "The mind is its own place"; nor are we anxious to arrive at the end of our journey. I can myself do the honors indifferently well to works of art and curiosity. I once took a party to Oxford with no mean *éclat*—showed them that seat of the Muses at a distance,

With glistering spires and pinnacles adorn'd—

descanted on the learned air that breathes from the grassy quadrangles and stone walls of halls and colleges—was at home in the Bodleian; and at Blenheim quite superseded the powdered Cicerone that attended us, and that pointed in vain with his wand to commonplace beauties in matchless pictures. As another exception to the above reasoning, I should not feel confident in venturing on a journey in a foreign country without a companion. I should want at intervals to hear the sound of my own language. There is an involuntary antipathy in the mind of an Englishman to foreign manners and notions that requires the assistance of social sympathy to carry it off. As the distance from home increases, this relief, which was at first a luxury, becomes a passion and an appetite. A person would almost feel stifled to find himself in the deserts of Arabia without friends and countrymen: there must be allowed to be something in the view of Athens or old Rome that claims the utterance of speech; and I own that the Pyramids are too mighty for any single contemplation. In such situations, so opposite to all one's ordinary train of ideas, one seems a species by one's-self, a limb torn off from society, unless one can meet with instant fellowship and support.—Yet I did not feel this want or craving very pressing once, when

I first set my foot on the laughing shores of France. Calais was peopled with novelty and delight. The confused, busy murmur of the place was like oil and wine poured into my ears; nor did the mariners' hymn, which was sung from the top of an old crazy vessel in the harbor, as the sun went down, send an alien sound into my soul. I only breathed the air of general humanity. I walked over "the vine-covered hills and gay regions of France," erect and satisfied; for the image of man was not cast down and chained to the foot of arbitrary thrones: I was at no loss for language, for that of all the great schools of painting was open to me. The whole is vanished like a shade. Pictures, heroes, glory, freedom, all are fled: nothing remains but the Bourbons and the French people!—There is undoubtedly a sensation in traveling into foreign parts that is to be had nowhere else; but it is more pleasing at the time than lasting. It is too remote from our habitual associations to be a common topic of discourse or reference, and, like a dream or another state of existence, does not piece into our daily modes of life. It is an animated but a momentary hallucination. It demands an effort to exchange our actual for our ideal identity; and to feel the pulse of our old transports revive very keenly, we must "jump" all our present comforts and connections. Our romantic and itinerant character is not to be domesticated. Dr. Johnson remarked how little foreign travel added to the facilities of conversation in those who had been abroad. In fact, the time we have spent there is both delightful, and in one sense instructive; but it appears to be cut out of our substantial, downright existence, and never to join kindly on to it. We are not the same, but another, and perhaps more enviable individual, all the time we are out of our own country. We are lost to ourselves, as well as our friends. So the poet somewhat quaintly sings,

Out of my country and myself I go.

Those who wish to forget painful thoughts, do well to absent themselves for a while from the ties and objects that recall them; but we can be said only to fulfil our destiny in the place that gave us birth. I should on this account like well enough to spend the whole of my life in traveling abroad, if I could anywhere borrow another life to spend afterwards at home!

"The Fight"

*In "The Fight" (New Monthly Magazine, 1822)
Hazlitt realistically captures the excitement of the
ring and the personality of boxers. "Brummelliana"
(London Weekly Review, 1828) pokes fun at a different kind of sport—the dandy.*

Where there's a will, there's a way.—I said so to myself,
as I walked down Chancery lane, about half-past six o'clock
on Monday the 10th of December, to inquire at Jack Randall's where the fight the next day was to be; and I found
"the proverb" nothing "musty" in the present instance. I
was determined to see this fight, come what would, and see
it I did, in great style. It was my *first fight,* yet it more than
answered my expectations. Ladies! it is to you I dedicate
this description; nor let it seem out of character for the fair
to notice the exploits of the brave. Courage and modesty
are the old English virtues; and may they never look cold
and askance on one another! Think, ye fairest of the fair,
loveliest of the lovely kind, ye practicers of soft enchantment, how many more ye kill with poisoned baits than ever
fell in the ring; and listen with subdued air and without
shuddering, to a tale tragic only in appearance, and sacred
to the FANCY!

I was going down Chancery lane, thinking to ask at
Jack Randall's where the fight was to be, when looking
through the glass-door of the *Hole in the Wall,* I heard a
gentleman asking the same question *at* Mrs. Randall, as
the author of *Waverley* would express it. Now Mrs. Randall stood answering the gentleman's question, with the
authenticity of the lady of the Champion of the Light
Weights. Thinks I, I'll wait till this person comes out, and
learn from him how it is. For to say a truth, I was not
fond of going into this house of call for heroes and philosophers, ever since the owner of it (for Jack is no gentleman)
threatened once upon a time to kick me out of doors for
wanting a mutton-chop at his hospitable board, when the
conqueror in thirteen battles was more full of *blue ruin*
than of good manners. I was the more mortified at this
repulse, inasmuch as I had heard Mr. James Simpkins,
hosier in the Strand, one day when the character of the
Hole in the Wall was brought in question, observe—"The

house is a very good house, and the company quite genteel: I have been there myself!" Remembering this unkind treatment of mine host, to which mine hostess was also a party, and not wishing to put her in unquiet thoughts at a time jubilant like the present, I waited at the door, when, who should issue forth but my friend Joe Toms, and turning suddenly up Chancery lane with that quick jerk and impatient stride which distinguishes a lover of the FANCY, I said, "I'll be hanged if that fellow is not going to the fight, and is on his way to get me to go with him." So it proved in effect, and we agreed to adjourn to my lodgings to discuss measures with that cordiality which makes old friends like new, and new friends like old, on great occasions. We are cold to others only when we are dull in ourselves and have neither thoughts nor feelings to impart to them. Give a man a topic in his head, a throb of pleasure in his heart, and he will be glad to share it with the first person he meets. Toms and I, though we seldom meet, were an *alter idem* on this memorable occasion, and had not an idea that we did not candidly impart; and "so carelessly did we fleet the time," that I wish no better, when there is another fight, than to have him for a companion on my journey down, and to return with my friend Jack Pigott, talking of what was to happen or of what did happen, with a noble subject always at hand, and liberty to digress to others whenever they offered. Indeed, on my repeating the lines from Spenser in an involuntary fit of enthusiasm,

> *What more felicity can fall to creature,*
> *Than to enjoy delight with liberty?*

my last-named ingenious friend stopped me by saying that this, translated into the vulgate, meant *"Going to see a fight."* Joe Toms and I could not settle about the method of going down. He said there was a caravan, he understood, to start from Tom Belcher's at two, which would go there *right out* and back again the next day. Now I never travel all night, and said I should get a cast to Newbury by one of the mails. Joe swore the thing was impossible, and I could only answer that I had made up my mind to it. In short, he seemed to me to waver, said he only came to see if I was going, had letters to write, a cause coming on the day after, and faintly said at parting (for I was bent on setting out that moment)—"Well, we meet at Philippi!" I made the best of my way to Piccadilly. The mail coach stand was bare. "They are all gone," said I—"this is always the way with me—in the instant I lose the future—if I had not stayed to pour out that last cup of tea, I should have been just in time;"—and cursing my folly and ill-luck together, without inquiring at the coach-office whether the mails were gone or not, I walked on in despite, and to punish my own dilatoriness and want of determination. At any rate, I would not turn back: I might get to Hounslow, or perhaps farther, to be on my road the next morning. I passed Hyde park corner (my Rubicon), and trusted to fortune. Suddenly I heard the clattering of a Brentford stage, and the fight rushed full upon my fancy. I argued (not unwisely) that even a Brentford coachman was better company than my own thoughts (such as they were just then) and at his invitation mounted the box with him. I immediately stated my case to him—namely, my quarrel with myself for missing the Bath or Bristol mail, and my determination to get on in consequence as well as I could, without any disparagement or insulting comparison between longer or shorter stages. It is a maxim with me that stage-coaches, and consequently stage-coachmen, are respectable in proportion to the distance they have to travel: so I said nothing on that subject to my Brentford friend. Any incipient tendency to an abstract proposition, or (as he might have construed it) to a personal reflection of this kind, was however nipped in the bud; for I had no sooner declared indignantly that I had missed the mails, than he flatly denied that they were gone along, and lo! at the instant three of them drove by in rapid, provoking, orderly succession, as if they would devour the ground before them. Here again I seemed in the contradictory situation of the man in Dryden who exclaims,

I follow Fate, which does too hard pursue!

If I had stopped to inquire at the White Horse Cellar, which would not have taken me a minute, I should now have been driving down the road in all the dignified unconcern and *ideal* perfection of mechanical conveyance. The Bath mail I had set my mind upon, and I had missed it, as I miss everything else, by my own absurdity, in putting the will for the deed, and aiming at ends without employing means. "Sir," said he of the Brentford, "the Bath mail will be up presently, my brother-in-law drives it, and I will engage to stop him if there is a place empty." I almost doubted my good genius; but, sure enough, up it drove like lightning, and stopped directly at the call of the Brentford Jehu. I would not have believed this possible, but the brother-in-law of a mail-coach driver is himself no mean man. I was transferred without loss of time from the top of one coach to that of the other, desired the guard to pay my fare to the Brentford coachman for me as I had no change, was accommodated with a great coat, put up my umbrella to keep off a drizzling mist, and we began to cut through the air like an arrow. The mile-stones disappeared one after another, the rain kept off; Tom Turtle, the trainer, sat before me on the coach-box, with whom I exchanged civilities as a gentleman going to the fight; the passion that had transported me an hour before was subdued to pensive regret and conjectural musing on the next day's battle; I was promised a place inside at Reading, and upon the whole, I thought myself a lucky fellow. Such is the force of imagination! On the outside of any other coach on the 10th of December, with a Scotch mist drizzling through the cloudy moonlight air, I should have been cold, comfortless, impatient, and, no doubt, wet through; but seated on the Royal mail, I felt warm and comfortable, the air did me good, the ride did me good, I was pleased with the progress we had made, and confident that all would go well through the journey. When I got inside at Reading, I found Turtle and a stout valetudinarian, whose costume bespoke him one of the FANCY, and who had risen from a three months' sick bed to get into the mail to see the fight. They were intimate, and we fell into a lively discourse. My friend the trainer was confined in his topics to fighting dogs and men, to bears and badgers; beyond this he was "quite chapfallen," had not a word to throw at a dog, or indeed very wisely fell asleep, when any other game was started. The whole art of training (I, however, learnt from him,) consists in two things, exercise and abstinence, abstinence and exercise, repeated alternately and without end. A yolk of an egg with a spoonful of rum in it is the first thing in a morning, and then a walk of six miles till breakfast. This meal consists of a plentiful supply of tea and toast and beefsteaks. Then another six or seven miles till dinner-time, and another supply of solid beef or mutton with a pint of porter, and perhaps, at the utmost, a couple of glasses of sherry. Martin trains on water, but this increases his infirmity on another very dangerous side. The Gas-man takes now and then a chirping glass (under the rose) to console him, during a six weeks' probation, for the absence of Mrs. Hickman—an agreeable woman, with (I understand) a pretty fortune of two hundred pounds. How matter presses on me! What stubborn things are facts! How inexhaustible is nature and art! "It is well," as I once heard Mr. Richmond observe, "to see a variety." He was speaking of cock-fighting as an edifying spectacle. I cannot deny but that one learns more of what *is* (I do not say of what *ought to be*) in this desultory mode of practical study, than from reading the same book twice over, even though it should be a moral treatise. Where was I? I was sitting at dinner with the candidate for the honors of the ring, "where good digestion waits on appetite, and health on both." Then follows an hour of social chat and native glee; and afterwards, to another breathing over heathy hill or dale. Back to supper, and then to bed, and up by six again—Our hero

> *Follows so the ever-running sun,*
> *With profitable* ardour——

to the day that brings him victory or defeat in the green fairy circle. Is not this life more sweet than mine? I was going to say; but I will not libel any life by comparing it to mine, which is (at the date of these presents) bitter as coloquintida and the dregs of aconitum!

The invalid in the Bath mail soared a pitch above the trainer, and did not sleep so sound, because he had "more figures and more fantasies." We talked the hours away merrily. He had faith in surgery, for he had had three ribs set right, that had been broken in a *turn-up* at Belcher's, but thought physicians old women, for they had no antidote in their catalogue for brandy. An indigestion is an excellent common-place for two people that never met before. By way of ingratiating myself, I told him the story of my doctor, who, on my earnestly representing to him that I thought his regimen had done me harm, assured me that the whole pharmacopeia contained nothing comparable to the prescription he had given me; and, as a proof of its undoubted efficacy, said, that "he had had one gentleman with my complaint under his hands for the last fifteen years." This anecdote made my companion shake the rough sides of his three great coats with boisterous laughter; and Turtle, starting out of his sleep, swore he knew how the fight would go, for he had had a dream about it. Sure enough the rascal told us how the three first rounds went off, but "his dream," like others, "denoted a foregone conclusion." He knew his men. The moon now rose in silver state, and I ventured, with some hesitation, to point out this object of placid beauty, with the blue serene beyond to the man of science, to which his ear he "seriously inclined," the more as it gave promise *d'un beau jour* for the morrow, and showed the ring undrenched by envious showers, arrayed in sunny smiles. Just then, all going on well, I thought on my friend Toms, whom I had left behind, and said innocently, "There was a blockhead of a fellow I left in town, who said there was no possibility of getting down by the mail, and talked of going by a caravan from Belcher's at two in the morning, after he had written some letters." "Why," said he of the lapels, "I should not wonder if that was the very person we saw running about like mad from one coach-door to another, and asking if any one had seen a friend of his, a gentleman going to the fight, whom he had missed stupidly enough by staying to write a note." "Pray, Sir," said my fellow-traveler, "had he a plaid-cloak on?"—"Why, no," said I, "not at the time I left him, but he very well might afterwards, for he offered to lend me one." The plaid-cloak and the letter decided the thing. Joe, sure enough, was in the Bristol mail, which preceded us by about fifty yards. This was droll enough. We had now but a few miles to our place of destination, and the first thing I did on alighting at Newbury, both coaches stopping at the same time, was to call out, "Pray, is there a gentleman in that mail of the name of Toms?" "No," said Joe, borrowing something of the vein of Gilpin, "for I have just got out." "Well!" says he, "this is lucky; but you don't know how vexed I was to miss you; for," added he, lowering his voice, "do you know when I left you I went to Belcher's to ask about the caravan, and Mrs. Belcher said very obligingly, she couldn't tell about that, but there were two gentlemen who had taken places by the mail and were gone on in a laudau, and she could frank us. It's a pity I didn't meet with you; we could then have got down for nothing. But *mum's the word*." It's the devil for anyone to tell me a secret, for it is sure to come out in print. I do not care so much to gratify a friend, but the public ear is too great a temptation to me.

Our present business was to get beds and a supper at an inn; but this was no easy task. The public-houses were full, and where you saw a light at a private house, and people poking their heads out of the casement to see what was going on, they instantly put them in and shut the window, the moment you seemed advancing with a suspicious overture for accommodation. Our guard and coachman thundered away at the outer gate of the Crown for some time without effect—such was the greater noise within;—and when the doors were unbarred, and we got admittance, we found a party assembled in the kitchen round a good hospitable fire, some sleeping, others drinking, others talking on politics and on the fight. A tall English yeoman (something like Matthews in the face, and quite as great a wag)—*A lusty man to ben an abbot able,*—was making such a prodigious noise about rent and taxes, and the price of corn now and formerly, that he had prevented us from being heard at the gate. The first thing I heard him say was to a shuffling fellow who wanted to be off a bet for a shilling glass of brandy and water—"Confound it, man, don't be *insipid!*" Thinks I, that is a good phrase. It was a good omen. He kept it up so all night, nor flinched with the approach of morning. He was a fine fellow, with sense, wit, and spirit, a hearty body and a joyous mind, free-spoken, frank, convivial—one of that true English breed that went with Harry the Fifth to the siege of Harfleur—"standing like greyhounds in the slips," &c. We ordered tea and eggs (beds were soon found to be out of the question) and this fellow's conversation was *sauce piquante.* It did one's heart good to see him brandish his oaken towel and to hear him talk. He made mince-meat of a drunken, stupid, red-faced, quarrelsome, *frowsy* farmer, whose nose "he moralized into a thousand similes," making it out a firebrand like Bardolph's. "I'll tell you what, my friend," says he, "the landlady has only to keep you here to save fire and candle. If one was to touch your nose, it would go off like a piece of charcoal." At this the other only grinned like an idiot, the sole variety in his purple face being his little peering grey eyes and yellow teeth; called for another glass, swore he would not stand it; and after many attempts to provoke his humorous antagonist to single combat, which the other turned off (after working him up to a ludicrous pitch of choler) with great adroitness, he fell quietly asleep with a glass of liquor in his hand, which he could not lift to his head. His laughing persecutor made a speech over him, and turning to the opposite side of the room, where they were all sleeping in the midst of this "loud and furious fun," said, "There's a scene, by G—d, for Hogarth to paint. I think he and Shakespeare were our two best men at copying life." This confirmed me in my good opinion of him. Hogarth, Shakespeare and Nature, were just enough for him (indeed for any man) to know. I said, "You read Cobbett, don't you? At least," says I, "you talk just as well as he writes." He seemed to doubt this. But I said, "We have an hour to spare: if you'll get pen, ink, and paper, and keep on talking, I'll write down what you say; and if it doesn't make a capital 'Political Register,' I'll forfeit my head. You have kept me alive to-night, however. I don't know what I should have done without you." He did not dislike this view of the thing, nor my asking if he was not about the size of Jem Belcher; and told me soon afterwards, in the confidence of friendship, that "the circumstance which had given him nearly the greatest concern in his life, was Cribb's beating Jem after he had lost his eye by racket playing."—The morning dawns; that dim but yet clear light appears, which weighs like solid bars of metal on the sleepless eyelids; the guests drop down from their chambers one by one—but it was too late to think of going to bed now (the clock was on the stroke of seven), we had nothing for it but to find a barber's (the pole that glittered in the morning sun lighted us to his shop), and then a nine miles' march to Hungerford. The day was fine, the sky was blue, the mists were retiring from the marshy ground, the path was tolerably dry, the sitting-up all night had not done us much harm—at least the cause was good; we talked of this and that with amicable difference, roving and sipping of many subjects, but still invariably we returned to the fight. At length, a mile to the left of Hungerford, on a gentle eminence, we saw the ring surrounded by covered carts, gigs, and carriages, of which hundreds had passed us on the road; Toms gave a youthful shout, and we hastened to the scene of action.

Reader, have you ever seen a fight? If not, you have a pleasure to come, at least if it is a fight like that between the Gas-man and Bill Neate. The crowd was very great when we arrived on the spot; open carriages were coming up, with streamers flying and music playing, and the country-people were pouring in over hedge and ditch in all directions, to see their hero beat or be beaten. The odds were still on Gas, but only about five to four. Gully had been down to try Neate, and had backed him considerably, which was a damper to the sanguine confidence of the adverse party. About two hundred thousand pounds were pending. The Gas says, he has lost 3000£ which were promised him by different gentlemen if he had won. He had presumed too much on himself, which had made others presume on him. This spirited and formidable young fellow seems to have taken for his motto the old maxim, that "there are three things necessary to success in life—*Impudence! Impudence! Impudence!*" It is so in matters of opinion, but not in the FANCY, which is the most practical of all things, though even here confidence is half the battle, but only half. Our friend had vapored and swaggered too much, as if he wanted to grin and bully his adversary out of the fight. "Alas! the Bristol man was not so tamed!" —"This is *the grave-digger*" (would Tom Hickman exclaim in the moments of intoxication from gin and success, showing his tremendous right hand), "this will send many of them to their long homes; I haven't done with them yet!" Why should he—though he had licked four of the best men within the hour, yet why should he threaten to inflict dishonorable chastisement on my old master Richmond, a veteran going off the stage and who has borne his sable honors meekly? Magnanimity, my dear Tom, and bravery, should be inseparable. Or why should he go up to his antagonist, the first time he ever saw him at the Fives Court, and measuring him from head to foot with a glance of contempt, as Achilles surveyed Hector, say to him, "What, are you Bill Neate? I'll knock more blood out of that great carcase of thine, this day fortnight, than you ever knock'd out of a bullock's!" It was not manly, 'twas not fighter-like. If he was sure of the victory (as he was not), the less said about it the better. Modesty should accompany the FANCY as its shadow. The best men were always the best behaved. Jem Belcher, the Game Chicken (before whom the Gas-man could not have lived) were civil, silent men. So is Cribb, so is Tom Belcher, the most elegant of sparrers, and not a man for every one to take by the nose. I enlarged on this topic in the mail (while Turtle was asleep), and said very wisely (as I thought) that impertinence was a part of no profession. A boxer was bound to beat his man, but not to thrust his fist, either actually or by implication, in every one's face. Even a highwayman, in the way of trade, may blow out your brains, but if he uses foul language at the same time, I should say he was no gentleman. A boxer, I would infer, need not be a blackguard or a coxcomb, more than another. Perhaps I press this point too much on a fallen man —Mr. Thomas Hickman has by this time learnt that first of all lessons, "That man was made to mourn." He has lost nothing by the late fight but his presumption; and that every man may do as well without! By an over-display of this quality, however, the public had been prejudiced against him, and the *knowing-ones* were taken in. Few but those who had bet on him wished Gas to win. With my own prepossessions on the subject, the result of the 11th of December appeared to me as fine a piece of poetical justice as I had ever witnessed. The difference of weight between the two combatants (14 stone to 12) was nothing to the sporting men. Great, heavy, clumsy, long-armed Bill Neate kicked the beam in the scale of the Gas-man's vanity. The amateurs were frightened at his big words, and thought they would make up for the difference of six feet and five feet nine. Truly, the FANCY are not men of imagination. They judge of what has been, and cannot conceive of anything that is to be. The Gas-man had won hitherto; therefore he must beat a man half as big again as himself— and that to a certainty. Besides, there are as many feuds, factions, prejudices, pedantic notions in the FANCY as in the state or in the schools. Mr. Gully is almost the only cool, sensible man among them, who exercises an unbiased discretion, and is not a slave to his passions in these matters. But enough of reflections, and to our tale. The day, as I have said, was fine for a December morning. The grass was wet, and the ground miry, and ploughed up with multitudinous feet, except that, within the ring itself, there was a spot of virgin-green closed in and unprofaned by vulgar tread, that shone with dazzling brightness in the mid-day sun. For it was now noon, and we had an hour to wait. This is the trying time. It is then the heart sickens, as you think what the two champions are about, and how short a time will determine their fate. After the first blow is struck, there is no opportunity for nervous apprehensions; you are swallowed up in the immediate interest of the scene—but

> *Between the acting of a dreadful thing*
> *And the first motion, all the interim is*
> *Like a phantasma, or a hideous dream.*

I found it so as I felt the sun's rays clinging to my back, and saw the white wintry clouds sink below the verge of the horizon. "So," I thought, "my fairest hopes have faded from my sight!—so will the Gas-man's glory, or that of his adversary, vanish in an hour." The *swells* were parading in their white box-coats, the outer ring was cleared with some bruises on the heads and shins of the rustic assembly (for the *cockneys* had been distanced by the sixty-six miles); the time drew near; I had got a good stand; a bustle, a buzz, ran through the crowd; and from the opposite side entered Neate, between his second and bottle-holder. He rolled along, swathed in his loose great coat, his knock-knees bending under his huge bulk; and, with a modest cheerful air, threw his hat into the ring. He then just looked round, and began quietly to undress; when from the other side there was a similar rush and an opening made, and the Gas-man came forward with a conscious air of antici-pated triumph, too much like the cock-of-the-walk. He strutted about more than became a hero, sucked oranges with a supercilious air, and threw away the skin with a toss of his head, and went up and looked at Neate, which was an act of supererogation. The only sensible thing he did was, as he strode away from the modern Ajax, to fling out his arms, as if he wanted to try whether they would do their work that day. By this time they had stripped, and presented a strong contrast in appearance. If Neate was like Ajax, "with Atlantean shoulders, fit to bear" the pugilistic reputation of all Bristol, Hickman might be compared to Diomed, light, vigorous, elastic, and his back glistened in the sun, as he moved about, like a panther's hide. There was now a dead pause—attention was awe-struck. Who at that moment, big with a great event, did not draw his breath short—did not feel his heart throb? All was ready. They tossed up for the sun, and the Gas-man won. They were led up to the *scratch*—shook hands, and went at it.

In the first round every one thought it was all over. After making play a short time, the Gas-man flew at his adversary like a tiger, struck five blows in as many seconds, three first, and then following him as he staggered back, two more, right and left, and down he fell, a mighty ruin. There was a shout, and I said, "There is no standing this." Neate seemed like a lifeless lump of flesh and bone, round which the Gas-man's blows played with the rapidity of electricity or lightning, and you imagined he would only be lifted up to be knocked down again. It was as if Hickman held a sword or a fire in that right hand of his, and directed it against an unarmed body. They met again, and Neate seemed, not cowed, but particularly cautious. I saw his teeth clenched together and his brows knit close against the sun. He held out both his arms at full length straight before him, like two sledge-hammers, and raised his left an inch or two higher. The Gas-man could not get over this guard—they struck mutually and fell, but without advantage on either side. It was the same in the next round; but the balance of power was thus restored—the fate of the battle was suspended. No one could tell how it would end. This was the only moment in which opinion was divided; for, in the next, the Gas-man aiming a mortal blow at his adversary's neck, with his right hand, and failing from the length he had to reach, the other returned it with his left at full swing, planted a tremendous blow on his cheek-bone and eye-brow, and made a red ruin of that side of his face. The Gas-man went down, and there was another shout—a roar of triumph as the waves of fortune rolled tumultuously from side to side. This was a settler. Hickman got up, and "grinned horrible a ghastly smile," yet he was evidently dashed in his opinion of himself; it was the first time he had ever been so punished; all one side of his face was perfect scarlet, and his right eye was closed in dingy blackness, as he advanced to the fight, less confident, but still determined. After one or two rounds, not receiving another such remembrancer, he rallied and went at it with his former impetuosity. But in vain. His strength had been weakened,—his blows could not tell at such a distance,—he was obliged to fling himself at his adversary, and could not strike from his feet; and almost as regularly as he flew at him with his right hand, Neate warded the blow, or drew back out of its reach, and felled him with the return of his left. There was little cautious sparring—no half-hits—no tapping and trifling, none of the *petitmaitreship* of the art—they were almost all knock-down blows:—the fight was a good stand-up fight. The wonder was the half-minute time. If there had been a minute or more allowed between each round, it would have been intelligible how they should by degrees recover strength and resolution; but to see two men smashed to the ground, smeared with gore, stunned, senseless, the breath beaten out of their bodies; and then, before you recover from the shock, to see them rise up with new strength and courage, stand ready to inflict or receive mortal offense, and rush upon each other "like two clouds over the Caspian"—this is the most astonishing thing of all:—this is the high and heroic state of man! From this time forward the event became more certain every round; and about the twelfth it seemed as if it must have been over. Hickman generally stood with his back to me; but in the scuffle, he had changed positions, and Neate just then made a tremendous lunge at him, and hit him full in the face. It was doubtful whether he would fall backwards or forwards; he hung suspended for a second or two, and then fell back, throwing his hands in the air, and with his face lifted up to the sky. I never saw any thing more terrific than his aspect just before he fell. All traces of life, of natural expression, were gone from him. His face was like a human skull, a death's head, spouting blood. The eyes were filled with blood, the nose streamed with blood, the mouth gaped blood. He was not like an actual man, but like a preternatural, spectral appearance, or like one of the figures in Dante's *Inferno*. Yet he fought on after this for several rounds, still striking the first desperate blow, and Neate standing on the defensive, and using the same cautious guard to the last, as if he had still all his work to do; and it was not till the Gas-man was so stunned in the seventeenth or eighteenth round, that his senses forsook him, and he could not come to time, that the battle was declared over. Ye who despise the FANCY, do something to show as much *pluck,* or as much self-possession as this, before you assume a superiority which you have never given a single proof of by any one action in the whole course of your lives!—When the Gas-man came to himself, the first words he uttered were, "Where am I? What is the matter?"—"Nothing is the matter, Tom,—you have lost the battle, but you are the bravest man alive." And Jackson whispered to him, "I am collecting a purse for you, Tom."—Vain sounds, and unheard at that moment! Neate instantly went up and shook him cordially by the hand, and seeing some old acquaintance, began to flourish with his fists, calling out, "Ah! you always said I couldn't fight—What do you think now?" But all in good humor, and without any appearance of arrogance; only it was evident Bill Neate was pleased that he had won the fight. When it was over, I asked Cribb if he did not think it was a good one? He said, *"Pretty well!"* The carrier-pigeons now mounted into the air, and one of them flew with the news of her husband's victory to the bosom of Mrs. Neate. Alas, for Mrs. Hickman!

Mais au revoir, as Sir Fopling Flutter says. I went down with Toms; I returned with Jack Pigott, whom I met on the ground. Toms is a rattle-brain; Pigott is a sentimentalist. Now, under favor, I am a sentimentalist too—therefore I say nothing, but that the interest of the excursion did not flag as I came back. Pigott and I marched along the causeway leading from Hungerford to Newbury, now observing the effect of a brilliant sun on the tawny meads or moss-colored cottages, now exulting in the fight, now digressing to some topic of general and elegant literature. My friend was dressed in character for the occasion, or like one of the FANCY; that is, with a double portion of great coats, clogs, and overhauls: and just as we had agreed with a couple of country-lads to carry his superfluous wearing-apparel to the next town, we were overtaken by a return post-chaise, into which I got, Pigott preferring a seat on the bar. There were two strangers already in the chaise, and on their observing they supposed I had been to the fight, I said I had, and concluded they had done the same. They appeared, however, a little shy and sore on the subject; and it was not till after several hints dropped, and questions put, that it turned out that they had missed it. One of these friends had undertaken to drive the other there in his gig: they had set out, to make sure work, the day before at three in the afternoon. The owner of the one-horse vehicle scorned to ask his way, and drove right on to Bagshot, instead of turning off at Hounslow: there they stopped all night, and set off the next day across the country to Reading, from whence they took coach, and got down within a mile or two of Hungerford, just half an hour after the fight was over. This might be safely set down as one of the miseries of human life. We parted with these two gentlemen who had been to see the fight, but had returned as they went, at Wolhampton, where we were promised beds (an irresistible temptation, for Pigott had passed the preceding night at Hungerford as we had done at Newbury), and we turned into an old bow-windowed parlor with a carpet and a snug fire; and after devouring a quantity of tea, toast, and eggs, sat down to consider, during an hour of philosophic leisure, what we should have for supper. In the midst of an Epicurean deliberation between a roasted fowl and mutton chops with mashed potatoes, we were interrupted by an inroad of Goths and Vandals—*O procul este profani*—not real flash-men, but interlopers, noisy pretenders, butchers from Tothill-fields, brokers from Whitechapel, who called immediately for pipes and tobacco, hoping it would not be disagreeable to the gentlemen, and began to insist that it was *a cross*. Pigott withdrew from the smoke and noise into another room, and left me to dispute the point with them for a couple of hours *sans intermission* by the dial. The next morning we rose refreshed; and on observing that Jack had a pocket volume in his hand, in which he read in the intervals of our discourse, I inquired what it was, and learned to my particular satisfaction that it was a volume of the *New Eloise*. Ladies, after this, will you contend that a love for the FANCY is incompatible with the cultivation of sentiment?—We jogged on as before, my friend setting me up in a genteel drab great coat and green silk handkerchief (which I must say became me exceedingly), and after stretching our legs for a few miles, and seeing Jack Randall, Ned Turner, and Scroggins, pass on the top of one of the Bath coaches, we engaged with the driver of the second to take us to London for the usual fee. I got inside, and found three other passengers. One of them was an old gentleman with an aquiline nose, powdered hair, and a pigtail, and who looked as if he had played many a rubber at the Bath rooms. I said to myself, he is very like Mr. Windham; I wish he would enter into conversation, that I might hear what fine observations would come from those finely-turned features. However, nothing passed, till stopping to dine at Reading, some inquiry was made by the company about the fight, and I gave (as the reader may believe) an eloquent and animated description of it. When we got into the coach again, the old gentleman, after a graceful exordium, said, he had, when a boy, been to a fight between the famous Broughton and George Stevenson, who was called the *Fighting Coachman*, in the year 1770, with the late Mr. Windham. This beginning flattered the spirit of prophecy within me, and riveted my attention. He went on—"George Stevenson was coachman to a friend of my father's. He was an old man when I saw him some years afterward. He took hold of his own arm and said, 'there was muscle here once, but now it is no more than this young gentleman's.' He added, 'well, no matter; I have been here long, I am willing to go hence, and I hope I have done no more harm than another man.' Once," said my unknown companion, "I asked him if he had ever beat Broughton? He said Yes; that he had fought with him three times, and the last time he fairly beat him, though the world did not allow it. 'I'll tell you how it was, master. When the seconds lifted us up in the last round, we were so exhausted that neither of us could stand, and we fell upon one another, and as Master Broughton fell uppermost, the mob gave it in his favor, and he was said to have won the battle. But the fact was, that as his second (John Cuthbert) lifted him up, he said to him, "I'll fight no more, I've had enough;" which,' says Stevenson, 'you know gave me the victory. And to prove to you that this was the case, when John Cuthbert was on his death-bed, and they asked him if there was any thing on his mind which he wished to confess, he answered, "Yes, that there was one thing he wished to set right, for that certainly Master Stevenson won that last fight with Master Broughton; for he whispered him as he lifted him up in the last round of all, that he had had enough." ' This," said the Bath gentleman, "was a bit of human nature;" and I have written this account of the fight on purpose that it might not be lost to the world. He also stated as a proof of the candor of mind in this class of men, that Stevenson acknowledged that Broughton could have beat him in his best day; but that he (Broughton) was getting old in their last rencounter. When we stopped in Piccadilly, I wanted to ask the gentleman some questions about the late Mr. Windham, but had not courage. I got out, resigned my coat and green silk handkerchief to Pigott (loth to part with these ornaments of life), and walked home in high spirits.

P.S. Toms called upon me the next day, to ask me if I did not think the fight was a complete thing? I said I thought it was. I hope he will relish my account of it.

On Beau Brummell

We look upon Beau Brummell as the greatest of small wits. Indeed, he may in this respect be considered, as Cowley says of Pindar, as "a species alone," and as forming a class by himself. He has arrived at the very *minimum* of wit, and reduced it, "by happiness or pains," to an almost invisible point. All his *bon mots* turn upon a single circumstance, the exaggerating of the merest trifles into matters of importance, or treating everything else with the utmost *nonchalance* and indifference, as if whatever pretended to pass beyond those limits was a *bore,* and disturbed the serene air of high life. We have heard of

A sound so fine,
That nothing lived 'twixt it and silence.

So we may say of Mr. Brummell's jests, that they are of a meaning so attenuated that "nothing lives 'twixt them and nonsense": they hover on the very brink of vacancy, and are in their shadowy composition next of kin to nonentities. It is impossible for anyone to go beyond him without falling flat into insignificance and insipidity: he has touched the *ne plus ultra* that divides the dandy from the dunce. . . . We shall not go deeply into the common story of Mr. Brummell's asking his servant, as he was going out for the evening, "Where do I dine to-day, John?" This is little more than the common cant of a multiplicity of engagements, so as to make it impossible to bear them all in mind, and of an utter disinclination to all attention to one's own affairs; but the following is brilliant and original. Sitting one day at table between two other persons, Mr. Brummell said to his servant, who stood behind his chair—"John!" "Yes, Sir." "Who is this at my right hand?" "If you please, sir, it's the Marquis of Headfort." "And who is this at my left hand?" "It's my Lord Yarmouth." "Oh, very well!" and the Beau then proceeded to address himself to the persons who were thus announced to him. Now, this is surely superb, and "high fantastical." No, the smallest fold of that nicely adjusted cravat was not to be deranged, the least deviation from that select posture was not to be supposed possible. Had his head

been fastened in a vise, it could not have been more im-
movably fixed than by the "great idea in his mind," of how
a coxcomb should sit; the air of fashion and affectation
"bound him with Styx nine times round him"; and the Beau
preserved the perfection of an attitude—like a piece of incomprehensible *still-life*—the whole of dinner-time. The
ideal is everything, even in frivolity and folly.

It is not one of the least characteristic of our hero's answers to a lady, who asked him if he never tasted vegetables
—"Madam, I once ate a pea!" This was reducing the quantity of offensive grossness to the smallest assignable fraction:
anything beyond *that* his imagination was oppressed with;
and even this he seemed to confess to, with a kind of remorse, and to hasten from the subject with a certain mono-
syllabic brevity of style. . . . There is something piquant
enough in his answer to a city-fashionable, who asked him if
he would dine with him on a certain day—"Yes, if you
won't mention it to anyone"; and in an altercation with the
same person afterwards, about obligations, the assumption
of superiority implied in the appeal—"Do you count my
having *borrowed* a thousand pounds of you for nothing?"
soars immediately above commonplace.

On Byron

The most celebrated writers of their day, Byron and Scott are contrasted in this chapter from The Spirit of the Age.

Lord Byron and Sir Walter Scott are among writers now living, the two who would carry away a majority of suffrages as the greatest geniuses of the age. The former would, perhaps, obtain the preference with the fine gentlemen and ladies (squeamishness apart)—the latter with the critics and the vulgar. We shall treat of them in the same connection, partly on account of their distinguished pre-eminence, and partly because they afford a complete contrast to each other. In their poetry, in their prose, in their politics, and in their tempers, no two men can be more unlike. If Sir Walter Scott may be thought by some to have been "born universal heir to all humanity," it is plain Lord Byron can set up no such pretension. He is, in a striking degree, the creature of his own will. He holds no communion with his kind; but stands alone, without mate or fellow—

> *As if a man were author of himself,*
> *And owned no other kin.*

He is like a solitary peak, all access to which is cut off not more by elevation than distance. He is seated on a lofty eminence, cloud-capt, or reflecting the last rays of setting suns; and in his poetical moods, reminds us of the fabled Titans, retired to a ridgy steep, playing on their Pan's-pipes, and taking up ordinary men and things in their hands with haughty indifference. He raises his subject to himself, or tramples on it; he neither stoops to, nor loses himself in it. He exists not by sympathy, but by antipathy. He scorns all things, even himself. Nature must come to him to sit for her picture—he does not go to her. She must consult his time, his convenience, and his humor; and wear a somber or a fantastic garb, or his Lordship turns his back upon her. There is no ease, no unaffected simplicity of manner, no "golden mean." All is strained, or petulant in the extreme. His thoughts are sphered and crystalline; his style "prouder than when blue Iris bends"; his spirit fiery, impatient, wayward, indefatigable. Instead of taking his impressions from without, in entire and almost unimpaired masses, he molds them according to his own temperament, and heats the materials of his imagination in the furnace of his passions. Lord Byron's verse glows like a flame, consuming everything in its way; Sir Walter Scott's glides like a river, clear, gentle, harmless. The poetry of the first scorches, that of the last scarcely warms. The light of the one proceeds from an internal source, ensanguined, sullen, fixed; the other reflects the hues of Heaven, or the face of nature, glancing vivid and various. The productions of the Northern Bard have the rust and the freshness of antiquity about them; those of the Noble Poet cease to startle from their extreme ambition of novelty, both in style and matter. Sir Walter's rhymes are "silly sooth"—

> *And dally with the innocence of thought,*
> *Like the old age—*

his Lordship's Muse spurns *the olden time,* and affects all the supercilious airs of a modern fine lady and an upstart. The object of the one writer is to restore us to truth and nature: the other chiefly thinks how he shall display his own power, or vent his spleen, or astonish the reader either by starting new subjects and trains of speculation, or by expressing old ones in a more striking and emphatic manner than they have been expressed before. He cares little what it is he says, so that he can say it differently from others. This may account for the charges of plagiarism which have been repeatedly brought against the Noble Poet—if he can borrow an image or sentiment from another, and heighten it by an epithet or an allusion of greater force and beauty than is to be found in the original passage, he thinks he shows his superiority of execution in this in a more marked manner than if the first suggestion had been his own. It is not the value of the observation itself he is solicitous about; but he wishes to shine by contrast—even nature only serves as a foil to set off his style. He therefore takes the thoughts of others (whether contemporaries or not) out of their mouths, and is content to make them his own, to set his stamp upon them, by imparting to them a more meretricious gloss, a higher relief, a greater loftiness of tone, and a characteristic inveteracy of purpose. Even in those collateral ornaments of modern style, slovenliness, abruptness, and eccentricity (as well as in terseness and significance), Lord Byron, when he pleases, defies competition and surpasses all his contemporaries. Whatever he does, he must do in a more decided and daring manner than anyone else—he lounges with extravagance, and yawns so as to alarm the reader! Self-will, passion, the love of singularity, a disdain of himself and of others (with a conscious sense that this is among the ways and means of procuring admiration) are the proper categories of his mind: he is a lordly writer, is above his own reputation, and condescends to the Muses with a scornful grace!

Lord Byron, who in his politics is a *liberal,* in his genius is haughty and aristocratic: Walter Scott, who is an aristocrat in principle, is popular in his writings, and is (as it were) equally servile to nature and to opinion. The genius of Sir Walter is essentially imitative, or "denotes a foregone conclusion": that of Lord Byron is self-dependent; or at least requires no aid, is governed by no law, but the impulses of its own will. We confess, however much we may admire independence of feeling and erectness of spirit in general or practical questions, yet in works of genius we prefer him who bows to the authority of nature, who appeals to actual objects, to moldering superstitions, to history, observation, and tradition, before him who only consults the pragmatical and restless workings of his own breast, and gives them out as oracles to the world. We like a writer (whether poet or prose-writer) who takes in (or is willing to take in) the range of half the universe in feeling, character, description, much better than we do one who obstinately and invariably shuts himself up in the Bastile of his own ruling passions. In short, we had rather be Sir Walter Scott (meaning thereby the author of *Waverley*) than Lord Byron, a hundred times over. And for the reason just given, namely, that he casts his descriptions in the mold of nature, ever-varying, never tiresome, always interesting and always instructive, instead of casting them constantly in the mold of his own individual impressions. He gives us man as he is, or as he was, in almost every variety of situation, action, and feeling. Lord Byron makes men after his own image, woman after his own heart; the one is a capricious tyrant, the other a yielding slave; he gives us the misanthrope and the voluptuary by turns; and with these two characters, burning or melting in their own fires, he makes out everlasting centos of himself. He hangs the cloud, the film of his existence over all outward things —sits in the center of his thoughts, and enjoys dark night, bright day, the glitter and the gloom "in cell monastic"— we see the mournful pall, the crucifix, the death's heads, the faded chaplet of flowers, the gleaming tapers, the agonized brow of genius, the wasted form of beauty—but we are still imprisoned in a dungeon, a curtain intercepts our view, we do not breathe freely the air of nature or of our own thoughts—the other admired author draws aside the curtain, and the veil of egotism is rent, and he shows us the crowd of living men and women, the endless groups, the landscape background, the cloud and the rainbow, and enriches our imaginations and relieves one passion by another, and expands and lightens reflection, and takes away that tightness at the breast which arises from thinking or wishing to think that there is nothing in the world out of a man's self! In this point of view, the author of *Waverley* is one of the greatest teachers of morality that ever lived, by emancipating the mind from petty, narrow, and bigoted prejudices: Lord Byron is the greatest pamperer of those prejudices, by seeming to think there is nothing else worth encouraging but the seeds or the full luxuriant growth of dogmatism and self-conceit. In reading the *Scotch Novels,* we never think about the author, except from a feeling of curiosity respecting our unknown benefactor: in reading Lord Byron's works, he himself is never absent from our minds. The coloring of Lord Byron's style, however rich and dipped in Tyrian dyes, is nevertheless opaque, is in itself an object of delight and wonder: Sir Walter Scott's is perfectly transparent. In studying the one, you seem to gaze at the figures cut in stained glass, which exclude the view beyond, and where the pure light of Heaven is only a means of setting off the gorgeousness of art: in reading the other, you look through a noble window at the clear and varied landscape without. Or to sum up the distinction in one word, Sir Walter Scott is the most *dramatic* writer now living; and Lord Byron is the least so. It would be difficult to imagine that the author of *Waverley* is in the smallest degree a pedant; as it would be hard to persuade ourselves that the author of *Childe Harold* and *Don Juan* is not a coxcomb, though a provoking and sublime one. In this decided preference given to Sir Walter Scott over Lord Byron, we distinctly include the prose works of the former, for we do not think his poetry alone by any means entitles him to that precedence. Sir Walter in his poetry, though pleasing and natural, is a comparative trifler: it is in his anonymous productions that he has shown himself for what he is!

Intensity is the great and prominent distinction of Lord Byron's writings. He seldom gets beyond force of style, nor has he produced any regular work or masterly whole. He does not prepare any plan beforehand, nor revise and retouch what he has written with polished accuracy. His only object seems to be to stimulate himself and his readers for the moment—to keep both alive, to drive away *ennui,* to substitute a feverish and irritable state of excitement for listless indolence or even calm enjoyment. For this purpose he pitches on any subject at random without much thought or delicacy—he is only impatient to begin—and takes care to adorn and enrich it as he proceeds with "thoughts that breathe and words that burn." He composes (as he himself has said) whether he is in the bath, in his study, or on horseback—he writes as habitually as others talk or think—and whether we have the inspiration of the Muse or not, we always find the spirit of the man of genius breathing from his verse. He grapples with his subject, and moves, penetrates, and animates it by the electric force of his own feelings. He is often monotonous, extravagant, offensive; but he is never dull, or tedious, but when he writes prose. Lord Byron does not exhibit a new view of nature, or raise insignificant objects into importance by the romantic associations with which he surrounds them; but generally takes commonplace thoughts and events, and endeavors to express them in stronger and statelier language than others. His poetry stands like a Martello tower by the side of his subject. He does not, like Mr. Wordsworth, lift poetry from the ground, or create a sentiment out of nothing. He does not describe a daisy or a periwinkle, but the cedar or the cypress: not "poor men's cottages, but princes' palaces." His *Childe Harold* contains a lofty and impassioned review of the great events of history, of the mighty objects left as wrecks of time, but he dwells chiefly on what is familiar to the mind of every schoolboy; has brought out few new traits of feeling or thought; and has done no more than justice to the reader's preconceptions by the sustained force and brilliancy of his style and imagery.

Lord Byron's earlier productions, *Lara*, the *Corsair*, &c. were wild and gloomy romances put into rapid and shining verse. They discover the madness of poetry together with the inspiration: sullen, moody, capricious, fierce, inexorable, gloating on beauty, thirsting for revenge, hurrying from the extremes of pleasure to pain, but with nothing permanent, nothing healthy or natural. The gaudy decorations and the morbid sentiments remind one of flowers strewed over the face of death! In his *Childe Harold* (as has been just observed) he assumes a lofty and philosophic tone, and "reasons high of providence, fore-knowledge, will, and fate." He takes the highest points in the history of the world and comments on them from a more commanding eminence: he shows us the crumbling monuments of time, he invokes the great names, the mighty spirit of antiquity. The universe is changed into a stately mausoleum: in solemn measures he chants a hymn to fame. Lord Byron has strength and elevation enough to fill up the molds of our classical and time-hallowed recollections, and to rekindle the earliest aspirations of the mind after greatness and true glory with a pen of fire. The names of Tasso, of Ariosto, of Dante, of Cincinnatus, of Caesar, of Scipio, lose nothing of their pomp or their lustre in his hands, and when he begins and continues a strain of panegyric on such subjects, we indeed sit down with him to a banquet of rich praise, brooding over imperishable glories. . . . Lord Byron's tragedies, *Faliero, Sardanapalus,* &c, are not equal to his other works. They want the essence of the drama. They abound in speeches and descriptions, such as he himself might make either to himself or others, lolling on his couch of a morning, but do not carry the reader out of the poet's mind to the scenes and events recorded. They have neither action, character, nor interest, but are a sort of gossamer tragedies, spun out, and glittering, and spreading a flimsy veil over the face of nature. Of all that he has done in this way *Heaven and Earth* is the best. We prefer it even to *Manfred. Manfred* is merely himself with a fancy-drapery on: but in the dramatic fragment published in the *Liberal,* the space between Heaven and Earth, the stage on which his characters have to pass to and fro, seems to fill his Lordship's imagination; and the Deluge, which he has so finely described, may be said to have drowned all his own idle humors.

His *English Bards and Scotch Reviewers* is dogmatical

and insolent, but without refinement or point. He calls people names, and tries to transfix a character with an epithet, which does not stick, because it has no other foundation than his own petulance and spite; or he endeavors to degrade by alluding to some circumstance of external situation. He says of Mr. Wordsworth's poetry that "it is his aversion." That may be; but whose fault is it? This is the satire of a lord, who is accustomed to have all his whims or dislikes taken for gospel, and who cannot be at pains to do more than signify his contempt or displeasure. If a great man meets with a rebuff which he does not like, he turns on his heel and this passes for a repartee. The Noble Author says of a celebrated barrister and critic, that he was "born in a garret sixteen stories high." The insinuation is not true; or if it were, it is low. The allusion degrades the person who makes, not him to whom it is applied. . . .

The *Don Juan* indeed has great power; but its power is owing to the force of the serious writing, and to the oddity of the contrast between that and the flashy passages with which it is interlarded. From the sublime to the ridiculous, there is but one step. You laugh and are surprised that any one should turn round and *travestie* himself: the drollery is in the utter discontinuity of ideas and feelings. He makes virtue serve as a foil to vice; *dandyism* is (for want of any other) a variety of genius. A classical intoxication is followed by the splashing of soda-water, by frothy effusions of ordinary bile. After the lightning and the hurricane, we are introduced to the interior of the cabin and the contents of wash-hand basins. The solemn hero of tragedy plays *Scrub* in the farce. This is "very tolerable and not to be endured." The Noble Lord is almost the only writer who has prostituted his talents in this way. He hallows in order to desecrate; takes a pleasure in defacing the images of beauty his hands have wrought; and raises our hopes and our belief in goodness to Heaven only to dash them to the earth again, and break them in pieces the more effectually from the very height they have fallen. It is not that Lord Byron is sometimes serious and sometimes trifling, sometimes profligate, and sometimes moral—but when he is most serious and most moral, he is only preparing to mortify the unsuspecting reader by putting a pitiful *hoax* upon him. . . .

On the French Revolution

An ardent champion of liberty, equality, and fraternity, Hazlitt devoted his last years to a Life of Napoleon (1828) which includes this study of the French Revolution.

Buonaparte was not quite twenty years old, when the French Revolution broke out in 1789. From the time of his being employed at the siege of Toulon and in the war of Italy which followed, he may be considered as its sword-arm. From that time, its fate became in a manner bound up with his. It awaited his appearance to triumph and to perish with him. It will be therefore not improper in this place to give some account of its origin and progress up to that period.

The French Revolution might be described as a remote but inevitable result of the invention of the art of printing. The gift of speech, or the communication of thought by words, is that which distinguishes man from other animals. But this faculty is limited and imperfect without the intervention of books, which render the knowledge possessed by every one in the community accessible to all. There is no doubt, then, that the press (as it has existed in modern times) is the great organ of intellectual improvement and civilization. It was impossible in this point of view, that those institutions, which were founded in a state of society and manners long anterior to this second breathing of understanding into the life of man, should remain on the same proud footing after it, with all their disproportions and defects. Many of these, indeed, must be softened by the lapse of time and influence of opinion, and give way of their own accord: but others are too deeply rooted in the passions and interests of men to be wrenched asunder without violence, or by the mutual consent of the parties concerned; and it is this which makes revolutions necessary, with their train of lasting good and present evil. When a government, like an old-fashioned building, has become crazy and rotten, stops the way of improvement, and only serves to collect diseases and corruption, and the proprietors refuse to come to any compromise, the community

221

proceed in this as in some other cases; they set summarily to work—"they pull down the house, they abate the nuisance." All other things had changed: why then should governments remain the same, an excrescence and incumbrance on the state? It is only because they have most power and most interest to continue their abuses. This circumstance is a reason why it is doubly incumbent on those who are aggrieved by them to get rid of them; and makes the shock the greater, when opinion at last becomes a match for arbitrary power.

The feudal system was in full vigor almost up to the period of the discovery of printing. Much had been done since that time: but it was the object of the French Revolution to get rid at one blow of the frame-work and of the last relics of that system. Before the diffusion of knowledge and inquiry, governments were for the most part the growth of brute force or of barbarous superstition. Power was in the hands of a few, who used it only to gratify their own pride, cruelty, or avarice, and who took every means to extend and cement it by fear and favor. The lords of the earth, disdaining to rule by the choice or for the benefit of the mass of the community, whom they regarded and treated as no better than a herd of cattle, derived their title from the skies, pretending to be accountable for the exercise or abuse of their authority to God only—the throne rested on the altar, and every species of atrocity or wanton insult having power on its side, received the sanction of religion, which it was thenceforth impiety and rebellion against the will of Heaven to impugn. This state of things continued and grew worse and worse, while knowledge and power were confined within mere local and personal limits. Each petty sovereign shut himself up in his castle or fortress, and scattered havoc and dismay over the unresisting country around him. In an age of ignorance and barbarism, when force and interest decided every thing, and reason had no means of making itself heard, what was to prevent this or act as a check upon it? The lord himself had no other measure of right than his own will: his pride and passions would blind him to every consideration of conscience or humanity; he would regard every act of disobedience as a crime of the deepest die, and to give unbridled sway to his lawless humors, would become the ruling passion and sole study of his life. How would it stand with those within the immediate circle of his influence or his vengeance? Fear would make them cringe, and lick the feet of their haughty and capricious oppressor: the hope of reward or the dread of punishment would stifle the sense of justice or pity; despair of success would make them cowards, habit would confirm them into slaves, and they would look up with bigoted devotion (the boasted *loyalty* of the good old times) to the right of the strongest as the only law. A king would only be the head of a confederation of such petty despots, and the happiness or rights of the people would be equally disregarded by them both. Religion, instead of curbing this state of rapine and licentiousness, became an accomplice and a party in the crime; gave absolution and plenary indulgence for all sorts of enormities; granting the forgiveness of Heaven in return for a rich jewel or fat abbey-lands, and setting up a regular (and what in the end proved an intolerable) traffic in violence, cruelty, and lust. As to the restraints of law, there was none but what resided in the breast of the *Grand Seigneur,* who hung up in his court-yard, without judge or jury, any one who dared to utter the slightest murmur against the most flagrant wrong. Such must be the consequence, as long as there was no common standard or impartial judge to appeal to; and this could only be found in public opinion, the offspring of books. As long as any unjust claim or transaction was confined to the knowledge of the parties concerned, the tyrant and the slave, which is the case in all unlettered states of society, *might* must prevail over *right;* for the strongest would bully, and the weakest must submit, even in his own defense, and persuade himself that he was in the wrong, even in his own despite: but the instant the world (that dread jury) are impanelled, and called to look on and be umpires in the scene, so that nothing is done by connivance or in a corner, then reason mounts the judgment-seat in lieu of passion or interest, and opinion becomes law, instead of arbitrary will; and farewell feudal lord and sovereign king!

From the moment that the press opens the eyes of the community beyond the actual sphere in which each moves, there is from that time inevitably formed the germ of a body of opinion directly at variance with the selfish and servile code that before reigned paramount, and approximating more and more to the manly and disinterested standard of truth and justice. Hitherto force, fraud, and fear decided every question of individual right or general reasoning; the possessor of rank and influence, in answer to any censure or objection to his conduct, appealed to God and to his sword:—now a new principle is brought into play which had never been so much as dreamt of, and before which he must make good his pretensions, or it will shatter his strongholds of pride and prejudice to atoms, as the pent-up air shatters whatever resists its expansive force. This power is public opinion, exercised upon men, things, and general principles, and to which mere physical power must conform, or it will crumble it to powder. Books alone teach us to judge of truth and good in the abstract: without a knowledge of things at a distance from us, we judge like savages or animals from our senses and appetites only; but by the aid of books and of an intercourse with the world of ideas, we are purified, raised, ennobled from savages into intellectual and rational beings. Our impressions of what is near to us are false, of what is distant feeble; but the last gaining strength from being united in public opinion, and expressed by the public voice, are like the congregated roar of many waters, and quail the hearts of princes. Who but the tyrant does not hate the tyrant? Who but the slave does not despise the slave? The first of these looks upon himself as a God, upon his vassal as a clod of the earth, and forces him to be of the same opinion: the philosopher looks upon them both as men, and instructs the world to do so. While they had to settle their pretensions by themselves, and in the night of ignorance, it is no wonder no good was done; while pride intoxicated the one, and fear stupefied the other. But let them be brought out of that dark cave of despotism and superstition, and let a thousand other persons, who have no interest but that of truth and justice, be called on to determine between them, and the plea of the lordly oppressor to make a beast of burden of his fellow-man becomes as ridiculous as it is odious. All that the light of philosophy, the glow of patriotism, all that the brain wasted in midnight study, the blood poured out upon the scaffold or in the field of battle can do or have done, is to take this question in all cases from before the first gross, blind, and iniquitous tribunal, where power insults over weakness, and place it before the last more just, disinterested, and in the end more formidable one, where each individual is tried by his peers, and according to rules and principles which have received the common examination and the common consent. A public sense is thus formed, free from slavish awe or the traditional assumption of insolent superiority, which the more it is exercised becomes the more enlightened and enlarged, and more and more requires equal rights and equal laws. This new sense acquired by the people, this new organ of opinion and feeling, is like bringing a battering-train to bear upon some old Gothic castle, long the den of rapine and crime, and must finally prevail against all absurd and antiquated institutions, unless it is violently suppressed. . . .

On Familiar Style

This famous lesson on the difficult art of writing with "propriety and simplicity" is taken from Table-Talk.

It is not easy to write a familiar style. Many people mistake a familiar for a vulgar style, and suppose that to write without affectation is to write at random. On the contrary, there is nothing that requires more precision, and, if I may so say, purity of expression, than the style I am speaking of. It utterly rejects not only all unmeaning pomp, but all low, cant phrases, and loose, unconnected, *slipshod* allusions. It is not to take the first word that offers, but the best word in common use; it is not to throw words together in any combinations we please, but to follow and avail ourselves of the true idiom of the language. To write a genuine familiar or truly English style, is to write as anyone would speak in common conversation who had a thorough command and choice of words, or who could discourse with ease, force, and perspicuity, setting aside all pedantic and oratorical flourishes. Or, to give another illustration, to write naturally is the same thing in regard to common conversation as to read naturally is in regard to common speech. It does not follow that it is an easy tning to give the true accent and inflection to the words you utter, because you do not attempt to rise above the level of ordinary life and colloquial speaking. You do not assume, indeed, the solemnity of the pulpit, or the tone of stage-declamation; neither are you at liberty to gabble on at a venture, without emphasis or discretion, or to resort to vulgar dialect or clownish pronunciation. You must steer a middle course. You are tied down to a given and appropriate articulation, which is determined by the habitual associations between sense and sound, and which you can only hit by entering into the author's meaning, as you must find the proper words and style to express yourself by fixing your thoughts on the subject you have to write about. Anyone may mouth out a passage with a theatrical cadence, or get upon stilts to tell his thoughts; but to write or speak with propriety and simplicity is a more difficult task. Thus it is easy to affect a pompous style, to use a word twice as big as the thing you want to express: it is not so easy to pitch upon the very word that exactly fits it. Out of eight or ten words equally common, equally intelligible, with nearly equal pretensions, it is a matter of some nicety and discrimination to pick out the very one the preferableness of which is scarcely perceptible, but decisive. The reason why I object to Dr. Johnson's style is that there is no discrimination, no selection, no variety in it. He uses none but "tall, opaque words," taken from the "first row of the rubric"—words with the greatest number of syllables, or Latin phrases with merely English terminations. If a fine style depended on this sort of arbitrary pretension, it would be fair to judge of an author's elegance by the measurement of his words and the substitution of foreign circumlocutions (with no precise associations) for the mother-tongue. How simple is it to be dignified without ease, to be pompous without meaning! Surely, it is but a mechanical rule for avoiding what is low, to be always pedantic and affected. It is clear you cannot use a vulgar English word if you never use a common English word at all. A fine tact is shown in adhering to those which are perfectly common, and yet never falling into any expressions which are debased by disgusting circumstances, or which owe their signification and point to technical or professional allusions. A truly natural or familiar style can never be quaint or vulgar, for this reason, that it is of universal force and applicability, and that quaintness and vulgarity arise out of the immediate connection of certain words with coarse and disagreeable, or with confined ideas. The last form what we understand by *cant* or *slang* phrases.—To give an example of what is not very clear in the general statement. I should say that the phrase *To cut with a knife,* or *To cut a piece of wood,* is perfectly free from vulgarity, because it is perfectly common; but to *cut an acquaintance* is not quite unexceptionable, because it is not perfectly common or intelligible, and has hardly yet escaped out of the limits of slang phraseology. I should hardly, therefore, use the word in this sense without putting it in italics as a license of expression, to be received *cum grano salis.* All provincial or bye-phrases come under the same mark of reprobation—all such as the writer transfers to the page from his fireside or a particular *coterie,* or that he invents for his own sole use and convenience. I conceive that words are like money, not the worse for being common, but that it is the stamp of custom alone that gives them circulation or value. I am fastidious in this respect, and would almost as soon coin the currency of the realm as counterfeit the King's English. I never invented or gave a new and unauthorized meaning to any word but one single one (the term *impersonal* applied to feelings), and that was in an abstruse metaphysical discussion to express a very difficult distinction. I have been (I know) loudly accused of revelling in vulgarisms and broken English. I cannot speak to that point; but so far I plead guilty to the determined use of acknowledged idioms and common elliptical expressions. I am not sure that the critics in question know the one from the other, that is, can distinguish any medium between formal pedantry and the most barbarous solecism. As an author I endeavor to employ plain words and popular modes of construction, as, were I a chapman and dealer, I should common weights and measures.

The proper force of words lies not in the words themselves, but in their application. A word may be a fine-sounding word, of an unusual length, and very imposing from its learning and novelty, and yet in the connection in which it is introduced may be quite pointless and irrelevant. It is not pomp or pretension, but the adaptation of the expression to the idea, that clenches a writer's meaning:—as it is not the size or glossiness of the materials, but their being fitted each to its place, that gives strength to the arch; or as the pegs and nails are as necessary to the support of the building as the larger timbers, and more so than the mere showy, unsubstantial ornaments. I hate anything that occupies more space than it is worth. I hate to see a load of band-boxes go along the street, and I hate to see a parcel of big words without anything in them. A person who does not deliberately dispose of all his thoughts alike in cumbrous draperies and flimsy disguises, may strike out twenty varieties of familiar everyday language, each coming somewhat nearer to the feeling he wants to convey, and at last not hit upon that particular and only one which may be said to be identical with the exact impression in his mind. This would seem to show that Mr. Cobbett is hardly right in saying that the first word that occurs is always the best. It may be a very good one; and yet a better may present itself on reflection or from time to time. It should be suggested naturally, however, and spontaneously, from a fresh and lively conception of the subject. We seldom succeed by trying at improvement, or by merely substituting one word for another that we are not satisfied with, as we cannot recollect the name of a place or person by merely plaguing ourselves about it. We wander farther from the point by persisting in a wrong scent; but it starts up accidentally in the memory when we least expected it, by touching some link in the chain of previous association.

There are those who hoard up and make a cautious display of nothing but rich and rare phraseology—ancient medals, obscure coins, and Spanish pieces of eight. They are very curious to inspect, but I myself would neither offer nor take them in the course of exchange. A sprinkling of archaisms is not amiss, but a tissue of obsolete expressions is more fit *for keep than wear*. I do not say I would not use any phrase that had been brought into fashion before the middle or the end of the last century, but I should be shy of using any that had not been employed by any approved author during the whole of that time. Words, like clothes, get old-fashioned, or mean and ridiculous, when they have been for some time laid aside. Mr. Lamb is the only imitator of old English style I can read with pleasure; and he is so thoroughly imbued with the spirit of his authors that the idea of imitation is almost done away. There is an inward unction, a marrowy vein, both in the thought and feeling, an intuition, deep and lively, of his subject, that carries off any quaintness or awkwardness arising from an antiquated style and dress. The matter is completely his own, though the manner is assumed. Perhaps his ideas are altogether so marked and individual as to require their point and pungency to be neutralized by the affectation of a singular but traditional form of conveyance. Tricked out in the prevailing costume, they would probably seem more startling and out of the way. The old English authors, Burton, Fuller, Coryate, Sir Thomas Browne, are a kind of mediators between us and the more eccentric and whimsical modern, reconciling us to his peculiarities. I do not, however, know how far this is the case or not, till he condescends to write like one of us. I must confess that what I like best of his papers under the signature of Elia (still I do not presume, amidst such excellence, to decide what is most excellent) is the account of *Mrs. Battle's Opinions on Whist*, which is also the most free from obsolete allusions and turns of expression—

"A well of native English undefiled. . . ."

On Keats and Shelley

As one of the first to recognize the "promise" of Keats and to assess Shelley's contribution to English poetry, Hazlitt helped to make their work known to the public. The following extracts are taken from Table-Talk, Select British Poets, *and "Shelley's Posthumous Poems" in* The Edinburgh Review *(July, 1824).*

I cannot help thinking that the fault of Mr. Keats' poems was a deficiency in masculine energy of style. He had beauty, tenderness, delicacy, in an uncommon degree, but there was a want of strength and substance. His *Endymion* is a very delightful description of the illusions of a youthful imagination, given up to airy dreams—we have flowers, clouds, rainbows, moonlight, all sweet sounds and smells, and Oreads and Dryads flitting by—but there is nothing tangible in it, nothing marked or palpable—we have none of the hardy spirit or rigid forms of antiquity. He painted his own thoughts and character; and did not transport himself into the fabulous and heroic ages. There is a want of action, of character, and so far, of imagination, but there is exquisite fancy. All is soft and fleshy, without bone or muscle. We see in him the youth, without the manhood of poetry. His genius breathed "vernal delight and joy." "Like Maia's son he stood and shook his plumes," with fragrance filled. His mind was redolent of spring. . . .

The reading of Mr. Keats' *Eve of Saint Agnes* lately made me regret that I was not young again. The beautiful and tender images there conjured up, "come like shadows—so depart." The "tiger-moth's wings," which he has spread over his rich poetic blazonry, just flit across my fancy; the gorgeous twilight window which he has painted over again in his verse to me "blushes" almost in vain "with blood of queens and kings." I know how I should have felt at one time in reading such passages; and that is all. . . . He gave the greatest promise of genius of any poet of his day. He displayed extreme tenderness, beauty, originality, and delicacy of fancy; all he wanted was manly strength and fortitude to reject the temptations of singularity in sentiment and expression. Some of his shorter and later pieces are, however, as free from faults as they are full of beauties.

Mr. Shelley's style is to poetry what astrology is to natural science—a passionate dream, a straining after impossibilities, a record of fond conjectures, a confused embodying of vague abstraction—a fever of the soul, thirsting and craving after what it cannot have, indulging its love of power and novelty at the expense of truth and nature, associating ideas by contraries, and wasting great powers by their application to unattainable objects.

Poetry, we grant, creates a world of its own; but it creates it out of existing materials. Mr. Shelley is the maker of his own poetry—out of nothing. Not that he is deficient in the true sources of strength and beauty, if he had given himself fair play but, in him, fancy, will, caprice, predominated over and absorbed the natural influences of things; and he had no respect for any poetry that did not strain the intellect as well as fire the imagination—and was not sublimed into a high spirit of metaphysical philosophy. Instead of giving a language to thought, or lending the heart a tongue, he utters dark sayings, and deals in allegories and riddles. His Muse offers her services to clothe shadowy doubts and inscrutable difficulties in a robe of glittering words, and to turn nature into a brilliant paradox. We thank him—but we must be excused. Where we see the dazzling beacon-lights streaming over the darkness of the abyss, we dread the quicksands and the rocks below. Mr. Shelley's mind was of "too fiery a quality" to repose (for any continuance) on the probable or the true—it soared "beyond the visible diurnal sphere," to the strange, the improbable, and the impossible. He mistook the nature of the poet's calling, which should be guided by involuntary, not by voluntary impulses. He shook off, as an heroic and praiseworthy act, the trammels of sense, custom, and sympathy, and became the creature of his own will. He was "all air," disdaining the bars and ties of mortal mold. He ransacked his brain for incongruities, and believed in whatever was incredible. Almost all is effort, almost all is extravagant, almost all is quaint, incomprehensible, and abortive, from aiming to be more than it is. Epithets are applied, because they do not fit: subjects are chosen, because they are repulsive: the colors of this style, for their gaudy, changeful, startling effect, resemble the display of fireworks in the dark, and, like them, have neither durability, nor keeping, nor discriminate form. Yet Mr. Shelley, with all his faults, was a man of genius; and we lament that uncontrollable violence of temperament which gave it a forced and false direction. He has single thoughts of great depth and force, single images of rare beauty, detached passages of extreme tenderness; and, in his smaller pieces, where he has attempted little, he has done most. If some casual and interesting idea touched his feelings or struck his fancy, he expressed it in pleasing and unaffected verse: but give him a larger subject, and time to reflect, and he was sure to get entangled in a system. The fumes of vanity rolled volumes of smoke, mixed with sparkles of fire, from the cloudy tabernacle of his thought. The success of his writings is therefore in general in the inverse ratio of the extent of his undertakings; inasmuch as his desire to teach, his ambition to excel, as soon as it was brought into play, encroached upon and outstripped his powers of execution. . . .

With all his faults, Mr. Shelley was an honest man. His unbelief and his presumption were parts of a disease, which was not combined in him either with indifference to human happiness, or contempt for human infirmities. There was neither selfishness nor malice at the bottom of his illusions. He was sincere in all his professions; and he practiced what he preached—to his own sufficient cost. He followed up the letter and the spirit of his theoretical principles in his own person, and was ready to share both the benefit and the penalty with others. He thought and acted logically, and was what he professed to be, a sincere lover of truth, of nature, and of human kind. To all the rage of paradox, he united an unaccountable candor and severity of reasoning: in spite of an aristocratic education, he retained in his manners the simplicity of a primitive apostle. An Epicurean in his sentiments, he lived with the frugality and abstemiousness of an ascetic. His fault was, that he had no deference for the opinions of others, too little sympathy with their feelings (which he thought he had a right to sacrifice, as well as his own, to a grand ethical experiment)—and trusted too implicitly to the light of his own mind, and to the warmth of his own impulses. He was indeed the most striking example we remember of the two extremes described by Lord Bacon as the great impediments to human improvement, the love of Novelty and the love of Antiquity. . . . Considered in this point of view, his career may not be uninstructive even to those whom it most offended; and might be held up as a beacon and warning no

less to the bigot than the sciolist. We wish to speak of the
errors of a man of genius with tenderness. His nature was
kind, and his sentiments noble; but in him the rage of free
inquiry and private judgment amounted to a species of
madness. Whatever was new, untried, unheard of, unauthorized, exerted a kind of fascination over his mind.
The examples of the world, the opinion of others, instead
of acting as a check upon him, served but to impel him
forward with double velocity in his wild and hazardous
career. Spurning the world of realities, he rushed into the
world of nonentities and contingencies, like air into a
vacuum. If a thing was old and established, this was with
him a certain proof of its having no solid foundation to
rest upon: if it was new, it was good and right. Every
paradox was to him a self-evident truth; every prejudice
an undoubted absurdity. The weight of authority, the sanction of ages, the common consent of mankind, were vouchers only for ignorance, error, and imposture. Whatever
shocked the feelings of others conciliated his regard; whatever was light, extravagant, and vain was to him a proportionable relief from the dullness and stupidity of established opinions. The worst of it however was, that he
thus gave great encouragement to those who believe in all
received absurdities, and are wedded to all existing abuses:
his extravagance seeming to sanction their grossness and
selfishness, as theirs were a full justification of his folly
and eccentricity. The two extremes in this way often meet,
jostle,—and confirm one another. . . .

Julian and Maddalo is a Conversation or Tale, full of
that thoughtful and romantic humanity, but rendered perplexing and unattractive by that veil of shadowy or of
glittering obscurity, which distinguished Mr. Shelley's writings. The depth and tenderness of his feelings seems often
to have interfered with the expression of them, as the sight
becomes blind with tears. A dull, waterish vapor clouds
the aspect of his philosophical poetry, like that mysterious
gloom which he has himself described as hanging over the
Medusa's Head of Leonardo da Vinci. The meter of this
poem, too, will not be pleasing to everybody. It is in the
antique taste of the rhyming parts of Beaumont and Fletcher and Ben Jonson—blank verse in its freedom and un-
broken flow, falling into rhymes that appear altogether
accidental—very colloquial in the diction—and sometimes

sufficiently prosaic. But it is easier showing than describing it. We give the introductory passage.

I rode one evening with Count Maddalo
Upon the bank of land which breaks the flow
Of Adria towards Venice: a bare strand
Of hillocks, heaped from ever-shifting sand,
Matted with thistles and amphibious weeds,
Such as from earth's embrace the salt ooze breeds
Is this: an uninhabited sea-side,
Which the lone fisher, when his nets are dried,
Abandons; and no other object breaks
The waste, but one dwarf tree and some few stakes
Broken and unrepaired, and the tide makes
A narrow space of level sand thereon,
Where 'twas our wont to ride while day went down.

The march of these lines is, it must be confessed, slow, solemn, sad: there is a sluggishness of feeling, a dearth of imagery, an unpleasant glare of lurid light. It appears to us that in some poets as well as in some painters the organ of color predominates over that of form; and Mr. Shelley is of the number. We have everywhere a profusion of dazzling hues, of glancing splendors, of floating shadows, but the objects on which they fall are bare, indistinct, and wild. There is something in the preceding extract that reminds us of the arid style and matter of Crabbe's versification, or that apes the labor and throes of parturition of Wordsworth's blank-verse. It is the preface to a story of Love and Madness—of mental anguish and philosophic remedies—not very intelligibly told, and left with most of its mysteries unexplained, in the true spirit of the modern metaphysical style—in which we suspect there is a due mixture of affection and meagerness of invention. This poem is, however, in Mr. Shelley's best and least mannered manner. If it has less brilliancy it has less extravagance and confusion. It is in his stanza-poetry, that his Muse chiefly runs riot and baffles all pursuit of common comprehension or critical acumen. The *Witch of Atlas*, the *Triumph of Life,* and *Marianne's Dream*, are rhapsodies or allegories of this description; full of fancy and of fire, with glowing allusions and wild machinery, but which it is difficult to read through, from the disjointedness of the materials, the incongruous metaphors and violent transitions, and of which, after reading them through, it is impossible, in most instances, to guess the drift or the moral. They abound in horrible imaginings, like records of a ghastly dream; life, death, genius, beauty, victory, earth, air, ocean, the trophies of the past, the shadows of the world to come, are huddled together in a strange and hurried dance of words, and all that appears clear is the passion and paroxysm of thought of the poet's spirit. The poem entitled the *Triumph of Life* is in fact a new and terrific *Dance of Death;* but it is thus Mr. Shelley transposes the appellations of the commonest things, and subsists only in the violence of contrast. How little this poem is deserving of its title, how worthy it is of its author, what an example of the waste of power, and of genius "made as flax" and devoured by its own elementary ardors, let the reader judge from the concluding stanzas.

> *The grove*
> *Grew dense with shadows to its inmost covers,*
> *The earth was grey with phantoms, and the air*
> *Was peopled with dim forms; as when there hovers*
> *A flock of vampire-bats before the glare*
> *Of the tropic sun, bringing, ere evening,*
> *Strange night upon some Indian vale; thus were*
> *Phantoms diffused around; and some did fling*
> *Shadows of shadows, yet unlike themselves,*
> *Behind them; some like eaglets on the wing*
> *Were lost in the white day; others like elves*
> *Danced in a thousand unimagined shapes*
> *Upon the sunny streams and grassy shelves; . . .*

Anything more filmy, enigmatical, discontinuous, unsubstantial than this, we have not seen; nor yet more full of morbid genius and vivifying soul. We cannot help preferring *The Witch of Atlas* to *Alastor, or the Spirit of Solitude;* for, though the purport of each is equally perplexing and undefined, (both being a sort of mental voyage through the unexplored regions of space and time), the execution of the one is much less dreary and lamentable than that of the other. In the "Witch," he has indulged his fancy more than his melancholy, and wantoned in the felicity of embryo and crude conceits even to excess. We give the description of the progress of the "Witch's" boat as a slight specimen of what we have said of Mr. Shelley's involved style and imagery.

And down the streams which clove those mountains vast,
Around their inland islets, and amid
The panther-peopled forests, whose shade cast
Darkness and odors, and a pleasure hid
In melancholy gloom, the pinnace past:
By many a star-surrounded pyramid
Of icy crag cleaving the purple sky,
And caverns yawning round unfathomably.

This we conceive to be the very height of wilful extravagance and mysticism. Indeed it is curious to remark everywhere the proneness to the marvelous and supernatural, in one who so resolutely set his face against every received mystery, and all traditional faith. Mr. Shelley must have possessed, in spite of all his obnoxious and indiscreet skepticism, a large share of credulity and wondering curiosity in his composition, which he reserved from common use, and bestowed upon his own inventions and picturesque caricatures. To every other species of imposture or disguise he was inexorable; and indeed it is only his antipathy to established creeds and legitimate crowns that ever tears the veil from his ideal idolatries, and renders him clear and explicit. Indignation makes him pointed and intelligible enough, and breathes into his verse a spirit very different from his own boasted spirit of Love. . . .

We pass on to some of Mr. Shelley's smaller pieces and translations which we think are in general excellent and highly interesting. His *Hymn of Pan* we do not consider equal to Mr. Keats' sounding lines in the *Endymion*. His *Mont Blanc* is full of beauties and of defects; but it is akin to its subject, and presents a wild and gloomy desolation. *Ginevra*, a fragment founded on a story in the first volume of the *Florentine Observer*, is like a troublous dream, disjointed, painful, oppressive, or like a leaden cloud, from which the big tears fall, and the spirit of the poet mutters deep-toned thunder. We are too much subject to these voluntary inflictions, these "moods of mind," these effusions of "weakness and melancholy" in the perusal of modern poetry. It has shuffled off, no doubt, its old pedantry and formality; but has at the same time lost all shape or purpose, except that of giving vent to some morbid feeling of the moment. The writer thus discharges a fit of the spleen or a paradox, and expects the world to admire and be satisfied. We are no longer annoyed at seeing the luxuriant growth of nature and fancy clipped into arm-chairs and peacocks' tails; but there is danger of having its stately products choked with unchecked underwood, or weighed down with gloomy nightshade, or eaten up with personality, like ivy clinging round and eating into the sturdy oak! The *Dirge,* at the conclusion of this fragment is an example of the manner in which this craving after novelty, this desire "to elevate and surprise," leads us to overstep the modesty of nature, and the bounds of decorum. The translations from Euripides, Calderon, and Goethe in this volume will give great pleasure to the scholar and to the general reader. They are executed with equal fidelity and spirit. . . .

On the Conversation
of Authors

Though written in a vein of irony, "On the Conversa-
tion of Authors" (London Magazine, 1820) and "On
the Ignorance of the Learned" (Edinburgh Magazine,
1818), are final lessons in praise of the critical intel-
lect developed through a unity of life and literature.

An author is bound to write—well or ill, wisely or fool-
ishly: it is his trade. But I do not see that he is bound to
talk, any more than he is bound to dance, or ride, or fence
better than other people. Reading, study, silence, thought,
are a bad introduction to loquacity. It would be sooner
learnt of chambermaids and tapsters. He understands the
art and mystery of his own profession, which is book-
making: what right has anyone to expect or require him
to do more—to make a bow gracefully on entering or
leaving a room, to make love charmingly, or to make a
fortune at all? In all things there is a division of labor. A
lord is no less amorous for writing ridiculous love-letters,
nor a General less successful for wanting wit and honesty.
Why, then, may not a poor author say nothing, and yet
pass muster? Set him on the top of a stagecoach, he will
make no figure; he is *mumchance,* while the slang-wit flies
about as fast as the dust, with the crack of the whip and the
clatter of the horses' heels: put him in a ring of boxers, he
is a poor creature—

And of his port as meek as is a maid.

Introduce him to a tea-party of milliners' girls, and they
are ready to split their sides with laughing at him: over his
bottle, he is dry: in the drawing-room, rude or awkward:
he is too refined for the vulgar, too clownish for the fashionable:—"he is one that cannot make a good leg, one that
cannot eat a mess of broth cleanly, one that cannot ride a
horse without spur-galling, one that cannot salute a woman, and look on her directly:"—in courts, in camps, in
town and country, he is a cypher or a butt: he is good for
nothing but a laughing-stock or a scarecrow. You can

238

scarcely get a word out of him for love or money. He knows nothing. He has no notion of pleasure or business, or of what is going on in the world; he does not understand cookery (unless he is a doctor in divinity), nor surgery, nor chemistry (unless he is a *Quidnunc*), nor mechanics, nor husbandry and tillage (unless he is as great an admirer of Tull's *Husbandry,* and has profited as much by it as the philosopher of Botley)—no, nor music, painting, the Drama, nor the Fine Arts in general.

"What the deuce is it then, my good sir, that he does understand, or know anything about?"

"BOOKS, VENUS, BOOKS!"

"What books?"

"Not receipt-books, Madona, nor account-books, nor books of pharmacy, or the veterinary art (they belong to their respective callings and handicrafts), but books of liberal taste and general knowledge."

"What do you mean by that general knowledge which implies not a knowledge of things in general, but an ignorance (by your own account) of every one in particular: or by that liberal taste which scorns the pursuits and acquirements of the rest of the world in succession, and is confined exclusively, and by way of excellence, to what nobody takes an interest in but yourself, and a few idlers like yourself? Is this what the critics mean by the *belles-lettres,* and the study of humanity?"

Book-knowledge, in a word, then, is knowledge *communicable by books:* and it is general and liberal for this reason, that it is intelligible and interesting on the bare suggestion. That to which anyone feels a romantic attachment, merely from finding it in a book, must be interesting in itself: that which he constantly forms a lively and entire conception of, from seeing a few marks and scratches upon paper, must be taken from common nature: that which, the first time you meet with it, seizes upon the attention as a curious speculation, must exercise the general faculties of the human mind. There are certain broader aspects of society and views of things common to every subject, and more or less cognizable to every mind; and these the scholar treats, and founds his claims to general attention upon them, without being chargeable with pedantry. The minute descriptions of fishing-tackle, of baits and flies in Walton's *Complete Angler,* make that work a great favorite with sportsmen: the alloy of an amiable humanity, and the modest but touching descriptions of familiar incidents and rural objects scattered through it, have made it an equal favorite with every reader of taste and feeling. Montaigne's *Essays,* Dilworth's *Spelling Book,* and Fearn's *Treatise on Contingent Remainders,* are all equally books, but not equally adapted for all classes of readers. The two last are of no use but to school-masters and lawyers: but the first is a work we may recommend to anyone to read who has ever thought at all, or who would learn to think justly on any subject. Persons of different trades and professions—the mechanic, the shop-keeper, the medical practitioner, the artist, etc., may all have great knowledge and ingenuity in their several vocations, the details of which will be very edifying to themselves, and just as incomprehensible to their neighbors: but over and above this professional and technical knowledge, they must be supposed to have a stock of common sense and common feeling to furnish subjects for common conversation, or to give them any pleasure in each other's company. It is to this common stock of ideas, spread over the surface, or striking its roots into the very center of society, that the popular writer appeals, and not in vain; for he finds readers. It is of this finer essence of wisdom and humanity "etherial mold, sky-tinctured," that books of the better sort are made. They contain the language of thought. It must happen that, in the course of time and the variety of human capacity, some persons will have struck out finer observations, reflections, and sentiments than others. These they have committed to books of memory, have bequeathed as a lasting legacy to posterity; and such persons have become standard authors. We visit at the shrine, drink in some measure of the inspiration, and cannot easily "breathe in other air less pure, accustomed to immortal fruits." Are we to be blamed for this because the vulgar and illiterate do not always understand us? The fault is rather in them who are "confined and cabin'd in" each in their own particular sphere and compartment of ideas, and have not the same refined medium of communication or abstracted topics of discourse. Bring a number of literary, or of illiterate persons together, perfect strangers to each other, and see which party will make the best company. "Verily, we have our reward." We have made our election, and have no reason to repent it, if we were wise. But the misfortune is, we wish to have all the advantages on one side. We grudge, and cannot reconcile it to ourselves, that anyone "should go about to cozen fortune, without the stamp of learning!" We think "because we are *scholars,* there shall be no more cakes and ale!" We don't know how to account for it, that bar-maids should gossip, or ladies whisper, or bullies roar, or fools laugh, or knaves thrive, without having gone through the same course of select study that we have! This vanity is preposterous, and carries its own punishment with it. Books are a world in themselves, it is true; but they are not the only world. The world itself is a volume larger than all the libraries in it. Learning is a sacred deposit from the experience of ages; but it has not put all future experience on the shelf, or debarred the common herd of mankind from the use of their hands, tongues, eyes, ears, or understandings. Taste is a luxury for the privileged few: but it would be hard upon those who have not the same standard of refinement in their own minds that we suppose ourselves to have, if this should prevent them from having recourse, as usual, to their old frolics, coarse jokes, and horse-play, and getting through the wear and tear of the world, with such homely sayings and shrewd helps as they may. Happy is it, that the mass of mankind eat and drink, and sleep, and perform their several tasks, and do as they like without us—caring nothing for our scribblings, our carpings, and our quibbles; and moving on the same, in spite of our fine-spun distinctions, fantastic theories, and lines of demarcation, which are like chalk-figures drawn on ballroom floors to be danced out before morning! In the field opposite the window where I write this, there is a country-girl picking stones: in the one next it, there are several poor women weeding the blue and red flowers from the corn: farther on, are two boys, tending a flock of sheep. What do they know or care about what I am writing about them, or ever will?—or what would they be the better for it, if they did? . . .

The conversation of authors is not so good as might be imagined: but, such as it is (and with rare exceptions) it is better than any other. The proof of which is, that, when you are used to it, you cannot put up with any other. That of mixed company becomes utterly intolerable—you cannot sit out a common tea and card party, at least, if they pretend to talk at all. You are obliged in despair to cut all your old acquaintances who are not *au fait* on the prevailing and most smartly contested topics, who are not imbued with the high gusto of criticism and *virtù*. You cannot bear to hear a friend whom you have not seen for many years, tell at how much a yard he sells his laces and tapes, when he means to move into his next house, when he heard last from his relations in the country, whether trade is alive or dead, or whether Mr. Such-a-one gets to look old. This sort of neighborly gossip will not go down after the high-raised tone of literary conversation. The last may be absurd, very unsatisfactory, and full of turbulence and heart-burnings; but it has a zest in it which more ordinary topics of news or family-affairs do not supply. Neither will the conversation of what we understand by *gentlemen* and men of fashion, do after that of men of letters. It is flat, insipid, stale, and unprofitable, in the comparison. They talk about much the same things—pictures, poetry, politics, plays; but they do it worse, and at a sort of vapid secondhand. They, in fact, talk out of newspapers and magazines, what *we write there*. They do not feel the same interest in the subjects they affect to handle with an air of fashionable condescension, nor have they the same knowledge of them, if they were ever so much in earnest in displaying it. If it were not for the wine and the dessert, no author in his senses would accept an invitation to a well-dressed dinner-party, except out of pure good-nature and unwillingness to disoblige by his refusal. Persons in high life talk almost entirely by rote. There are certain established modes of address, and certain answers to them expected as a matter of course, as a point of etiquette. The studied forms of politeness do not give the greatest possible scope to an exuberance of wit and fancy. The fear of giving offense destroys sincerity, and without sincerity there can be no true enjoyment of society, nor unfettered exertion of intellectual activity.—Those who have been accustomed to live with the great are hardly considered as conversible persons in literary society. They are not to be talked with, any more than puppets or echoes. They have no opinions but what will please; and you naturally turn away, as a waste of time and words, from attending to a person who just before assented to what you said, and whom you find the moment after, from something that unexpectedly or perhaps by design drops from him, to be of a totally different way of thinking. This *bush-fighting* is not regarded as fair play among scientific men. As fashionable conversation is a sacrifice to politeness, so the conversation of low life is nothing but rudeness. They contradict you without giving a reason, or if they do, it is a very bad one—swear, talk loud, repeat the same thing fifty times over, get to calling names, and from words proceed to blows. You cannot make companions of servants, or persons in an inferior station in life. You may talk to them on matters of business, and what they have to do for you (as lords talk to bruisers on subjects of *fancy,* or country squires to their grooms on horse-racing), but out of that narrow sphere, to any general topic, you cannot lead them; the conversation soon flags, and you go back to the old question, or are obliged to break up the sitting for want of ideas in common.

The conversation of authors is better than that of most professions. It is better than that of lawyers, who talk nothing but *double entendre*—than that of physicians, who talk of the approaching deaths of the College, or the marriage of some new practitioner with some rich widow—than that of divines, who talk of the last place they dined at—than that of University-men, who make stale puns, repeat the refuse of London newspapers, and affect an ignorance of Greek and mathematics; it is better than that of players, who talk of nothing but the Green-room, and rehearse the scholar, the wit, or the fine gentleman, like a part on the stage—or than that of ladies, who, whatever you talk of, think of nothing, and expect you to think of nothing, but themselves. It is not easy to keep up a conversation with women in company. It is thought a piece of rudeness to differ from them: it is not quite fair to ask them a reason for what they say. You are afraid of pressing too hard upon them: but where you cannot differ openly and unreservedly, you cannot heartily agree. It is not so in France. There the women talk of things in general, and reason better than the men in this country. They are mistresses of the intellectual foils. They are adepts in all the topics. They know what is to be said for and against all sorts of questions, and are lively and full of mischief into the bargain. They are very subtle. They put you to your trumps immediately. Your logic is more in requisition even than your gallantry. You must argue as well as bow yourself into the good graces of these modern Amazons. What a situation for an Englishman to be placed in!

The fault of literary conversation in general is its too great tenaciousness. It fastens upon a subject, and will not let it go. It resembles a battle rather than a skirmish, and

makes a toil of a pleasure. Perhaps it does this from necessity, from a consciousness of wanting the more familiar
graces, the power to sport and trifle, to touch lightly and
adorn agreeably, every view or turn of a question *en pas-
sant,* as it arises. Those who have a reputation to lose
are too ambitious of shining, to please. "To excel in conversation," said an ingenious man, "one must not be always
striving to say good things: to say one good thing, one
must say many bad, and more indifferent ones." This desire
to shine without the means at hand, often makes men
silent:—

The fear of being silent strikes us dumb.

A writer who has been accustomed to take a connected
view of a difficult question and to work it out gradually in
all its bearings, may be very deficient in that quickness
and ease which men of the world, who are in the habit of
hearing a variety of opinions, who pick up an observation
on one subject, and another on another, and who care
about none any farther than the passing away of an idle
hour, usually acquire. An author has studied a particular
point—he has read, he has inquired, he has thought a
great deal upon it: he is not contented to take it up
casually in common with others, to throw out a hint, to
propose an objection: he will either remain silent, uneasy,
and dissatisfied, or he will begin at the beginning, and go
through with it to the end. He is for taking the whole
responsibility upon himself. He would be thought to understand the subject better than others, or indeed would show
that nobody else knows anything about it. There are always three or four points on which the literary novice at
his first outset in life fancies he can enlighten every company, and bear down all opposition: but he is cured of
this Quixotic and pugnacious spirit, as he goes more into
the world, where he finds that there are other opinions and
other pretensions to be adjusted besides his own. When this
asperity wears off, and a certain scholastic precocity is
mellowed down, the conversation of men of letters becomes
both interesting and instructive. Men of the world have
no fixed principles, no groundwork of thought: mere scholars have too much an object, a theory always in view, to
which they wrest everything, and not unfrequently, common sense itself. By mixing with society, they rub off their

hardness of manner, and impracticable, offensive singularity, while they retain a greater depth and coherence of
understanding. There is more to be learnt from them than
from their books. This was a remark of Rousseau's, and it
is a very true one. In the confidence and unreserve of
private intercourse, they are more at liberty to say what
they think, to put the subject in different and opposite
points of view, to illustrate it more briefly and pithily by
familiar expressions, by an appeal to individual character
and personal knowledge—to bring in the limitation, to
obviate misconception, to state difficulties on their own
side of the argument, and answer them as well as they can.
This would hardly agree with the prudery, and somewhat
ostentatious claims of authorship. Dr. Johnson's conversation in Boswell's *Life* is much better than his published
works: and the fragments of the opinions of celebrated men,
preserved in their letters or in anecdotes of them, are justly
sought after as invaluable for the same reason. For instance, what a fund of sense there is in Grimm's *Memoirs!*
We thus get at the essence of what is contained in their
more labored productions, without the affectation or formality. Argument, again, is the death of conversation, if
carried on in a spirit of hostility: but discussion is a pleasant and profitable thing, where you advance and defend
your opinions as far as you can, and admit the truth of
what is objected against them with equal impartiality: in
short, where you do not pretend to set up for an oracle, but
freely declare what you really know about any question, or
suggest what has struck you as throwing a new light upon
it, and let it pass for what it is worth. This tone of conversation was well described by Dr. Johnson, when he said of
some party at which he had been present the night before
—"We had good talk, sir!" As a general rule, there is no
conversation worth anything but between friends, or those
who agree in the same leading views of a subject. Nothing
was ever learnt by either side in a dispute. You contradict
one another, will not allow a grain of sense in what your
adversary advances, are blind to whatever makes against
yourself, dare not look the question fairly in the face, so
that you cannot avail yourself even of your real advantages,
insist most on what you feel to be the weakest points of
your argument, and get more and more absurd, dogmatical,
and violent every moment. Disputes for victory generally
end to the dissatisfaction of all parties; and the one record-

ed in *Gil Blas* breaks up just as it ought. I once knew a very ingenious man, than whom, to take him in the way of common chit-chat or fireside gossip, no one could be more entertaining or rational. He would make an apt classical quotation, propose an explanation of a curious passage in Shakespeare's *Venus and Adonis,* detect a metaphysical error in Locke, would infer the volatility of the French character from the chapter in Sterne where the Count mistakes the feigned name of Yorick for a proof of his being the identical imaginary character in Hamlet (*Et vous êtes Yorick!*)—thus confounding words with things twice over—but let a difference of opinion be once hitched in, and it was all over with him. His only object from that time was to shut out common sense, and to be proof against conviction. He would argue the most ridiculous point (such as that there were two original languages) for hours together, nay, through the horologe. You would not suppose it was the same person. He was like an obstinate run-away horse, that takes the bit in his mouth, and becomes mischievous and unmanageable. He had made up his mind to one thing—not to admit a single particle of what any one else said for or against him. It was all the difference between a man drunk and sober, sane or mad. It is the same when he once gets the pen in his hand. He has been trying to prove a contradiction in terms for the last ten years of his life, viz., that the Bourbons have the same right to the throne of France that the Brunswick family have to the throne of England. Many people think there is a want of honesty or a want of understanding in this. There is neither. But he will persist in an argument to the last pinch; he will yield, in absurdity, to no man!

This litigious humor is bad enough: but there is one character still worse—that of a person who goes into company, not to contradict, but to *talk at* you. This is the greatest nuisance in civilized society. Such a person does not come armed to defend himself at all points, but to unsettle, if he can, and throw a slur on all your favorite opinions. If he has a notion that any one in the room is fond of poetry, he immediately volunteers a contemptuous tirade against the idle jingle of verse. If he suspects you have a delight in pictures, he endeavors, not by fair argument, but by a side-wind, to put you out of conceit with so frivolous an art. If you have a taste for music, he does not think much good is to be done by this tickling of the ears.

If you speak in praise of a comedy, he does not see the use of wit: if you say you have been to a tragedy, he shakes his head at this mockery of human misery, and thinks it ought to be prohibited. He tries to find out beforehand whatever it is that you take a particular pride or pleasure in, that he may annoy your self-love in the tenderest point (as if he were probing a wound) and make you dissatisfied with yourself and your pursuits for several days afterwards. A person might as well make a practice of throwing out scandalous aspersions against your dearest friends or nearest relations, by way of ingratiating himself into your favor. Such ill-timed impertinence is "villainous, and shows a pitiful ambition in the fool that uses it."

The soul of conversation is sympathy.—Authors should converse chiefly with authors, and their talk should be of books. "When Greek meets Greek, then comes the tug of war." There is nothing so pedantic as pretending not to be pedantic. No man can get above his pursuit in life: it is getting above himself, which is impossible. There is a Free-masonry in all things. You can only speak to be understood, but this you cannot be, except by those who are in the secret. Hence an argument has been drawn to supersede the necessity of conversation altogether; for it has been said, that there is no use in talking to people of sense, who know all that you can tell them, nor to fools, who will not be instructed. There is, however, the smallest encouragement to proceed, when you are conscious that the more you really enter into a subject, the farther you will be from the comprehension of your hearers—and that the more proofs you give of any position, the more odd and out-of-the-way they will think your notions. C[oleridge] is the only person who can talk to all sorts of people, on all sorts of subjects, without caring a farthing for their understanding one word he says—and *he* talks only for admiration and to be listened to, and accordingly the least interruption puts him out. I firmly believe he would make just the same impression on half his audiences, if he purposely repeated absolute nonsense with the same voice and manner and inexhaustible flow of undulating speech! In general, wit shines only by reflection. You must take your cue from your company—must rise as they rise, and sink as they fall. You must see that your good things, your knowing allusions, are not flung away, like the pearls in the adage. What a check it is to be asked a foolish question; to find that the first principles are not understood! You are thrown on your back immediately, the conversation is stopped like a country-dance by those who do not know the figure. But when a set of adepts, of *illuminati,* get about a question, it is worth while to hear them talk. They may snarl and quarrel over it, like dogs; but they pick it bare to the bone, they masticate it thoroughly.

This was the case formerly at L[amb]'s—where we used to have many lively skirmishes at their Thursday evening parties. Oh! for the pen of John Buncle to consecrate a *petit souvenir* to their memory!—There was L[amb] himself, the most delightful, the most provoking, the most witty and sensible of men. He always made the best pun, and the best remark in the course of the evening. His serious conversation, like his serious writing, is his best. No one ever stammered out such fine, piquant, deep, eloquent things in half a dozen half-sentences as he does. His jests scald like tears: and he probes a question with a play upon words. What a keen, laughing, hair-brained vein of home-felt truth! What choice venom! How often did we cut into the haunch of letters, while we discussed the haunch of mutton on the table! How we skimmed the cream of criticism! How we got into the heart of controversy! How we picked out the marrow of authors! "And, in our flowing cups, many a good name and true was freshly remembered." Recollect (most sage and critical reader) that in all this I was but a guest! Need I go over the names? They were but the old everlasting set—Milton and Shakespeare, Pope and Dryden, Steele and Addison, Swift and Gay, Fielding, Smollett, Sterne, Richardson, Hogarth's prints, Claude's landscapes, the Cartoons at Hampton Court, and all those things that, having once been, must ever be. The Scotch Novels had not then been heard of: so we said nothing about them. In general, we were hard upon the moderns. The author of the *Rambler* was only tolerated in Boswell's *Life* of him; and it was as much as anyone could do to edge in a word for *Junius.* L[amb] could not bear *Gil Blas.* This was a fault. I remember the greatest triumph I ever had was in persuading him, after some years' difficulty, that Fielding was better than Smollett. On one occasion, he was for making out a list of persons famous in history that one would wish to see again—at the head of whom were Pontius Pilate, Sir Thomas Browne, and Dr. Faustus—but we black-balled most of his list. But with what a gusto would he describe his favorite authors, Donne, or Sir Philip Sidney, and call their most crabbed passages *delicious!* He tried them on his palate as epicures taste olives, and his observations had a smack in them, like a roughness on the tongue. With what discrimination he hinted a defect in what he admired most —as in saying that the display of the sumptuous banquet in *Paradise Regained* was not in true keeping, as the simplest fare was all that was necessary to tempt the extremity of hunger—and stating that Adam and Eve in *Paradise Lost* were too much like married people. He has furnished many a text for C[oleridge] to preach upon. There was no fuss or cant about him: nor were his sweets or his sours ever diluted with one particle of affectation. I cannot say that the party at L[amb]'s were all of one description. There were honorary members, lay-brothers. Wit and good fellowship was the motto inscribed over the door. When a stranger came in, it was not asked, "Has he written anything?"—we were above that pedantry; but we waited to see what he could do. If he could take a hand at piquet, he was welcome to sit down. If a person liked anything, if he took snuff heartily, it was sufficient. He would understand, by analogy, the pungency of other things besides Irish blackguard or Scotch rappee. A character was good anywhere, in a room or on paper. But we abhorred insipidity, affectation, and fine gentlemen. There was one of our party who never failed to mark "two for his Nob" at cribbage, and he was thought no mean person. This was Ned P[hillips], and a better fellow in his way breathes not. There was R[ickman], who asserted some incredible matter of fact as a likely paradox, and settled all controversies by an *ipse dixit*, a *fiat* of his will, hammering out many a hard theory on the anvil of his brain—the Baron Munchausen of politics and practical philosophy: there was Captain [Burney], who had you at an advantage by never understanding you:—there was Jem White, the Author of *Falstaff's Letters*, who the other day left this dull world to go in search of more kindred spirits, "turning like the latter end of a lover's lute:"—there was A[yrton], who sometimes dropped in, the Will Honeycomb of our set— and Mrs. R[eynolds], who being of a quiet turn, loved to hear a noisy debate. An utterly uninformed person might have supposed this a scene of vulgar confusion and uproar. While the most critical question was pending, while the most difficult problem in philosophy was solving, P[hillips] cried out, "That's game," and M[artin] B[urney] muttered a quotation over the last remains of a veal-pie at a side table. Once, and once only, the literary interest overcame the general. For C[oleridge] was riding the high German horse, and demonstrating the Categories of the Transcendental Philosophy to the Author of the *Road to Ruin;* who insisted on his knowledge of German, and German metaphysics, having read the *Critique of Pure Reason* in the original. "My dear Mr. Holcroft," said C[oleridge], in a tone of infinitely provoking conciliation, "you really put me in mind of a sweet pretty German girl, about fifteen, that I met with in the Hartz forest in Germany—and who one day, as I was reading the *Limits of the Knowable and the Unknowable,* the profoundest of all his works, with great attention, came behind my chair, and leaning over, said, 'What, *you* read Kant? Why *I* that am a German born, don't understand him!' " This was too much to bear, and Holcroft, starting up, called out in no measured tone, "Mr. C[oleridge], you are the most eloquent man I ever met with, and the most troublesome with your eloquence!" P[hillips] held the cribbage-peg that was to mark him game, suspended in his hand; and the whist table was silent for a moment. I saw Holcroft downstairs, and, on coming to the landing-place at Mitre Court, he stopped me to observe, that "he thought Mr. C[oleridge] a very clever man, with a great command of language, but that he feared he did not always affix very precise ideas to the words he used." After he was gone, we had our laugh out, and went on with the argument on the nature of Reason, the Imagination, and the Will. I wish I could find a publisher for it: it would make a supplement to the *Biographia Literaria* in a volume-and-a-half octavo.

On the Ignorance of
the Learned

The description of persons who have the fewest ideas
of all others are mere authors and readers. It is better
to be able neither to read nor write than to be able to do
nothing else. A lounger who is ordinarily seen with a book
in his hand is (we may be almost sure) equally without
the power or inclination to attend either to what passes
around him or in his own mind. Such a one may be said
to carry his understanding about with him in his pocket,
or to leave it at home on his library shelves. He is afraid
of venturing on any train of reasoning, or of striking out
any observation that is not mechanically suggested to
him by passing his eyes over certain legible characters;
shrinks from the fatigue of thought, which, for want of
practice, becomes insupportable to him; and sits down
contented with an endless, wearisome succession of words
and half-formed images, which fill the void of the mind,
and continually efface one another. Learning is, in too
many cases, but a foil to common sense; a substitute for
true knowledge. Books are less often made use of as
"spectacles" to look at nature with, than as blinds to keep
out its strong light and shifting scenery from weak eyes
and indolent dispositions. The book-worm wraps himself
up in his web of verbal generalities, and sees only the
glimmering shadows of things reflected from the minds
of others. Nature *puts him out*. The impressions of real
objects, stripped of the disguises of words and voluminous
roundabout descriptions, are blows that stagger him; their
variety distracts, their rapidity exhausts him; and he turns
from the bustle, the noise, and glare, and whirling motion
of the world about him (which he has not an eye to follow
in its fantastic changes, nor an understanding to reduce to
fixed principles), to the quiet monotony of the dead languages, and the less startling and more intelligible combinations of the letters of the alphabet. It is well, it is
perfectly well. "Leave me to my repose," is the motto of
the sleeping and the dead. You might as well ask the
paralytic to leap from his chair and throw away his crutch,
or, without a miracle, to "take up his bed and walk," as

expect the learned reader to throw down his book and think for himself. He clings to it for his intellectual support; and his dread of being left to himself is like the horror of a vacuum. He can only breathe a learned atmosphere, as other men breathe common air. He is a borrower of sense. He has no ideas of his own, and must live on those of other people. The habit of supplying our ideas from foreign sources "enfeebles all internal strength of thought," as a course of dram-drinking destroys the tone of the stomach. The faculties of the mind, when not exerted, or when cramped by custom and authority, become listless, torpid, and unfit for the purposes of thought or action. Can we wonder at the languor and lassitude which is thus produced by a life of learned sloth and ignorance; by poring over lines and syllables that excite little more idea or interest than if they were the characters of an unknown tongue, till the eye closes on vacancy, and the book drops from the feeble hand! I would rather be a wood-cutter, or the meanest hind, that all day "sweats in the eye of Phœbus, and at night sleeps in Elysium," than wear out my life so, 'twixt dreaming and awake. The learned author differs from the learned student in this, that the one transcribes what the other reads. The learned are mere literary drudges. If you set them upon original composition, their heads turn, they don't know where they are. The indefatigable readers of books are like the everlasting copiers of pictures, who, when they attempt to do anything of their own, find they want an eye quick enough, a hand steady enough, and colors bright enough, to trace the living forms of nature.

Anyone who has passed through the regular gradations of a classical education, and is not made a fool by it, may consider himself as having had a very narrow escape. It is an old remark, that boys who shine at school do not make the greatest figure when they grow up and come out into the world. The things, in fact, which a boy is set to learn at school, and on which his success depends, are things which do not require the exercise either of the highest or the most useful faculties of the mind. Memory (and that of the lowest kind) is the chief faculty called into play in conning over and repeating lessons by rote in grammar, in languages, in geography, arithmetic, etc., so that he who has the most of this technical memory, with the least turn for other things, which have a stronger

and more natural claim upon his childish attention, will
make the most forward schoolboy. The jargon containing
the definitions of the parts of speech, the rules for casting
up an account, or the inflections of a Greek verb, can have
no attraction to the tyro of ten years old, except as they
are imposed as a task upon him by others, or from his
feeling the want of sufficient relish or amusement in
other things. A lad with a sickly constitution and no very
active mind, who can just retain what is pointed out to
him, and has neither sagacity to distinguish nor spirit to
enjoy for himself, will generally be at the head of his form.
An idler at school, on the other hand, is one who has high
health and spirits, who has the free use of his limbs, with
all his wits about him, who feels the circulation of his
blood and the motion of his heart, who is ready to laugh
and cry in a breath, and who had rather chase a ball or a
butterfly, feel the open air in his face, look at the fields
or the sky, follow a winding path, or enter with eagerness
into all the little conflicts and interests of his acquaintances
and friends, than doze over a musty spelling-book, repeat
barbarous distichs after his master, sit so many hours
pinioned to a writing-desk, and receive his reward for the
loss of time and pleasure in paltry prize-medals at Christmas and Midsummer. There is indeed a degree of stupidity
which prevents children from learning the usual lessons,
or ever arriving at these puny academic honors. But what
passes for stupidity is much oftener a want of interest,
of a sufficient motive to fix the attention and force a
reluctant application to the dry and unmeaning pursuits
of school-learning. The best capacities are as much above
this drudgery as the dullest are beneath it. Our men of
the greatest genius have not been most distinguished for
their acquirements at school or at the university.

Gray and Collins were among the instances of this wayward disposition. Such persons do not think so highly of
the advantages, nor can they submit their imaginations
so servilely to the trammels of strict scholastic discipline.
There is a certain kind and degree of intellect in which
words take root, but into which things have not power to
penetrate. A mediocrity of talent, with a certain slender-
ness of moral constitution, is the soil that produces the
most brilliant specimens of successful prize-essayists and
Greek epigrammatists. It should not be forgotten that the

least respectable character among modern politicians was the cleverest boy at Eton.

Learning is the knowledge of that which is not generally known to others, and which we can only derive at second-hand from books or other artificial sources. The knowledge of that which is before us, or about us, which appeals to our experience, passions, and pursuits, to the bosoms and businesses of men, is not learning. Learning is the knowledge of that which none but the learned know. He is the most learned man who knows the most of what is farthest removed from common life and actual observation, that is of the least practical utility, and least liable to be brought to the test of experience, and that, having been handed down through the greatest number of intermediate stages, is the most full of uncertainty, difficulties, and contradictions. It is seeing with the eyes of others, hearing with their ears, and pinning our faith on their understandings. The learned man prides himself in the knowledge of names and dates, not of men or things. He thinks and cares nothing about his next-door neighbors, but he is deeply read in the tribes and castes of the Hindoos and Calmuc Tartars. He can hardly find his way into the next street, though he is acquainted with the exact dimensions of Constantinople and Pekin. He does not know whether his oldest acquaintance is a knave or a fool, but he can pronounce a pompous lecture on all the principal characters in history. He cannot tell whether an object is black or white, round or square, and yet he is a professed master of the laws of optics and the rules of perspective. He knows as much of what he talks about as a blind man does of colors. He cannot give a satisfactory answer to the plainest question, nor is he ever in the right in any one of his opinions upon any one matter of fact that really comes before him, and yet he gives himself out for an infallible judge on all those points, of which it is impossible that he or any other person living should know anything but by conjecture. He is expert in all the dead and in most of the living languages; but he can neither speak his own fluently, nor write it correctly. A person of this class, the second Greek scholar of his day, undertook to point out several solecisms in Milton's Latin style; and in his own performance there is hardly a sentence of common English. Such was Dr. ———. Such is Dr. ———. Such was not Porson. He was an exception that confirmed the general rule,—a man that, by uniting talents and knowledge with learning, made the distinction between them more striking and palpable.

A mere scholar, who knows nothing but books, must be ignorant even of them. "Books do not teach the use of books." How should he know anything of a work who knows nothing of the subject of it? The learned pedant is conversant with books only as they are made of other books, and those again of others, without end. He parrots those who have parroted others. He can translate the same word into ten different languages, but he knows nothing of the *thing* which it means in any one of them. He stuffs his head with authorities built on authorities, with quotations quoted from quotations, while he locks up his senses, his understanding, and his heart. He is unacquainted with the maxims and manners of the world, he is to seek in the characters of individuals. He sees no beauty in the face of nature or of art. To him "the mighty world of eye and ear" is hid; and "knowledge," except at one entrance, "quite shut out." His pride takes part with his ignorance; and his self-importance rises with the number of things of which he does not know the value, and which he therefore despises as unworthy of his notice. He knows nothing of pictures,—"of the coloring of Titian, the grace of Raphael, the purity of Domenichino, the *corregioscity* of Correggio, the learning of Poussin, the airs of Guido, the taste of the Caracci, or the grand contour of Michael Angelo,"—of all those glories of the Italian and miracles of the Flemish school, which have filled the eyes of mankind with delight, and to the study and imitation of which thousands have in vain devoted their lives. These are to him as if they had never been, a mere dead letter, a by-word; and no wonder, for he neither sees nor understands their prototypes in nature. A print of Rubens' Watering-place, or Claude's Enchanted Castle, may be hanging on the walls of his room for months without his once perceiving them; and if you point them out to him he will turn away from them. The language of nature, or of art (which is another nature), is one that he does not understand. He repeats indeed the names of Apelles and Phidias, because they are to be found in classic authors, and boasts of their works as prodigies, because they no longer exist; or when he sees the finest remains of Grecian art actually before him in the Elgin Marbles, takes no other interest in them than as they lead to a learned dispute, and (which is the same thing) a quarrel about the meaning of a Greek particle. He is equally ignorant of music; he "knows no touch of it," from the strains of the all-accomplished Mozart to the shepherd's pipe upon the mountain. His ears are nailed to his books; and deadened with the sound of the Greek and Latin tongues, and the din and smithery of school-learning. Does he know anything more of poetry? He knows the number of feet in a verse, and of acts in a play; but of the soul or spirit he knows nothing. He can turn a Greek ode into English, or a Latin epigram into Greek verse; but whether either is worth the trouble he leaves to the critics. Does he understand "the act and practique part of life" better than "the theorique"? No. He knows no liberal or mechanic art, no trade or occupation, no game of skill or chance. Learning "has no skill in surgery," in agriculture, in building, in working in wood or in iron; it cannot make any instrument of labor, or use it when made; it cannot handle the plough or the spade, or the chisel or the hammer; it knows nothing of hunting or hawking, fishing or shooting, of horses or dogs, of fencing or dancing, or cudgel-playing, or bowls, or cards, or tennis, or anything else. The learned professor of all arts and sciences cannot reduce any one of them to practice, though he may contribute an account of them to an Encyclopedia. He has not the use of his hands or of his feet; he can neither run, nor walk, nor swim; and he considers all those who actually understand and can exercise any of these arts of body or mind as vulgar and mechanical men,—though to know almost any one of them in perfection requires long time and practice, with powers originally fitted, and a turn of mind particularly devoted to them. It does not require more than this to enable the learned candidate to arrive, by painful study, at a doctor's degree and a fellowship, and to eat, drink, and sleep the rest of his life!